MEDICATIONS & THE ELDERLY

A Guide for Promoting Proper Use

William Simonson, Pharm. D.

School of Pharmacy
Oregon State University

Foreword by
Claude Pepper

AN ASPEN PUBLICATION ®
Aspen Systems Corporation
Rockville, Maryland
Royal Tunbridge Wells
1984

Library of Congress Cataloging in Publication Data

Simonson, William.
Medications and the elderly.

Includes index and bibliographies.
1. Geriatric pharmacology. 2. Medication abuse—
Prevention. I. Title.
[DNLM: 1. Drug Therapy—In old
age. WT 100 56106m]
RC953.7.S55   1984   615.5′8′0880565   83-17182
ISBN: 0-89443-944-8

Publisher: John Marozsan
Editorial Director: Darlene Como
Executive Managing Editor: Margot Raphael
Editorial Services: Martha Sasser
Printing and Manufacturing: Debbie Collins

Library of Congress Catalog Card Number: 83-17182
ISBN: 0-89443-944-8

Printed in the United States of America

3 4 5

To my parents,
who have learned the art of aging gracefully

Table of Contents

Foreword ix

Preface xi

Acknowledgments xiii

Chapter 1—Introduction 1

Chapter 2—Medication Consumption Patterns in the Elderly 7

       Financial Considerations of Health Care and Medication
          Consumption 7
       Prescription Drug Consumption 11
       Nonprescription Drug Consumption 14
       Factors Influencing Medication Consumption 15
       Polypharmacy 32

Chapter 3—Generic Drugs and Their Implications in the Elderly .. 43

       Definitions 44
       Historical Perspective of Generic Drug Use 46
       Why Do Physicians Prescribe Brand Name Drugs? 50
       Patient Protection for Brand Name Drugs 52
       Economic Considerations 52
       Generic Equivalence Versus Therapeutic Equivalence ... 55
       Disadvantages of Generic Drug Use 57
       Why Aren't Generic Drugs Used More? 59
       Conclusions and Recommendations 62

Chapter 4—Compliance to Drug Therapy **65**

    Types of Noncompliance 65
    Incidence of Noncompliance 68
    Factors Contributing to Noncompliance 69
    Consequences of Noncompliance 74
    Detection of Noncompliant Patients 76
    Traits of Noncompliant Individuals 76
    Encouraging Proper Compliance 77
    The Use of "Child-Proof" Containers 79

Chapter 5—Medication Education and the Elderly Patient **83**

    Goals of Patient Medication Education 84
    What the Patient Should Know 84
    The Team Approach to Patient Medication Education 89
    The Effective Patient Educator 93
    Responsibilities of the Patient 93
    Responsibilities of Family and Friends 94
    Special Concerns in Medication Education
      for the Elderly 95
    Techniques for Facilitating Communication with the
      Elderly 97
    Appendix 5-1—Consumer-Oriented References on
      Medications 101

Chapter 6—The Effect of Aging on Medication Dosage **105**

    Definitions 106
    The Science of Pharmacokinetics 108
    Pharmacokinetic Changes That Occur with Age 110
    Conclusion 120

Chapter 7—Adverse Effects of Medications **125**

    Definitions 126
    Incidence of Adverse Drug Reactions 128
    Identifying the Patient at Risk 130
    Prescription Medications Commonly Causing
      Adverse Drug Reactions in the Elderly 132
    Nonprescription Medications Commonly Causing Adverse
      Drug Reactions in the Elderly 145

The Consequences of Adverse Reactions to Medications . .   146
Common Manifestations of Adverse Reactions to
    Medications   148
The Elderly Stereotype   153
The Danger of Not Recognizing an Adverse Drug
    Reaction   153
Role of Health Professionals   156
Role of Family Members   163

Chapter 8—Drug Interactions **167**

The Discovery of Drug Interactions   168
The Incidence of Drug Interactions   169
Drug Interactions in the Elderly   169
The Mechanisms of Drug Interactions   172
Drug-Alcohol Interactions   175
Consequences of Drug-Drug Interactions   175
Drug-Nutrient Interactions   176
Management of Drug Interactions by Health
    Professionals   180

Chapter 9—Sexual Implications of Drug Therapy in the Elderly . .   **185**

Patterns of Sexual Activity in the Elderly   187
Sexual Response in the Aging Male   188
Sexual Response in the Aging Female   188
Disease Conditions Interfering with Sexuality   189
Sexual Impotence   196
Inhibition of Sexual Response in the Female   198
Drug-Induced Gynecomastia   200
Medications Used for Their Positive Effect on Sexuality . .   202
Interventions by Health Professionals   204

Chapter 10—The Use of Unproven Remedies by the Elderly **209**

Theories of Aging   210
Interventions in the Aging Process   211
The Impact of an Extended Life Span   213
Why Do People Use Unproven Remedies?   213
What Are Unproven Remedies Treating?   217
Common Unproven Remedies   219

DMSO 223
EDTA 226
Dangers of Unproven Remedies 226

Index **231**

Foreword

I am concerned about the serious and growing problem of drug misuse among the elderly. When drugs are used incorrectly, the cost to the patient and society in human and monetary terms can be devastating.

At hearings of my Subcommittee on Health and Long-Term Care, senior citizens have brought in large plastic bags filled with pills of every variety. These were medications that had been prescribed for them, and which they were supposedly taking simultaneously. One elderly woman told me that she was admitted to the hospital and nearly lost her physical and mental health before she was weaned from the drugs.

When drug reactions are experienced, the average hospital stay is nearly doubled. The estimated cost of these drug-induced hospitalizations is almost $24 billion a year. The Medicare system, which is already in financial trouble, cannot bear such unnecessary expense.

There are three major reasons for drug misuse and adverse drug reactions among the elderly. First, many senior citizens are simply not aware of the possible dangers of their medications. They swap drugs, take more medication than is needed, and use out-of-date drugs. Second, drugs are often not manufactured, tested, or monitored to take into account the problems of the elderly patient. Senior citizens can and do react differently than young people to the same drug. The Food and Drug Administration needs to consider that. And third, few physicians and other health care professionals receive specific training in the administration of drugs to the elderly.

I am confident that this book will help people who work with the elderly to better understand the confusing and complex topic of the elderly and drugs. I commend the author for this valuable and much needed book.

Claude Pepper
Member of Congress
Washington, D.C.

Preface

The subject of the use and misuse of medication by the elderly is one that stirs a great deal of interest among individuals who work with the elderly in many different capacities. It can be a very complex and confusing subject, especially to those who have not had formal training in medicine or pharmacology.

Textbooks and professional journals addressing this subject have been published, but they are almost universally written with highly technical terminology, under the assumption that the reader will have a thorough knowledge of the theory and terminology of pharmacology. Therefore, reference material that is "understandable" to anyone but physicians or other medically trained individuals is lacking.

Medication and the Elderly has been written primarily for those individuals who work with or are interested in the elderly and who do not have extensive training or knowledge of the principles of medication use by this segment of the population. Considerable input from gerontologists and health care professionals was obtained to aid in the selection of the chapter topics, which cover the important theoretical and practical aspects of drug therapy in the elderly.

The many problems older citizens have with the use of medications are examined in a positive way, first by identifying them, then by discussing their significance, and finally by providing suggestions and guidelines for their proper management. It is hoped that this book will provide an understandable look at the subject for "nonmedical" gerontologists such as health care administrators, activity directors, physical therapists, social workers, and psychologists. The material presented will also be of interest to nurses and pharmacists who would like to learn more about why elderly patients use and misuse medications.

Acknowledgments

I would like to thank the following people for their assistance in the preparation of this book: Dr. Sharon Boston for her valuable comments and suggestions on the first draft; Janet Crooks for her assistance with the tedious task of locating and evaluating reference material; Sarah Allen, Donna Taylor, Rose Anne Stuempel, and Elaine Plaggert for their superb word processing skills; and Dean Arthur C. Glasser for his generosity during my sabbatical visit to the University of Cincinnati.

Chapter 1

Introduction

The study of gerontology and geriatrics is finally coming of age, as evidenced by the rapidly growing memberships of gerontological societies and organizations and by a number of excellent medical, nursing, and pharmacy journals that are either partially or entirely devoted to the study of aging.

In recent years it has been my pleasure to attend a number of national professional meetings of gerontologists, pharmacists, physicians, nurses, and others who work with the elderly. I have been amazed and pleased by the amount of enthusiasm that these professionals have for their work, and I am overwhelmed by the attendance figures that these meetings generate. In fact, one particular annual meeting is attended by several thousand gerontologists, health professionals, and senior citizens.

On a local scale, the same enthusiasm and devotion to gerontology exists, as evidenced by the formation of interdisciplinary gerontological societies along with community-oriented nursing home task forces and groups of professionals such as physical therapists, activity leaders, and nurse practitioners who gather for local and regional seminars to discuss the care of the elderly patient.

Another extremely significant development in the field of aging, which has gone largely unnoticed, is the formation of the geriatrics advisory panel of the United States Pharmacopeia (U.S.P.). Although the fame of the U.S.P. is not widespread, its influence is significant, since it is the one organization that sets the official standards of strength, quality, and purity of prescription and nonprescription medications used in the United States. The U.S.P. also produces a number of publications and references for the purpose of developing and establishing a common data base for drug information for both the consumer and for health professionals. It is hoped that this geriatric advisory panel, which first met in 1982, can help to identify and perhaps standardize certain drug-related considerations that are pertinent to the care of the elderly patient. This accomplishment would greatly benefit both the elderly patient and the caregiver by specifying precautions

1

and potential adverse drug reactions that are of greater significance in the elderly patient and by identifying the specific medications that should be given to the elderly in reduced dosages.

Although a great deal of interest in geriatrics exists among the professionals who work with the elderly, formal academic programs in the clinical aspects of geriatrics are still relatively uncommon in professional schools of medicine, nursing, and pharmacy. There are, however, a considerable number of excellent gerontology programs that are primarily designed to train workers in the social sciences.

One area of study that is particularly deficient in any of the gerontology programs in both the clinical and the social sciences is that of medication use and misuse. This deficiency is underscored by findings of a survey of pharmacy schools in the United States that revealed that fewer than one third of these schools had academic courses that could be considered to devote even a minimally sufficient amount of attention to the subject.

The attention given to this subject by social science-oriented gerontology programs is even more deficient. A nationwide review of gerontology programs in 1976 revealed that no program offered a ''Drugs and the Elderly'' course exclusively to nonpharmacists, such as social workers, health care administrators, and others who work with the elderly. In 1980 it was found that only one U.S. school of pharmacy offered such a course to nonpharmacy students enrolled in various programs in the area of gerontology or geriatrics. It was also found that 21 percent of the existing geriatric courses were open for enrollment to nonpharmacy students, who were, however, almost exclusively medical students. Even if most existing geriatric pharmacy courses were open to enrollment by students and professionals from other disciplines of the study of aging, most of these students would lack the background in physiology, pharmacokinetics, and other prerequisite fields to benefit from these courses.

The irony of the situation is that although the persons who work with the ''nonmedical'' aspects of the elderly significantly outnumber the clinicians and have more interactions with the elderly than do physicians, pharmacists, and nurses, their formal training does not usually provide them with the opportunity to learn about the profound effect that medications may have in the elderly individuals with whom they work.

Physical, psychological, and social changes occur with age, but since these changes occur gradually throughout life, it is impossible to say at what age they become significant. For some they occur earlier than others; however, since the precedent to define *elderly* as 65 years of age or older has already been established, I will adhere to that definition throughout this book. It is imperative that the reader appreciate the fact that not everyone over 65 years of age will have problems with medications and not everyone under age 65 will be problem free.

I do not believe that the subject of drug use and misuse by the elderly is inherently difficult to understand, but rather it seems that persons who are more familiar with the technical aspects of medication use, such as physicians and pharmacists, do not usually appreciate the fact that the ''nonexperts'' have a tremendous desire and need to be familiar with this material. In addition, when the ''experts'' do attempt to write or lecture on the subject they frequently use language that is full of technical terms, assuming that their audience has a basic knowledge of pharmacology. This situation has resulted, in my view, in a critical lack of reference material about medication use and misuse by the elderly that is understandable to the majority of persons who work with, or provide care for, the elderly.

Although a number of books on geriatric pharmacology are now available, they tend to be written for the reader who has extensive clinical experience and a sophisticated background in pharmacology, thus essentially limiting their audience to physicians, pharmacists, and some nurses. I frequently hear the complaint that these books are too technical to be easily understood, that the significance of the drug-related information presented is usually lost in a flurry of pharmacological terms and technical nomenclature, and that these books do not deal with the social or the practical considerations of the use and misuse of medications by the elderly.

Some of the chapters in this book, by the nature of their content, tend to be more technical than others. For example, in Chapter 6, in which considerations for decreased medication dosages in the elderly are discussed, it is necessary to review some of the important principles of the science of pharmacokinetics as they pertain to the age-related medication requirements in the elderly. Because pharmacokinetics is such a complex science, I am certain that some of the readers will find this discussion more complex than they would like; however, in order to truly understand the principles of altered medication dosage requirements in the elderly, it is imperative to at least be familiar with the general principles of pharmacokinetics.

This book is written with the understanding that although most of the readers will have had little or no formal training in terminology related to pharmacology and medication, they have an interest in, and a need for, information about the use and misuse of medications by the elderly. For example, most nursing home administrators do not know a great deal about the mechanisms behind drug interactions; however, they should be aware that serious drug interactions could occur in elderly patients residing in their facilities. They should also know that although elderly patients may indeed be at a significant risk of experiencing an adverse drug reaction, the staff of the facility can take the appropriate steps to decrease the chance of this occurrence.

The selection of topics for the chapters in the book was based on considerable input from persons who work with the elderly. To determine this information, my colleague Dr. Clara C. Pratt, director of the Oregon State University Program on

Gerontology, and I surveyed almost 500 persons who work with the elderly in various professional capacities, including nursing, nursing home administration, social work, counseling, and other areas. We asked these people what they wanted to know about the use and misuse of medications by the elderly and what they thought was important information for both themselves and their professional colleagues to understand. In addition to this information, I have included the observations of my experience working with the elderly and of my university teaching and my lecturing on the subject to various groups of health professionals and gerontologists. Consequently, I feel that the final choice of chapter topics provides valuable and interesting information that individuals will be able to apply to their work with the elderly.

By examining the table of contents it will be noticed that the chapters mostly concern aspects of medication use and misuse that could pertain to younger patients as well as the elderly. Although this observation is true, each chapter is written with a specific emphasis on the relationship of the material as it relates to the elderly person, rather than to the general population.

For example, in Chapter 7, Adverse Effects of Medications in the Elderly, the emphasis on the elderly is more apparent. Although basic introductory material describing adverse drug reactions is presented, most of the chapter deals directly with the occurrence of adverse drug reactions in the elderly, including their incidence and the reasons why adverse reactions occur more frequently in this age-group.

On the other hand, Chapter 5, Medication Education and the Elderly Patient, contains a greater amount of information that is pertinent to the entire population. Although most of the information in this chapter does not exclusively pertain to the elderly, there is no doubt that it is extremely important for elderly patients to be fully educated about the medications that they take.

My formal training has been as a pharmacist, and my professional experiences have included work in a number of community pharmacies, hospitals, nursing homes, and major medical centers, where I have had the frequent opportunity to observe many elderly patients who were being treated with medications. As a result of this experience, I will frequently mention the responsibilities of the pharmacist, as well as other health professionals, in the care of the elderly patient. My support of the pharmacist in this role stems from my belief that although pharmacists are probably underused as resource persons, they nonetheless are drug experts who can have a significant impact on the improvement of the care of the elderly patient.

I do realize that many persons believe that pharmacists are primarily interested in selling greeting cards, cosmetics, and other nonmedicinal paraphernalia, a nonprofessional image that has largely been the fault of the profession itself. However, an exciting and viable clinical role is developing for the pharmacist as a health professional who has a unique expertise and who is willing to share that

2

expertise with the other members of the health care team for the benefit of the patient.

The reader may notice that I have chosen not to include a chapter devoted to the abuse of alcohol by the elderly. This is not meant to deemphasize the importance of the problems of alcohol abuse by the elderly but rather because numerous texts and journal articles already discuss the subject far more eloquently and completely than I could ever hope to. I have, however, included reference to this potentially lethal drug in the respect that it may cause significant interactions with other drugs and may cause adverse effects of its own.

To lend a better perspective to the discussions in this book, and with the assumption that not every reader will be familiar with the generic names of medications but may be familiar with some of the brand names of medications that are more commonly used by the elderly, I have included in parentheses an example of a common brand name drug after each generic name is mentioned. My choice of brand name is based solely on my estimation of which brand name will be most familiar to the reader. I have no favorite drug companies, and I own no stock.

The term *medication* is frequently used throughout this book in preference to the word *drug* because I think that it is a more appropriate term to describe a medicine and because, to some, the word *drug* evokes connotations of evil and of drug abuse. *Drug* is still used occasionally, however, and unless specifically used in reference to drugs of abuse, it is simply meant to be synonymous with the term *medication*.

Chapter 2

Medication Consumption Patterns in the Elderly

The fact that the elderly take more medications than the young should not be judged as an indication of their irresponsibility. This pattern of increased consumption is influenced by many valid and invalid factors. Certainly patients' perceptions of their need for medication have a significant influence on their consumption of medications; however, many of these factors are external in nature, making it difficult to counter their influence. Some factors influencing these consumption patterns include the presence of disease, the individual's access to health care, the effect of commercial advertisement, and the advice or opinion of various health professionals or family members who could influence the individual's medication-taking behavior. In any case, an awareness of the multiplicity of interrelating factors influencing the consumption of medication is crucial to understanding the types and amounts of medications that the elderly take and their reasons for taking them.

FINANCIAL CONSIDERATIONS OF HEALTH CARE AND MEDICATION CONSUMPTION

As a group, the elderly are major consumers of the dollars spent on health care in the United States, accounting for approximately 30 percent of all health-related expenses. As these expenditures continue to increase from the estimated 1981 total of $251.4 billion (U.S. Government Printing Office, 1982, p. 299), it is likely that both the total amount and the percentage of that total that is devoted to the elderly will continue to increase.

Long-Term Care

The cost of nursing home care, which in 1981 amounted to $22 billion, represents a significant portion of the total amount spent for health care in the

United States (U.S. Government Printing Office, 1982, p. 300). Since approximately 90 percent of all nursing home patients are 65 years of age or older (U.S. Government Printing Office, 1982, p. 306), most of this figure represents an expense of care for the elderly.

Additionally, based on current trends, the present number of nursing home residents of approximately 1.3 million is predicted to increase to 1.95 million by the year 2000 and to 2.95 million by 2030 (Table 2-1), with a corresponding increase in expenditures (U.S. Health Care Financing Administration, 1981a, p. 13).

Hospital Care

Expenses for hospital care in the United States rose to an estimated $115.8 billion in 1981 (U.S. Government Printing Office, 1982, p. 300), and although these expenses were accrued by persons of all ages, much of this can be attributed to care of the elderly, who in 1979 accounted for 25 percent of the total number of hospital stays and approximately 40 percent of the total number of inpatient hospital days in short-stay hospitals in 1978 (U.S. Government Printing Office, 1982, pp. 304-305). This pattern is reflected by 1978 figures showing a discharge rate from short-stay hospitals of 184 per 1,000 population for all ages and a substantially higher number of 362 per 1,000 population for those individuals 65 years of age or older, increasing to 507 per 1,000 population for patients aged 85 and older (Office of Human Development Services, 1981, p. 41) (Table 2-2).

These figures indicate a substantially higher hospitalization rate among the elderly. It has also been determined that the median length of stay for patients older than 65 years old and discharged from short-stay hospitals is approximately 8 days, compared with 4 days for the general population (Office of Human Development Services, 1981, pp. 48-49), with the average duration of stay in patients aged 75 and older greater than 11 days (U.S. Government Printing Office, 1982, p. 305).

With the adjusted expenses of community hospitals in the United States amounting to an average of $245 per inpatient day in 1980 (American Hospital

---

Table 2-1 U.S. Nursing Home Population: Present and Projected

Year	Number of residents
1980	1.3 million
2000	1.95 million
2030	2.95 million

Source: Reprinted from *Long term care: Background and future directions* (Publication No. HCFA 81-20047) by the U.S. Health Care Financing Administration, Washington, D.C., 1981.

Table 2-2 Discharge Rate from Short-Stay Hospitals by Patient Age

Age	Discharges per 1,000 population
Total population	184
65 and older	362
85 and older	507

Source: Reprinted from *Need for long term care: Information and issues. A chartbook of the Federal Council on the Aging, 1981* (Publication No. OHDS 81-20704) by the Office of Human Development Services, 1981.

Association, 1981) and with patients' hospital bills frequently running much higher than that, it is obvious that hospitalization expenses for the elderly are considerable.

Physician Visits

Health care expenditures are also experienced by the elderly through an increase in their number of visits to physicians. Persons under the age of 65 have an average of 3.2 physician visits per year. This figure increases to 4.8 annual visits for individuals between the ages of 65 and 74 and to 5.1 visits for those who are 75 and older, with 80 percent of all persons aged 65 and older seeing a physician at least once a year (U.S. Government Printing Office, 1982, pp. 294, 306).

Medication Expenses

In 1981, expenses for prescription and nonprescription drugs and for durable medical equipment reached $21.5 billion (U.S. Government Printing Office, 1982, p. 301). Approximately 57 percent of this amount was for prescription drugs, 31 percent was for nonprescription drugs, and the remainder was for nondrug items (Gibson & Waldo, 1981). Although that total represents an increase over previous years, it amounts to 8.8 percent of the total U.S. health care expenditures, which is down from more than 12 percent in 1965 (U.S. Government Printing Office, 1982, p. 301). The elderly make up approximately 11.5 percent of the population of the United States (U.S. Government Printing Office, 1982, p. 2), but their use of medication accounts for 25 to 30 percent of the U.S. drug expenditures.

It is important to note that Medicare does not cover prescription or nonprescription medications purchased on an outpatient basis. This places a significant financial burden on the elderly patient, necessitating some elderly individuals to purchase their prescription drugs with personal funds. Approximately two thirds of the elderly's total expenditures for health services are paid by public expenditures (Gfroerer & Young, 1979; Shanas & Maddox, 1976), but only 25 percent of the elderly's prescription expenses were so reimbursed. In fact, almost 20 percent of the elderly's out-of-pocket (nonreimbursed) health expenditures are for medications (Lamy, 1980). Out-of-pocket prescription medication expenses per year increase with age and are consistently higher in women than in men (Lamy, 1980). As demonstrated in Table 2-3, 15.7 percent of persons aged 65 and older have annual expenses ranging from $100 to $249 compared with 3.9 percent of the general population having expenses in this range. Three and three-tenths percent of the elderly spend $250 or more, compared with 0.8 percent of the total population (Kasper, 1982).

With the average prescription cost in 1981 reported to be $8.63, a 12.7 percent increase over 1980 prices ("Top 200 Drugs," 1982), accompanied by the increased medication consumption patterns of the average elderly patient, it is easy to understand how prescription drug expenditures can become considerable. Although an out-of-pocket expense of $100 or $200 may not seem unduly high to a middle-aged employed individual, it may represent a large portion of the spendable income of elderly persons who are receiving a fixed income, perhaps consisting solely of their social security allowance.

If such individuals with limited financial resources are faced with a significant medication expenditure, they may be forced to decide whether to purchase their medications or to devote their resources toward rent, utilities, or food. This may result in the patients neglecting to have certain prescriptions filled, or it may alter the amount of medication that is taken. It has been estimated that three to six percent of prescriptions written by physicians are never obtained by the patient (Blackwell, 1972; Boyd, Covington, & Stanaszek, 1974). Although many reasons

---

Table 2-3 Out-of-Pocket Expenses for Prescribed Medicines: Percent Distribution of Persons with and without Prescribed Medicines by Intervals of Out-of-Pocket Expense

Age of patient	None	$1-49	$50-99	$100-249	$250 or more
Under 6	10.6	51.0	3.4	0.4	0.0
6 to 18	7.7	34.7	1.6	0.5	0.0
19 to 24	8.9	40.1	3.2	0.8	0.1
25 to 54	7.9	41.7	5.8	3.2	0.5
55 to 64	6.9	40.5	10.2	9.3	2.2
65 or older	6.6	34.7	14.8	15.7	3.3
Total population	8.0	39.8	5.7	3.9	0.8

Source: Reprinted from *Prescribed medicines: Use, expenditures, and source of payment* (Data Preview 9. National Health Care Expenditure Study, U.S. Department of Health and Human Services, Publication No. [PHS] 82-3320) by J.A. Kasper, 1982.

may exist for this behavior (see Chapter 4), undoubtedly some of this is due to the inability of the patient to afford the prescription drugs.

In an effort to economize on prescription expenses, elderly individuals may take their prescription medications less frequently than prescribed. Unfortunately these efforts to reduce prescription expenditures by neglecting to have prescriptions filled or by trying to ''stretch'' their prescriptions may have the opposite effect if this ill-advised behavior results in the need for further treatment or even in institutionalization.

Even though prescription costs are increasing, it should be pointed out that they are increasing more slowly than other health care expenditures. The 1980 consumer price index for prescription drugs was 155.8, compared with a 1967 base of 100, while the corresponding consumer price index for all medical care in 1980 was 267.2 (U.S. Department of Health and Human Services, 1981, p. 198).

PRESCRIPTION DRUG CONSUMPTION

Annual Prescription Acquisitions

The percentage of the adult population taking prescription medications increases with age and is the highest in persons 65 years of age and older. Data for 1977 demonstrating a steady age-related increase in the percentage of the non-institutionalized population with at least one prescription acquisition (with slightly over 75 percent of patients greater than age 65 taking at least one prescription medication) are shown in Table 2-4.

Additional 1977 data of elderly individuals who were enrolled in the Supplemental Medical Insurance (S.M.I.) option of the U.S. Medicare program indicate

Table 2-4 Use of Prescribed Medicines: Percent of Adults in the United States with Prescribed Medicines in 1977

Age in years	Percentage with at least one prescribed medicine
19 to 24	53.2
25 to 54	59.1
55 to 64	69.1
65 or older	75.2
Total population	58.2

Source: Reprinted from *Prescribed medicines: Use, expenditures, and source of payment* (Data Preview 9. National Health Care Expenditure Study, U.S. Department of Health and Human Services, Publication [PHS] 82-3320) by J.A. Kasper, 1982.

a similar but slightly higher figure of 81 percent of the enrolled population using at least one prescription medication (U.S. Health Care Financing Administration, 1981b).

Although the mean number of prescription medications (both new prescriptions and refills) obtained by noninstitutionalized persons in the United States in 1977 was 4.3, the mean number of prescription medications obtained annually by individuals 65 years of age and older was 10.7 for the entire noninstitutionalized elderly population, including the minority of those who took no prescription drugs, and 14.2 prescriptions per year among all of those elderly persons who had acquired at least one prescription drug (Table 2-5).

An even higher usage rate in the population enrolled in the S.M.I. is indicated in Table 2-6. In 1977, enrollees obtained an average of 17.9 prescriptions each, including both new and refill prescriptions. This rate of use reflects a gradual increase since 1967, when there were only 13.4 prescriptions per aged S.M.I. enrollee.

The data were further broken down to reveal that in 1977 elderly women in this population acquired 19.6 prescriptions, while their male counterparts acquired 15.3 prescriptions (U.S. Health Care Financing Administration, 1981b). The reasons for this greater use by women are most likely numerous, but they could partially be attributed to an increased incidence of certain medical problems, such as simple urinary tract infections, which commonly require one or more prescription drugs for their management.

These figures demonstrate that prescription use is the rule rather than the exception in the elderly patient. The majority of the elderly acquire at least one prescription medication per year, and many acquire a significantly greater number of new or refill prescriptions.

Table 2-5 Use of Prescribed Medicines: Mean Number of Prescribed Medicines per Noninstitutionalized Person and per Person with at Least One Prescribed Medicine, by Patient Age

Age in years	Prescriptions per person	Prescriptions per person with at least one prescribed medicine
19 to 24	2.6	4.9
25 to 54	4.2	7.0
55 to 64	8.2	11.9
65 or older	10.7	14.2
Total population	4.3	7.5

Source: Reprinted from *Prescribed medicines: Use, expenditures, and source of payment* (Data Preview 9. National Health Care Expenditure Study, U.S. Department of Health and Human Services, Publication No. [PHS] 82-3320) by J.A. Kasper, 1982.

Table 2-6 Average Number of Prescriptions per Aged Supplemental
Medical Insurance User

Year	Prescriptions per year
1967	13.4
1968	14.9
1969	16.1
1970	16.8
1971	16.0
1972	16.9
1973	16.7
1974	17.6
1975	17.3
1976	17.5
1977	17.9

Source: Reprinted from *Medicare: Use of Prescription Drugs by Aged Persons Enrolled for Supplemental Medical Insurance 1967-77* by U.S. Health Care Financing Administration, March 1981.

Number of Different Medications Consumed

The fact that an elderly individual may have ten or more prescription acquisitions per year does not mean that ten different medications are being used at any one time. Rather, this represents the number of prescriptions acquired, including refills of existing prescriptions. For example, a person with 15 prescription acquisitions may be taking only three different medications and getting each one refilled five times each year.

Another valuable way to look at prescription drug consumption is to determine the number of different medications that an elderly person is taking at any one time. This is especially important because the number of different types of drugs that a person takes has a direct bearing on the incidence of adverse drug reactions, drug interactions, poor compliance to prescribed therapy, and other drug-related problems, which tend to be more common in the elderly population.

Numerous studies have been performed to determine the number of different medications taken by the elderly at any one time. Unfortunately, the findings of such studies rarely agree, largely due to differences between studies, such as patient population, methodology and statistics, definitions, and duration of study.

It is evident that patients who are institutionalized, primarily in nursing homes, generally consume a greater amount of prescription medication than noninstitutionalized patients. Based on the combined results of a number of studies, it appears that the average nursing home resident is taking four to seven different prescription medications at any one time, although this number will tend to vary significantly, depending on a large number of modifying factors, which will be discussed later in this chapter. One confusing factor regarding the consumption of prescription medications within nursing homes and other institutions is that state law and facility policy frequently require that a prescription order be written for every medication that a patient is to take, even if the drug is traditionally considered to be a nonprescription drug. Thus, a patient taking milk of magnesia in a nursing home environment requires a prescription, although technically it is not a prescription drug. Although perhaps appearing unduly restrictive to some, this policy is highly beneficial because by preventing the excessive use of nonprescription medications, or the use of these drugs without the knowledge of the patient's physician, pharmacist, or nurse, serious problems such as medication toxicity and drug interactions can be averted.

Noninstitutionalized elderly patients take fewer prescription medications than those who are in institutions. Based on a summary of studies performed to determine the medication consumption patterns of this population subgroup, it appears that the average elderly outpatient uses two to four different prescription drugs at any one time.

These figures cover a rather broad range, yet it is important that one be familiar with them so that individuals who are taking excessive amounts of medications can be identified and the situation corrected. Although uncommon, a situation may arise in which an elderly patient may be taking 15, 20, or even more different medications concurrently. There is almost no possible justification for this type of excessive use, which has been called *polypharmacy* and is a direct threat to the patient's well-being. Polypharmacy, its causes, common features, and how it can be prevented, is discussed in detail later in this chapter.

NONPRESCRIPTION DRUG CONSUMPTION

Relatively little information is available concerning the percentage of non-institutionalized elderly individuals who routinely take nonprescription (over-the-counter) medications.

As is the case with prescription medications, nonprescription medications are also used frequently by the elderly, with estimates of the percentage of elderly individuals using nonprescription medications ranging up to 75 percent (Shipp & Saffles, 1979). In my observations, and as a result of my experience in speaking with elderly consumers of medication, I would estimate that this figure is probably accurate and may even be an underestimation. The overwhelming majority of elderly patients with whom I have spoken take nonprescription medications at least occasionally, and not infrequently I have observed elderly individuals who routinely use six, ten, or even more of these drugs.

The apparently common use of nonprescription drugs is supported by the fact that approximately one third of all expenditures for medications by the elderly is for nonprescription drugs (Gibson & Waldo, 1981, p. 10), making the amount spent on nonprescription drugs in the United States during 1981 approximately $7 billion! Since nonprescription medications are generally less expensive than prescription drugs it is obvious that a great number of these medications must be purchased to result in that considerable expenditure.

FACTORS INFLUENCING MEDICATION CONSUMPTION

A large number of factors may affect both the amount and types of medications that are used by the elderly. These factors may relate to the patient's health status, to a variety of socioeconomic reasons, or to the effect of other persons such as health professionals, friends, or family members. Some of these factors, such as health status, are inherent to the population and difficult to alter, yet some, such as attitudes toward the elderly, can be modified, if recognized.

Occurrence of Disease

Perhaps the single most influential factor affecting the consumption of medications by the elderly is the incidence of disease in this group. "Old age" must never be considered to be a disease in itself, but it is true that the incidence of chronic disease conditions does increase with age, with greater than 80 percent of older persons experiencing at least one such condition. The manifestations of disease-related conditions occurring in the elderly may range from minor to severe and may result in varying degrees of inconvenience or disability. These conditions may range from problems such as dry skin to those relating to serious diseases, such as arthritis, diabetes, congestive heart failure, stroke, and many others (Exhibit 2-1).

Accordingly, prescription medications, nonprescription medications, and/or nondrug items may be used to resolve or manage these chronic problems. Relatively minor chronic conditions such as the loss of teeth due to poor dentition may require an individual to use products such as denture cleansers and adhesives. Potentially more severe problems, such as congestive heart failure, may often require the use of potent prescription medications, such as digitalis or diuretics.

Many of these disease conditions may be managed by one or more prescription or nonprescription medications and as so often happens in the elderly, multiple disease states may occur concurrently, necessitating the use of numerous medications, which understandably will be related to the types of conditions for which they are being used.

The types of both prescription and nonprescription medications taken by the elderly relate to the types of diseases that occur most commonly in older persons, as discussed earlier in this chapter. The major characteristics of these disease states

Exhibit 2-1 Selected Chronic Health-Related Conditions in the Elderly

Arthritis
Diabetes mellitus
Heart conditions
Visual impairments
Hearing disorders
Stroke
Cancer
Dental diseases
Diseases of the skin
Alcoholism
Nutritional disorders
Osteoporosis (softening of the bones)
Atherosclerosis (hardening of the arteries)
Gastrointestinal disorders
Urinary tract disorders
Reproductive system disorders

are that they tend to be chronic and are frequently manageable by one or more medications. A brief discussion of some selected disease states that occur in the elderly follows, along with a synopsis of the medications that may routinely be used in their management.

Congestive Heart Failure

Congestive heart failure (CHF) occurs relatively commonly in the elderly. Like most diseases, its degree of severity may range from mild to severe.

In CHF the force of contraction of the heart decreases. This may result from a number of different causes, including insufficient oxygen supply to the heart; improper function of one or more heart valves as a result of their calcification or degeneration; and calcification of the aorta, the main vessel through which blood leaves the heart. As a result of its weakened beat, the heart pumps blood less efficiently. Blood may "back up" into the vessels that carry it from the right side to the left side of the heart. Since these vessels pass through the lungs, this "back up" may result in fluid accumulation, or congestion, in the lungs.

The accumulation of fluid may cause wheezing and coughing and may make it difficult for the individual to breathe. It may also cause edema (swelling) of the ankles, although ankle edema may occur in the elderly as a result of a number of causes unrelated to CHF. The poor circulation of blood that results from the inefficient pumping of the heart may cause other symptoms, such as weakness and confusion, and it is possible that CHF may be mistakenly diagnosed as another condition, such as pneumonia.

The main therapeutic objectives of the management of CHF are to strengthen the contractility of the heart and to eliminate excess fluid from the body. Cardiac contractility, or the force of the contractions of the heart, may be strengthened by using one of the digitalis compounds, which include digitalis leaf, digoxin (Lanoxin®), and digitoxin (Crystodigin®). Diuretics, sometimes referred to by the lay term *water pills,* are frequently used to eliminate excess body fluids that accumulate as a result of the inefficiency of the cardiac muscle. Two main types of diuretics may be used: (1) the potassium-sparing diuretics, which tend to eliminate excess fluid without significant loss of potassium from the body, and (2) the potassium-wasting diuretics, which are usually very effective but occasionally result in the excessive loss of potassium from the body.

Commonly used diuretics include the potassium-sparing types such as spironolactone (Aldactone®) and triamterene (Dyrenium®) and the potassium-wasting types such as hydrochlorothiazide (HydroDIURIL®) or furosemide (Lasix®).

Many patients who take potassium-wasting diuretics may require correction of this potassium loss through the use of orally administered potassium salts. When the patient is found to be deficient in potassium, supplemental potassium may be provided to the patient as potassium chloride in liquid (Kaochlor®), tablet (Slow-K®), effervescent tablet (Klorvess®), or powder (K-Lor®) form.

Arthritis

Arthritis is a collective term that refers to a wide spectrum of disease processes involving the connective tissues of the body, primarily the cartilage, tendons, and ligaments. A variety of aches and pains ranging from mildly uncomfortable to severe may result from these conditions. Although the causes and clinical features of the various arthritic diseases can be extremely complex, two of the more commonly occurring types, rheumatoid arthritis and osteoarthritis, will be discussed here.

Rheumatoid arthritis may develop in elderly individuals who have not had the disease before; however, when seen in the elderly, it is usually a problem that began earlier in their life, with the effects of the disease process becoming more severe and more noticeable in old age. Rheumatoid arthritis is a complex autoimmune process in which the defense system of the body, which is designed to protect against infection and other problems, is stimulated by a variety of causes to attack and destroy its own tissue. The disease may cause the all too familiar destruction and severe deformity of the joints of the fingers and other joints of the body.

Osteoarthritis differs from rheumatoid arthritis in that it is the result of wear and tear and repeated injury. The predominant feature of osteoarthritis is the destruction and loss of cartilage that covers and protects the surfaces of bones where they have contact with other bones. This condition occurs most commonly in the larger "weight bearing" joints such as the knee, ankle, hip, and shoulder. With the destruction or loss of the protective cartilage, the function of the joint may be affected and considerable pain and discomfort may result.

The management of arthritis is based on the reduction of inflammation and on the treatment of pain and may vary considerably, depending on the type of arthritis and its severity. Rheumatoid arthritis may require the chronic ingestion of aspirin. Frequently 10 to 16 tablets may be taken during a 24-hour period. Severe cases may even require the use of corticosteroid drugs, such as prednisone (Deltasone®) or hydrocortisone. Many patients, especially those with osteoarthritis, may use another type of medication known as nonsteroidal antiinflammatory agents (noncortisone drugs). Examples of these nonsteroidal drugs include indomethacin (Indocin®), ibuprofen (Motrin®), and piroxicam (Feldene®).

Diabetes

Diabetes mellitus is a disorder of sugar metabolism that prevents the body from properly regulating the amount of sugar in the blood. Diabetes may lead to serious physiological effects, including kidney failure, heart attack, and blindness. This disease results from a decrease or cessation of insulin production by the pancreas. Since insulin is instrumental in regulating sugar metabolism, a deficiency of insulin will allow the concentration of sugar in the blood to rise above the normal level.

The most common form of diabetes that occurs in the older adult is known as type II or age-onset diabetes. This form of the disease is generally easier to control than juvenile diabetes, which is the type of diabetes that occurs in children. The control of juvenile diabetes usually requires injections of insulin, while adult-onset diabetes rarely requires insulin therapy and may often be managed by proper diet alone. A class of prescription medications, known as oral hypoglycemics, may be used to effectively control age-onset diabetes. It is important to understand that these drugs are not the same as insulin but in fact stimulate the pancreas to produce insulin. Examples of oral hypoglycemic medications that may be used by elderly diabetics include tolbutamide (Orinase®) and chlorpropamide (Diabinese®).

The occurrence of complications resulting from diabetes relates to the duration that the person has had the disease. Although age-onset diabetes may be no more than a minor inconvenience in some individuals, others may experience serious complications, such as skin disorders, foot ulcers, nerve damage, and loss of vision.

High Blood Pressure

High blood pressure, also known as hypertension, may occur in all age groups, but it is especially significant in the elderly for two reasons. First, it may occur in elderly individuals and therefore be the reason that they must take a number of different prescription medications, and, second, elderly individuals may be suffering from some of the serious complications that have resulted from high blood pressure that developed when they were younger.

These complications, especially kidney failure, stroke, heart attack, and loss of vision, are likely to occur if a patient's high blood pressure is left untreated, and they may be the cause of severe physical limitations in some elderly persons.

The most common form of high blood pressure is known as *essential hypertension,* which means that its actual cause is unknown. However, treatment with a low salt diet, exercise, reduction of stress, and drugs is usually successful to bring the patient's blood pressure down to normal levels, thus preventing most of the complications of this disease. Numerous types of medications can be used to control high blood pressure, including diuretics such as hydrochlorothiazide (HydroDIURIL®) or furosemide (Lasix®), which will lower blood pressure both by eliminating excess body fluids and by dilating blood vessels. Some of the many other medications that may be used to control high blood pressure include propranolol (Inderal®), methyldopa (Aldomet®), and clonidine (Catapres®).

Stroke

A stroke, which is more properly known as a cerebrovascular accident (CVA), is a major dysfunction of the central nervous system resulting from a decrease in the blood supply to a certain area or areas of the brain. A stroke may cause a significant physical deficit such as weakness, or it may result in inability to use the limbs of one side of the body. The patient may also be unable to speak, or there may be facial weakness or drooping. Coma and even death may result.

Because of the nerve pathways that exist in the brain, the deficits caused by a stroke occur on the side of the body that is opposite the side of the body where the stroke occurred. For example, if a person suffered a stroke in the left half of their brain, the physical deficits that result will occur on the right side of the body.

The causes of a stroke may be numerous but usually there is a sudden occlusion of a blood vessel that supplies blood to the brain. This occlusion could be caused by a small piece of fatty "plaque" in a person with hardening of the arteries, or it could be caused by a small aggregation of platelets formed on a defective heart valve, which when broken off follows the bloodstream to the brain.

Once a stroke has occurred there is no effective drug therapy to resolve it; however, proper medication management of certain diseases that predispose the patient to the occurrence of stroke, such as high blood pressure and diabetes, may decrease the chances of the occurrence of a stroke. Various medications may be used in stroke patients to manage other conditions that may make recovery from stroke more difficult. These conditions include anemia, heart attack, and thyroid disease.

Evidence exists that aspirin, used alone or in conjunction with dipyridamole (Persantine®), may reduce the chance of developing a stroke. This type of therapy may be most effective in preventing strokes that are caused by clumps of platelets, since these medications decrease the "stickiness" of platelets, making them less likely to clump together. In fact, I know of some physicians who take one aspirin tablet every day with the belief that it may decrease their chances of experiencing a stroke, although the actual effectiveness of this practice has yet to be conclusively proven.

Glaucoma

Glaucoma is characterized by an increased pressure within the eyeball that is caused by a restriction in the normal flow of the aqueous humor from within the eye outward to the general circulation. This pressure buildup results in damage to the optic nerve and eventual blindness if not treated. Glaucoma can usually be successfully treated with the use of eye drops of pilocarpine (Pilocar®) or timolol (Timoptic®).

The preceding examples are not provided to present a detailed summary of the major disease states occurring in the elderly but rather are meant to underscore the fact that the concurrent presence of two or three of these or other disease states in one patient may appropriately necessitate the use of four or five different medications or more (Table 2-7)!

In examining the prescription and nonprescription medications that are most commonly used by the elderly, an obvious relationship between the types of drugs used and the disease states and health-related conditions that commonly occur in the elderly is seen. These medications are primarily those used for chronic conditions and may be used continuously for many years (Table 2-8). The non-prescription medications used most commonly by the elderly include laxatives, antacids, analgesics, vitamins, and skin preparations (Table 2-9).

The Influence of Health Professionals

The amount and types of medications taken by the elderly may be influenced significantly by health professionals, especially physicians, pharmacists, and nurses.

Physicians

As the primary prescribers of medication, physicians have an obvious influence on what prescription drugs their patients will be taking. It is obvious to almost anyone who has worked in any aspect of health care that individual prescribing habits vary tremendously among physicians. Some physicians prescribe freely,

Table 2-7 Selected Disease Conditions Occurring in the Elderly and Selected Medications Commonly Used in Their Management

	Medications Used	
Disease condition	*Generic name*	*Brand name*
Congestive heart failure	Digoxin	Lanoxin®
	Digitoxin	Crystodigin®
	Spironolactone	Aldactone®
	Triamterene	Dyrenium®
	Hydrochlorothiazide	HydroDIURIL®
	Furosemide	Lasix®
Arthritis	Aspirin	
	Indomethacin	Indocin®
	Ibuprofen	Motrin®
	Prednisone	Deltasone®
Diabetes	Insulin	
	Tolbutamide	Orinase®
	Chlorpropamide	Diabinese®
High blood pressure	Hydrochlorothiazide	HydroDIURIL®
	Furosemide	Lasix®
	Propranolol	Inderal®
	Methyldopa	Aldomet®
	Clonidine	Catapres®
Glaucoma	Pilocarpine	Pilocar®
	Timolol	Timoptic®

without apparent hesitation, whenever a patient experiences a new complaint or symptom, while other physicians give considerable consideration to alternatives to drug therapy, such as diet and exercise, before prescribing medications, and even then they prescribe the fewest number of medications possible at the lowest effective dosage. The existence of this apparent dichotomy of practice does not necessarily indicate that physicians who prescribe medications more heavily are irresponsible. What it does reflect, however, is that there are many factors, both external and internal, that influence the prescribing habits of physicians.

For example, the education and formal training of some physicians may have stressed extreme prudence when prescribing medications, therefore establishing conservative prescribing patterns, which are incorporated into their practices following the completion of their formal training. After entering practice, physicians may be influenced to alter their prescribing habits as a result of subtle or overt pressure from their professional peers. Thus, when a physician who would be considered to be a relatively "heavy prescriber" of medication enters a group

Table 2-8 Medications Commonly Prescribed for the Elderly, with Generic Name, Brand Name Example, and Common Reasons for Their Use

Medication		
Generic Name	Brand Name	Condition(s) for which commonly used*
Belladonna alkaloids	Donnatal®	Gastro-intestinal complaints
Chlorthalidone	Hygroton®	Congestive heart failure, high blood pressure
Diazepam	Valium®	Anxiety, restlessness
Digoxin	Lanoxin®	Congestive heart failure, cardiac arrhythmias
Flurazepam	Dalmane®	Insomnia
Furosemide	Lasix®	Congestive heart failure, high blood pressure
Hydrochlorothiazide	HydroDIURIL®	Congestive heart failure, high blood pressure
Ibuprofen	Motrin®	Arthritis
Methyldopa	Aldomet®	High blood pressure
Potassium Chloride	Slow-K®	Used with diuretics for potassium replacement
Propranolol	Inderal®	High blood pressure, angina
Reserpine	Serpasil®	High blood pressure
Sulindac	Clinoral®	Arthritis
Theophylline	Theo-Dur®	Lung diseases
Triamterine	Dyrenium®	Congestive heart failure, high blood pressure

*Some medications listed may have multiple uses, some of which may not be listed.

Table 2-9 Selected Categories of Nonprescription Medications Commonly Used by the Elderly, with Examples

Category	Example
Analgesics	Aspirin
	Acetaminophen (Tylenol®)
Laxatives	Milk of magnesia
	Phenolphthalein (Ex-Lax®)
Antacids	Magnesium-aluminum hydroxide (Maalox®)
	Magnesium-aluminum hydroxide-simethicone (Mylanta®)
Skin preparations	Moisturizing cream (Lubriderm®, Keri®)
Cold medicine	Chlorpheniramine (Chlor-Trimeton®)
Vitamins	

practice with colleagues who prescribe more prudently, his or her prescribing patterns may be modified by peer influence.

Commercial advertising represents another factor that may influence the prescribing habits of physicians. Nonprescription medications are commonly advertised on television, in newspapers, in magazines, and on the radio, but prescription drug advertising is commonly found in many different professional medical, pharmacy, and nursing journals, in newsletters, and in other publications. Although nonprescription drug advertising often seems to be designed to convince viewers of their need for a particular product with the aid of flashy logos or catchy phrases, the advertising for prescription drugs is somewhat different. Ideally, prescription drug advertising should serve the purpose of educating health professionals to the availability and important clinical considerations of prescription drug products. These advertisements certainly do provide some degree of education in areas such as indications (reasons for use), toxicity, and dosage; however, by its very nature advertising is designed to sell a product, and specifically in the case of prescription drug advertising it is designed to convince the prescriber that a particular brand or type of medication has advantages over its competitors.

There is evidence to indicate that the advertising and promotion of prescription medications is at least somewhat successful in its goal, because pharmaceutical companies devote significant amounts of money for this purpose. In 1981, pharmaceutical companies (Rogers, 1982) spent over $215 million for drug advertising in professional journals. It is uncertain exactly how much of an effect this advertising has on prescribing habits; however, it is certain to have some effect, and it is important that physicians not be unfairly influenced or misled by these promotional efforts but rather that they use the information that is provided to determine a rational prescription regimen for each patient.

Do Physicians Overprescribe on Purpose? Contrary to the belief of some health professionals and lay persons with whom I have spoken, I do not perceive that most physicians are colluding purposefully to overmedicate the elderly population. I have observed that many physicians, in general, are aware of the problems that overmedication can create. In discussions that I have had with physicians concerning the issue of overprescribing to elderly patients, the physicians frequently raise the point that elderly individuals often exert a significant amount of pressure on them to prescribe a medication that the patients themselves desire. In this day of increased availability of medication information, numerous patients understand medications well enough to request a prescription for a specific medication and perhaps even a specific dosage. I believe that this type of situation presents the prescriber with a significant problem that is not widely appreciated by the public. The physician must handle individuals who have unreasonable requests for medication with tact and diplomacy, because meeting unreasonable demands for prescription medication would be inexcusable; however, to discount completely the patient's request by failing to make an effort to understand such a request or why the patient believes that such a medication is needed may seriously damage the prescriber-patient relationship.

One component of this relationship involves the dynamics of prescription writing, which are both interesting and complex. Muller (1972) describes these dynamics in the following statement:

> Prescribing is, theoretically at least, a means of terminating the interview in a fashion that satisfies both doctor and patient. . . . The prescription is a signal for the approaching end of the encounter, it both summarizes and carries forward the relationship, it is an expression of concern, and it deals with interests of both parties in a manner perceived as equitable. (p. 490)

Some patients may perceive that the prescription is the fulfillment of the unwritten "contract" between themselves and their physicians. Also, some patients may feel that if the physician does not prescribe a medication they are not actually doing anything for the patient, owing to lack of concern or because the patient's problem is "untreatable."

It may be difficult for some elderly patients, especially those who have numerous somatic complaints and who have a great preoccupation with their self-perceived declining health, to accept a pat on the shoulder by the physician, saying "there is really nothing major that is wrong with you so I am not going to give you any medications this time."

Perceptions and Understanding of the Elderly Patient. Another factor that may influence the prescription practices of physicians is their attitude toward the elderly. Sufficient evidence exists to indicate that the paucity of the study of geriatrics in medical school curricula creates a significant deficit in the physician's understanding of the unique aspects of the elderly patient. One study has indicated that 34,000 to 53,000 geriatric-trained physicians will be needed in the United States by the year 2010; however, at present only about 600 physicians in the United States describe themselves as having an expertise in the field of geriatrics (U.S. Government Printing Office, 1982, pp. 339-340). If physicians do not develop an appreciation for the unique medication-related aspects of the elderly patient either through their formal training or postgraduate education, the likelihood of improper prescribing will remain. For example, if physicians are not fully aware of the fact that elderly patients may be more sensitive to both the therapeutic and toxic effect of medications, improper dosages may be prescribed and toxicity may result. It is also extremely important for physicians to understand that old age is not by itself an incurable disease and that many of the chronic disease-related complaints and problems that occur in the elderly are amenable to appropriate drug therapy and should not be interpreted as an acceptable and incurable facet of aging.

Pharmacists

Elderly individuals frequently rely on their pharmacist for many of their routine health care needs, such as information on the expected side effects or toxicities of prescription and nonprescription medications and advice on health care appliances and drug-related items. As the patient's primary nonprescription drug advisor, the pharmacist may also serve a triage function when contacted by an elderly patient for advice concerning the need for the use of a nonprescription medication. In this instance the pharmacist can determine whether patients should attempt to manage the particular medical problem themselves or if they should be referred to a physician.

Since many elderly patients hold the advice of the pharmacist in high regard, it is important that pharmacists make a sincere effort to determine the reason why the patient is considering the use of a nonprescription medication and what the patient hopes to gain from this therapy. The recommendations of the pharmacist should be sincere and not influenced by the thought of commercial gain, that is, the pharmacist should not use this opportunity to make a "quick sale" by recommending that the elderly patient use nonprescription medications that are not truly indicated.

The influence of the pharmacist may also be reflected by the use of prescription medications by the elderly. The pharmacist can encourage the use of appropriate medications by advising patients to take their medications as prescribed and by discouraging the use of unnecessary medications, perhaps by reassuring elderly patients that medications are good only when used for the appropriate conditions and may not always be the best option.

Pharmacists' personal perceptions of the value of medications and the need for their use also may have a significant effect on whether they recommend that a patient rely on drug therapy in an attempt to manage a health-related problem or whether they would recommend nondrug therapy. For example, a patient complaining of constipation could be given a stool softener and a stimulant laxative or could be told to consume a greater amount of vegetables or bran and perhaps get more exercise.

Pharmacists' perceptions of both the aging process and the elderly patient may also influence the recommendations that they provide regarding patients' use of medications. A pharmacist who dreads the aging process, perhaps perceiving it as a generalized debilitation characterized by the degeneration of body systems and the presence of multiple symptomatology, might tend to be more prone to recommend the use of medications, whereas a pharmacist who views the aging process as an acceptable and natural part of the life cycle may be more concerned with helping elderly patients improve the quality of their lives through nondrug means, such as improved nutrition, exercise, and companionship. The pharmacist should also realize that any recommendation for additional drug therapy in their elderly patients may result in drug-related problems such as adverse drug reactions or drug interactions that may cause the patient some discomfort or perhaps even require the use of additional medications.

Nurses

Nursing personnel may also significantly influence the amount of medications that an elderly person may take, especially with medications that are ordered on an "as needed" (p.r.n.) basis (Aycock, 1981; Howard, Strong, & Strong, 1977; Miller, 1982). All p.r.n. medication orders should specify the drug to be given, the route of administration, the dose, the frequency of administration, and the reason(s) for administration. Some p.r.n. orders are very explicit and assessable on objective criteria, such as an order for aspirin, 325 mg by mouth every four hours, for a temperature greater than 102°F. Since temperature can be accurately and objectively measured there is little question what this order means. Some p.r.n. orders may be more difficult to assess, such as an order for morphine sulfate, 2 to 4 mg I.M. (intramuscular) p.r.n. pain. Since a patient's pain cannot be quantitatively measured, a subjective evaluation must be used in the decision to give the morphine. This decision is usually based on both the patient's description of the pain that they are experiencing and on the nurse's interpretation of the patient's pain. Since the tolerance to pain can be extremely variable among individuals, it may understandably have an effect on the administration of medications in this type of situation. For example, one nurse responsible for administering the morphine to this patient may have a low tolerance for pain, sympathizing with the patient who is experiencing the pain and administering the morphine at the maximum dosage as frequently as possible; another nurse who happens to have a high tolerance for pain may perceive that the patient is a "complainer" who is exaggerating the need for pain medication and consequently may give the patient smaller morphine doses at less frequent intervals.

The importance of the proper interpretation of p.r.n. orders is underscored by a joke that states "when a drug is ordered p.r.n. anxiety, it is meant for the patient's anxiety, not the nurse's."

All p.r.n. orders provide a considerable degree of flexibility, which may be necessary, especially in institutional settings such as long-term care facilities. However, this flexibility may also be abused. One example of this type of situation would be in a nursing home where the majority of patients have existing orders for p.r.n. sleep medications, such as chloral hydrate (Noctec®), 500 mg p.r.n. sleep. I do not dispute the need for the prescription of a sleep-inducing agent for certain patients, but facilities where all or most of the patients with existing orders for sleep medications receive those medications routinely with no real effort to assess the need for them are occasionally seen. In this example, the nurse who is administering the medications may have decided that every patient with an existing order for sleep-inducing medications should receive them at 8 P.M. Perhaps a more appropriate approach to the situation might be a more specific p.r.n. order, such as "Chloral hydrate, 500 mg by mouth. Administer at patient's request only, and do not administer before 10 P.M." Another approach could be the development of a nursing policy that prohibits the routine anticipation that patients will not be able to sleep properly, rather than waiting to see if they cannot get to sleep by themselves.

Nurses may also have a significant impact on the medications that an elderly patient is taking by the suggestions provided to the patient's physicians. On numerous occasions I have seen nurses in long-term care facilities contact a patient's physician, notifying him or her of the patient's condition and providing a suggestion for the addition of a particular medication to the patient's medication regimen. I have been impressed at the frequency at which physicians accept this type of suggestion and think that it reflects the physician's respect for the nurses' opinion and evaluation; however, I think it appropriate to remind nurses that their therapeutic suggestions may have major consequences to the patient's condition, especially if those recommendations are inappropriate.

From this example and others it can be shown that nurses may have a significant effect on the medications that their elderly patients may take, thus emphasizing the importance that nurses understand the problems and principles of drug therapy in the elderly.

The Influence of the Patient

In addition to the influence of health professionals, the medication consumption patterns of the elderly may also be strongly influenced by the individual's own attitudes and personal perceptions of the need for and importance of medication.

Obviously the patients' perceptions of their own health status and medication needs have a profound effect on their consumption of medication. Some patients tend to be very concerned with the many somatic complaints that they and other elderly individuals may experience, such as muscle pain, arthritis pain, constipation, gastrointestinal upset, skin problems, and insomnia. Some patients may devote too much concern to these complaints and may consequently request numerous unnecessary prescription medications from their physicians, or they may purchase excessive amounts of nonprescription medications in an attempt to self-medicate these problems.

I have seen many examples of this type of personality. Medication-dependent persons may perceive themselves to be sicker than they actually are. They may request medications from their physicians or pharmacists and sometimes seem to languish in the attention that they get while playing the "sick role." Some of these patients seem to think that they can titrate their illnesses with the external aid of medications.

It may be difficult to convince these patients that they may be taking too much medication. I have seen such individuals enter the hospital or nursing home with a shoe box or shopping bag full of the various prescription and nonprescription medications that they have brought from home.

Occasionally, patients may manipulate prescribers in order to obtain the medications that they desire, perhaps by visiting numerous physicians without the knowledge of other physicians or by visiting multiple pharmacies in an effort to conceal blatantly abusive medication consumption.

I have observed an elderly male patient who actually lied about his symptoms in order to be admitted to a major medical center to get specific prescription medications that his family physician would no longer prescribe for him. I believe that this is an extreme example of manipulative behavior and medication abuse, and I do not mean to imply that incidents of this magnitude occur commonly.

In contrast, there are patients who perceive themselves as basically healthy in spite of numerous physical ailments. They tend to avoid the use of medications as the first treatment alternative and may in fact have a healthy respect for the potential toxic effects of medications. I have frequently encountered this type of patient when performing medication histories in patients who were recently admitted to hospitals. When asked if he or she takes any medications the patient may respond by saying, "No, I try to stay away from all kinds of pills unless I really need them."

Although prescription medication is traditionally obtained through formal processes in the health care system, occasionally friends may offer their leftover prescription medications to another. This practice is both unwise and dangerous and is frequently based on the assumption that "if it worked for me, it may work for you, too!" Patients should be discouraged from sharing prescription medications with those for whom it was not intended, owing to the possibility of drug interactions, aggravation of disease states that may exist in one individual but not the other, drug allergies, and many other reasons.

If elderly patients learn of a medication that they think may help them, it is better that they first check with their physician to discuss the matter, rather than borrowing the drug from a friend and trying it without the knowledge of their physician or pharmacist.

The Influence of Family Members

Family members may also have an effect on a person's consumption of medication. Ideally the spouse, and other family members who may or may not be living in the same household as the patient, should discourage the excessive or improper medication practices of the patient. However, this may not always be possible. Sometimes the spouse or family member may intervene in the relationship between the patient and their physician. I have seen this occur in instances in which the elderly patient is suffering from a chronic illness such as osteoporosis, which is a disease characterized by a softening of the bones. In spite of the fact that there is no clearly effective therapy for this sometimes debilitating disease, family members in a sincere effort to aid the patient might be tempted to persuade the physician to "try something," rather than just to let the patient suffer.

Socioeconomic Factors

The medication consumption patterns of the elderly may also be affected by various socioeconomic factors, including lack of access to health care, the health care environment, method of reimbursement, and others.

Access to Health Care

The medication consumption patterns of some elderly persons may be influenced by their access to health care. For example, individuals with considerable physical problems that limit their mobility may find it difficult to make routine physician visits. This could be especially limiting to the patient if adequate home health care services were not available, which is frequently the case. Lack of transportation could also be a problem, especially if the patients live a great distance from the nearest physician or pharmacy. These and other factors limiting the patients' mobility may decrease their access to their physician or pharmacist, resulting in a decrease in the number of prescriptions that are written for them and a decrease in the use of prescription or nonprescription drugs.

Increased Physician Visits

As mentioned earlier in this chapter, the average number of annual physician visits increases with age. Persons under 65 years of age are responsible for 3.2 annual visits, with this figure increasing to 4.8 visits for persons aged 65 to 74 and to 5.1 for those aged 75 and above.

Since 59 percent of physician visits result in a prescription being written (Gibson & Waldo, 1981), it could be reasoned that the more physician visits that a person has, the greater the chance that a prescription will be written.

This may be especially true where the increased visits of an elderly individual are the result of visits to different physicians rather than repeat visits to the same physician. By visiting a variety of physicians with different schools of thought and different specialties, the situation may arise that one physician may find it necessary to prescribe medications to treat the unwanted or toxic effects of a medication that was prescribed by another physician, or one physician may believe that a particular medication is necessary whereas another may disagree.

Commercial Advertising

Commercial advertising directed toward the consumer is another factor that may influence the medication consumption patterns of the elderly. Nonprescription medications are heavily advertised in the public media, using various techniques such as the endorsement of a respected or well-liked actor to instill trust in a particular product and to encourage its use. Advertisements may also be slightly misleading and therefore may confuse the elderly consumer. One example of a misleading advertisement is that for an "extra strength" nonprescription pain reliever that claims to be better than plain aspirin but somehow fails to mention that its own main active ingredient is in fact aspirin. Responsible commercial advertising can serve the purpose of educating the elderly consumer to the availability of nonprescription medications; however, elderly individuals should make an effort, perhaps by speaking with a pharmacist, to find out more about a particular product that they are taking and should not allow themselves to be convinced by a friendly face, or misleading commercial, that they need a medication.

Method of Reimbursement

An interesting relationship between the consumption of medications in nursing homes and the method of reimbursement was discovered in a seven-year nursing home study (Strandberg, 1980), which revealed that patients who were supported by third-party payment consumed a significantly greater amount of medication than patients in the same facilities who were liable for their own financial responsibilities (see Table 2-10). Although this relationship needs to be explored further, it is possible to speculate on some of the reasons for this pattern of consumption. One possibility may be that medical, pharmacy, and nursing staff might be more willing to accept a higher medication utilization rate in patients "who aren't paying for it anyway." Another reason for this disparity between "private" patients (those who are responsible for paying their own expenses) and "public" patients (those on Medicaid or welfare) may be that "private" patients are more likely to decline the use of a medication because of its cost or may be more prone to questioning the necessity of additional or expensive medications. In any case it is curious and disturbing that the type of reimbursement system would have a significant impact on the use of medications in two apparently otherwise similar groups of patients.

Health Care Environment

The health care environment of patients may also affect their medication consumption patterns. Patients in long-term care facilities tend to take more medications than patients who live at home; however, this difference may be because institutionalized patients are sicker and simply require more complex drug therapies.

Table 2-10 Medication Consumption and Average Monthly Medication Bill by Year in Three Nursing Homes with Comprehensive Pharmaceutical Services

Year	Mean number of prescription drugs	Mean monthly bill (dollars) Private	Welfare	All patients
1970	4.48	27.79	37.87	31.15
1971	3.86	26.61	33.71	29.61
1972	3.67	24.22	37.64	29.22
1973	3.55	22.28	35.97	27.23
1974	2.87	14.72	31.76	20.62
1975	2.70	16.68	28.67	20.28
1976	3.22	27.49	45.05	32.04
1977	2.57	23.09	26.42	23.68

Source: Adapted from *Effect of Comprehensive Pharmaceutical Services on Drug Use in Long Term Care Facilities* by L.R. Strandberg, G.W. Dawson, D. Mathieson, J. Rawlings, and B.G. Clark in *American Journal of Hospital Pharmacy,* Vol. 37, No. 1, pp. 92-94, 1980, with permission of the American Society of Hospital Pharmacists, Washington, D.C., © 1982.

Part of the observed differences in consumption between nursing home patients and individuals living at home is certainly because many patients who are ill enough to be institutionalized have disease-related problems that warrant the use of a greater number of medications than those for whom institutionalization was unnecessary, although a portion of this increased consumption could be because institutional care by itself may be a contributing factor to increased and sometimes unnecessary medication use. For example, institutionalized patients who may spend a considerable amount of time in bed, or involved with other sedentary behaviors, may find it necessary to take stool softeners or bowel evacuants to counter the constipation that frequently results from this decrease in activity. There may also be a tendency to medicate institutionalized patients for sleep when they do not follow the facility's accepted sleep routines, therefore upsetting the smooth operation of the facility by disturbing other residents or staff, as opposed to patients who live at home and who may be used to reading or watching television at 2 A.M.

The health care environment of patients can also have a significant effect on their medication consumption as a result of the professional services that are provided to the patients in that environment. This can best be demonstrated by describing the effect of two very different pharmaceutical services on separate nursing homes.

The first example is shown in a group of three nursing homes with both skilled and intermediate care beds. Under the supervision of a consultant pharmacist, a program of comprehensive pharmaceutical services was adopted in 1970. Services included routine medication stop-order policies, 24-hour unit-dose drug distribution, review of the patients' charts by the pharmacist, the provision of drug information to the staff, team meetings with nurses and other facility staff members, and additional services.

It was found that over a 7-year period between the initiation of these services in 1970 and a detailed evaluation of their impact in 1977, this comprehensive system resulted in a 42.8 percent decrease in the number of prescription drugs consumed and a 24 percent decrease in the patient's average monthly medication bill, from $31.15 in 1970 to $23.68 in 1977, in spite of a 20.9 percent increase in prescription drug prices during the same time period (Strandberg, 1980) (Table 2-10).

In stark contrast to this situation is a 50-bed nursing home (intermediate-care facility) that I had the opportunity to visit. The pharmaceutical services provided to this facility were minimal, and all of its medications were obtained in large, multiple-dose vials, rather than the more desirable unit-dose system. A pharmacist never visited the facility for clinical functions such as chart review or drug interaction detection, and the lack of such services was evident in that patients were consuming approximately eight medications each, which is higher than the four to six medications consumed by the average nursing home resident and considerably higher than the consumption patterns described in the previous example.

POLYPHARMACY

One pattern of medication consumption occasionally seen in elderly patients is that of polypharmacy, which is the excessive and unnecessary use of medication. Polypharmacy can occur to many degrees. One simple example of polypharmacy is the excessive use of a stool softener and stimulant laxative in a patient who is experiencing constipation caused by a pain medication, such as codeine (in Tylenol® with Codeine No. 3), when a nonconstipating analgesic such as aspirin would have been sufficient to treat the patient's pain.

Polypharmacy can also be represented by the nursing home patient who has orders for 15 different medications, some of which are unnecessary since they duplicate the effects of other medications that the patient is taking. Extreme examples of polypharmacy may also be cited in which the patient may be taking amounts and types of medications that are inappropriate beyond all comprehension, such as one patient I observed who possessed 75 prescription and nonprescription medications and was using them all on a fairly regular basis! Extreme examples such as this one do not occur very frequently, but they do receive considerable publicity and attention when discovered and are a very memorable example that may give the false impression that this extreme abuse occurs more often than it actually does.

Polypharmacy may be initiated by the patient or the physician or may result from a multifaceted interaction involving the patient, the physician, and other health professionals.

Identification of Features of Polypharmacy

Although rigid criteria labeling a medication pattern as polypharmacy do not exist, there are certain common features that may help in its identification.

Use of Medications That Have No Apparent Indication

For example, a patient may be taking the cardiac glycoside digoxin (Lanoxin®) without ever having a diagnosis of heart disease. This disturbing practice is not uncommon in elderly patients, especially in those who were started on medications by individual physicians who have since died or retired or for some other reason are no longer taking care of the patient. I have seen this practice occur frequently with newly admitted nursing home patients who are continued on medications that they were taking prior to their admission, perhaps for many years, without these medications being reevaluated to assess their continued appropriateness.

Use of Duplicate Medications

Occasionally drug therapy may be unnecessarily duplicated by the concurrent use of different medications with similar or identical pharmacological effects. For example, the patient may be taking two or three different laxatives or two or more sedatives to aid in sleep when one laxative or sleeping medication, when used properly, would be more appropriate.

Concurrent Use of Interacting Medications

The patient may be using medications that, when taken concurrently, have the potential of modifying each other's effect, resulting in a drug interaction. One example of this is the patient who is taking digoxin (Lanoxin®) and kaolin-pectin (Kaopectate®) suspension at the same time. Since these drugs interact, resulting in a decrease in the amount of digoxin absorbed into the bloodstream, the patient should alternate the administration times of these medications in order to prevent this interaction. A patient may also be taking two medications with opposite physiological effects, such as a laxative and an antidiarrheal agent, when the most appropriate action might very well be to discontinue both medications. Medications may also result in interactions with nutrients (see Chapter 8 for a more detailed discussion of drug interactions).

Use of Contraindicated Medications

Patients may be taking medications that are not appropriate for their particular disease condition. For example, patients with congestive heart failure may develop further cardiac decompensation with the concurrent administration of a beta-receptor blocker such as propranolol (Inderal®), owing to the inhibiting effect that this drug has on the heart. Patients may also have an existing order for a medication such as penicillin to which they are truly allergic, or they may receive a prescription for a medication that has caused them some type of adverse effect or toxicity in the past.

Use of Inappropriate Dosage

The patient's drug therapy regimen may include medications that are being given in inappropriate dosages. The administration of the drug may be too frequent, that is, a drug that is usually given once a day may be mistakenly ordered to be given two or three times a day, or it may be that the dosage is too great for the patient's physical stature or that the ability to eliminate the drug from the body is impaired owing to age-related decreases in kidney or liver function. Although specific geriatric dosage recommendations do not exist for most medications, smaller than average doses are frequently necessary, and a dose that would appear to be "normal" for most patients may actually be too high for the elderly patient.

Use of Drug Therapy to Treat Adverse Drug Reactions

One feature that may account for the initiation of many instances of polypharmacy is the occurrence of adverse drug reactions and the subsequent management of these adverse reactions by the addition of still more medications. This practice can add significantly to the occurrence of polypharmacy because some medications may have two or more side effects that could possibly be treated or modified with additional drugs. A medication that is used to treat a drug-induced side effect or toxicity may have its own side effects, resulting in the use of still more medications, which may have side effects of their own, thus continuing the spiral of polypharmacy.

Improvement Following Discontinuation of Medications

Another interesting feature, underscoring the significance of polypharmacy, is the observation that in many instances the condition of patients may actually improve following the discontinuation of most or all of their medications. Sometimes the practice of discontinuing all of a patient's medications is used when the therapy of a patient becomes so complicated that it is extremely unclear as to whether the medications are providing any benefit at all or whether they are in fact creating more problems than they are alleviating. When this point is reached, it may sometimes be beneficial for the physician to discontinue all of the patient's medications, gradually restarting selected drugs to determine which, if any, the patient actually needs.

I have seen instances in which patients themselves have discontinued their own polypharmacy, with a resultant improvement in their health status. However, since it is likely that at least some of an individual's medications are beneficial they should not be discontinued without the knowledge and supervision of their physician.

Consequences of Polypharmacy

The development of polypharmacy is not usually a rapidly occurring phenomenon but rather occurs insidiously, as additional medications are incorporated into the patient's drug therapy, and its development may not be recognized until it is fairly well advanced. The consequences of polypharmacy may be numerous.

Adverse Drug Reactions

As the patient takes more medications, the chances of experiencing adverse drug reactions to one or more of those medications increase. These adverse reactions may result in relatively minor problems such as nausea or constipation, which would primarily be an inconvenience to the patient, but they may also result in drowsiness or dizziness, possibly resulting in a catastrophic fall.

Drug Interactions

With the consumption of increased amounts and types of medications comes the increased chance that one or more of the medications that the patient is ingesting may interact either with another medication that the patient is taking or perhaps with one or more of the nutrients that the patient is ingesting. Drug interactions may occur between both prescription and nonprescription medications and may be lethal. The subject of drug interactions is covered more completely in Chapter 8.

Financial Expense

Because drugs and drug-related items represent a significant expense to the elderly patient, any increase in this expense will increase the financial burden that the elderly patient must bear. Since most elderly individuals are on fixed incomes, increased personal expenditures for medications may mean that less money is available for food or utilities. It is not likely that the overall effect of any drug therapy will be positive if the patient is placed in the position of not being able to afford sufficient nutrition or heat in order to pay for medications.

Diagnostic Consequences

The manifestations of medication toxicity can present in many varied ways and in different degrees of severity. Such toxicity can appear to mimic certain diseases that occur more commonly in the elderly, such as congestive heart failure or pulmonary embolism, or they may present as signs of confusion or depression that may mimic certain psychological conditions that may occur in the elderly. The difficulty that sometimes occurs is the determination of whether a particular symptom or disease presentation is caused by an actual disease process or is the result of a medication toxicity. The best way to treat a medication-induced problem would, of course, be to discontinue the offending agent, perhaps switching to an alternate drug. If a drug-induced problem is not recognized, attempts may be made to "treat" the problem as if it were a manifestation of a disease. This pattern would serve only to complicate the patient's medication regimen even further and worsen the vicious cycle of polypharmacy, because any additional medication possesses the potential of causing still more toxicity.

Decreased Sensorium

Many of the medication-related toxicities that occur in elderly patients may cause effects that will serve to decrease their acuity of perception of the world about them. Confusion, depression, and drowsiness may decrease the ability to communicate with others and may impede the ability to interact appropriately with the environment, perhaps resulting in the patients becoming unable to manage their medications or creating difficulties in their ability to clean or feed themselves or to take care of other personal responsibilities.

Prevention of Polypharmacy

Polypharmacy is a phenomenon that is potentially extremely detrimental to the patient; yet, while it is not necessarily that common, it need not occur as often as it does. The best way to decrease polypharmacy is to prevent its occurrence. This can be accomplished through a cooperative effort of the health care team and a logical evaluation of the patient's medication therapy.

Most importantly, everyone involved with the care of the individual must cooperate to prevent polypharmacy. Physicians, being the primary prescribers of medications, must be aware of what medications the patient is taking and must take care not to add unnecessary or duplicate medications that would complicate the patient's therapeutic regimen.

Polypharmacy in Nursing Homes

Evidence exists that some physicians may be less aware of potential drug incompatibilities than others and less attentive to patients in skilled nursing facilities than to office or hospital patients (Segal, Thompson, & Floyd, 1979), therefore placing these patients at a higher risk of polypharmacy. Largely because of the unique requirements and potential neglect of these nursing facility patients the role of pharmacists has become more formalized and extensive in these facilities.

Since 1974, U.S. government conditions for participation of skilled nursing facilities in Medicare/Medicaid programs have specified that a registered pharmacist must provide a number of clinically oriented services, including the monthly monitoring of patients' drug therapy (Standards for Certification, 1974). One purpose of this review is to prevent or reverse polypharmacy, and although the specific functions making up this drug therapy are not precisely defined in those guidelines, a fairly common format for this review has evolved through the efforts of pharmaceutical societies. These functions have also been described in professional publications. A discussion of some of the more important components of drug therapy review follows.

Determination of the Number of Medications a Patient Is Taking

Studies have determined that nursing home patients consume, on the average, four to seven different medications during a one-month period. Determining the number of medications taken by patients in a skilled nursing facility can help to identify individual patients or entire nursing facilities where polypharmacy may be present, although it must be remembered that some patients may have a legitimate requirement for a greater than average number of medications, owing to the number or severity of their existing disease conditions.

Determination of Whether Medications Used Are Properly Indicated

Evaluating whether medications are properly indicated can be accomplished by examining the use of each medication individually to determine whether a valid indication exists. This procedure can be particularly effective in identifying medications that are being used inappropriately. For example, I have seen elderly patients who were taking digoxin (Lanoxin®) admitted to a nursing home or hospital without the diagnosis of either congestive heart failure or atrial fibrillation, the two major indications for the use of this cardiac glycoside. After questioning the patient, the physician, or both, it is frequently determined that the patient was placed on this drug years ago for some unclear reason, perhaps by a physician who is no longer in practice. I have found that in many cases the drug could be discontinued without any detrimental effect on the patient. The administration of medications without an appropriate indication has been found to increase the incidence of adverse drug reactions. This review and justification process should routinely be applied to all of the medications that the patient is taking in order to determine whether they are necessary or whether they are providing no therapeutic benefit and simply contributing to the patient's polypharmacy.

Determination of the Effectiveness of Each Medication

Even though the patient may be taking a medication for an appropriate condition, periodic review should address the question of whether or not the medication is helping to improve the condition of the patient or whether the use of the medication is superfluous. Since there is a tremendous variation in the way that patients respond to medications, there is no guarantee that a medication that is approved for use with a particular problem that the patient has is necessarily going to have any therapeutic effect. In cases such as this, when the medication is found to be ineffective, the medication in question should be discontinued and either an effective agent should be used or the condition should be left untreated if it is of little or no consequence to the patient. This practice is based on the assumption that the continuation of ineffective medications will not help patients and may in fact place them at a higher risk of experiencing some form of toxicity.

Determination of Whether the Patient Is Experiencing an Adverse Drug Reaction

Since the elderly are more prone to experiencing adverse reactions to medications than younger persons, they should continuously be monitored for this occurrence. I believe that one of the more effective methods of accomplishing this can be performed when the patient develops a new problem, either subjective or objective, or new complaint. One member of the health care team, most likely the pharmacist, can assume the role of "devil's advocate" and attempt to attribute the patient's newly developed problems to one or more of the individual's medications, rather than as a manifestation of a new or existing disease. Admittedly, the majority of the patient's complaints will not be due to the adverse effects of medications; however, this monitoring technique will effectively identify and reduce the occurrence of medication toxicity when it does occur. More importantly, it will also decrease the instances in which additional medication is added to treat the adverse effects of existing medications, rather than discontinuing the offending agent.

Determination of Whether Drug Interactions Are Present

The risk of drug interactions increases with the number of medications a person takes. Therefore, the consumption of an increased number of medications is likely to increase the patient's chance of experiencing such an interaction. Interactions can occur between medications or between medications and the patient's nutritional intake. Interactions are usually of a relatively minor clinical significance in the elderly patient; however, the consequences may also be serious and even lethal. Some of the more commonly occurring drug interactions can be memorized and prevented by identifying medication orders for offending agents as soon as they are prescribed, although the existence of thousands of potential interactions precludes the reliance of our memories as an effective screening tool. Various methods such as manual screening devices, interaction charts, and computer programs have been successfully used in the effort to detect and reduce the incidence of occurrence of this aspect of polypharmacy.

Role of Nurses in the Prevention of Polypharmacy

As integral members of the health care team, the nursing staff may help to decrease the incidence of polypharmacy by being aware of the fact that the use of unnecessary medications in the elderly may be detrimental. Nurses should also be alert to signs of medication-induced illness and other instances of medication misuse. Since nurses have such an extensive contact with the patient, both on an inpatient and outpatient basis, they can provide valuable information regarding the patient's response to medications.

The concept of the use of the team approach to reduce polypharmacy has been demonstrated by the study published in 1980 and described earlier in this chapter that examined the effect of a pharmacy-based system of drug distribution and drug therapy review in a group of three nursing homes (Strandberg et al., 1980). This system, which incorporated routine communication between the physician, pharmacist, and nurse was found to reduce the use of prescription drugs by 42.8 percent.

Self-Induced Polypharmacy

Certainly not all polypharmacy is the fault of the medical community, since it is the choice of some patients. I have seen some individuals with somatic complaints, or the unfounded belief that they were sick, take far more medications than necessary for their actual condition. Although it is not a common occurrence, some patients visit numerous physicians without the knowledge of the others to obtain multiple prescriptions for their various perceived or contrived needs. These individuals may also have their prescriptions filled at a number of different pharmacies in order to avoid detection by an alert pharmacist.

This type of behavior leading to polypharmacy in community-based patients may sometimes be best detected by various nonmedical personnel who might be providing care for the patient, such as social workers, home health care aides, or family members. If this type of behavior is detected, notification of the patient's primary physician would be an appropriate step in an effort to reverse this potentially destructive behavior and to develop a more rational pattern of medication use for the individual.

REFERENCES

American Hospital Association. *Hospital statistics: Trends among U.S. registered hospitals.* Chicago: Author, 1981.

Aycock, E.K. PRN drug use in nursing homes. *American Journal of Hospital Pharmacy,* 1981, *38,* 105.

Blackwell, B. The drug defaulter. *Clinical Pharmacology and Therapeutics,* 1972, *13,* 841-848.

Boyd, J.R., Covington, T.R., Stanaszek, W.F., & Coussons, R.T. Drug defaulting: Part ii: Analysis of noncompliance patterns. *American Journal of Hospital Pharmacy,* 1974, *31,* 485-491.

Gfroerer, J., & Young, C.A. Utilization of health resources. In *Sourcebook on aging* (2nd ed.). Chicago: Marquis Academic Media, 1979.

Gibson, R.M., & Waldo, D.R. National health expenditures, 1980. *Health Care Financing Review,* 1981, *3,* 1-54.

Howard, J.B., Strong, K.E., Sr., & Strong, K.E., Jr. Medication procedures in a nursing home: Abuse of PRN orders. *Journal of the American Geriatrics Society,* 1977, *25,* 83-84.

Kasper, J.A. *Prescribed medicines: Use, expenditures, and source of payment* (Data Preview 9, National Health Care Expenditure Study, U.S. Department of Health and Human Services, Publication No. [PHS] 82-3320), April 1982.

Lamy, P.P. Health care expenditures and drugs. In *Prescribing for the elderly.* Littleton, Mass.: Publishing Sciences Group, 1980.

Miller, C.A. PRN drugs . . . to give or not to give? *Geriatric Nursing,* 1982, *3,* 37-38.

Muller, C. The overmedicated society: Forces in the marketplace for medical care. *Science,* 1972, *176,* 488-492.

Office of Human Development Services. *Need for long term care: Information and issues: A chartbook of the Federal Council on the Aging,* 1981 (Publication No. OHDS 81-20704).

Rogers, J.V. Personal communication (Pharmaceutical Manufacturers Association), 1982.

Segal, J.L., Thompson, J.F., & Floyd, R.A. Drug utilization and prescribing patterns in a skilled nursing facility: The need for a rational approach to therapeutics. *Journal of the American Geriatrics Society,* 1979, *27,* 117-122.

Shanas, E., & Maddox, G.L. Aging, health, and the organization of health resources. In R.H. Binstock & E. Shanas (Eds.), *Handbook of aging and the social sciences.* New York: Van Nostrand Reinhold, 1976.

Shipp, L., & Saffles, J. An analysis of laxative use in extended care facilities. *Contemporary Pharmacy Practice,* 1979, *2,* 206-207.

Standards for certification and participation in Medicare and Medicaid programs. *Federal Register,* Thursday, January 17, 1974.

Strandberg, L.R., Dawson, G.W., Mathieson, D., Rawlings, J., & Clark, B.G. Effect of comprehensive pharmaceutical services on drug use in long-term care facilities. *American Journal of Hospital Pharmacy,* 1980, *37,* 92-94.

Top 200 Drugs in 1981. *Pharmacy Times,* 1982, *48*(4), 23-32.

U.S. Department of Health and Human Services. *Health—United States 1981* (DHHS Publication No. [PHS] 82-1232). December 1981.

U.S. Government Printing Office. Part IV Health. In *Developments in Aging: A report of the Special Committee on Aging, United States Senate* (Vol. 1) Washington, D.C.: Author, 1982.

U.S. Health Care Financing Administration. *Long term care: Background and future directions* (Publication No. HCFA 81-20047). Washington, D.C., 1981.(a)

U.S. Health Care Financing Administration. *Medicare: Use of prescription drugs by aged persons enrolled for Supplemental Medical Insurance 1967-77*. March 1981.(b)

Chapter 3

Generic Drugs and Their Implications in the Elderly

The issue of generic prescription drugs has been well publicized, especially in the 1970s, during which many of the state laws prohibiting pharmacists from substituting generic drugs for brand name prescription drugs were repealed. The entire subject elicited emotional responses, with irate consumers fearing that they were being taken advantage of by a collusion between pharmacists who were making unfair profits and their physician "buddies."

The issue also had strong political overtones when active consumer groups lobbied and pressured state lawmakers to allow generic drug substitution. The consumers who were perhaps most active in these efforts were senior citizens, who, because of their low, fixed incomes and their high medication consumption rates, stood to gain the most from the financial savings that could result from the use of generic drugs.

The political aspects of the use of generic drugs also included the consideration of patients' rights because some consumers felt that as patients they should have some say as to which brand of drug they would be putting into their own bodies. The political concerns of physicians also had to be considered because some physicians feared that the use of generic drugs could represent a possible erosion of their exclusive power to decide on a patient's drug therapy.

Consumers are now becoming more familiar with the availability of generic products in general, ranging from canned tomatoes to beer to motor oil. However, it may not be possible, and in fact it may be unwise, to draw a direct correlation between these generic products and generic prescription medications, owing to the important therapeutic and toxic implications involved. If patients purchase generically labeled cans of tomatoes that are of poorer quality than the brand name product, the individual stands to lose nothing but the aesthetic quality of the food; however, if they take a generic drug that is of poorer quality than its brand name counterpart, they may experience toxicity or they may suffer the consequences of inadequate treatment of their disease.

Today nearly every state allows for some form of generic drug substitution and most of the turmoil surrounding this issue has subsided. However, it remains important for health professionals who work with the elderly to be familiar with this subject, including the terminology, history, and implications of generic drugs and the risks and benefits that are also associated with the use of generic drugs.

DEFINITIONS

In order to understand the subject of generic drugs it is necessary to review the definitions and specialized terminology that apply to this subject. Although some of these terms may have multiple meanings, the following definitions relate to their application to this subject:

chemical name. The chemical or chemicals that make up the active ingredients of each medication have specific names that actually describe the drug in chemical terms. The chemical name tends to be very complex and is not frequently used by health professionals and therefore could be considered to be of no practical value to consumers, although the use of this complex terminology is necessary by chemists and other scientists who are involved with the chemical aspects of medications. The following is an example of the chemical name of a drug: 7-chloro-2-methylamino-5-phenyl-3H-1,4-benzodiazepine-4-oxide hydrochloride.

generic name (also called official name or nonproprietary name). This is a shortened and simplified version of the chemical name of a drug. Medications that are chemically identical, yet sold by different companies, will have the same generic name, although they will have different brand names. The generic name of the drug, whose chemical name is listed above, is chlordiazepoxide hydrochloride.

brand name (also called trade name or proprietary name). This is a registered trademark used by a pharmaceutical company to identify their brand of a specific medication. Although a particular brand name is used only by the company that has the rights to that name, more than one company may assign their own unique brand names to the same medication as long as one company does not hold exclusive patent rights for the sale of that drug; thus the same drug may be marketed under different brand names. An example of two different brand names representing chlordiazepoxide hydrochloride are Librium® and A-Poxide® (Figure 3-1).

chemical equivalence. When two or more medications contain the same chemical(s) as active ingredients then they are chemically equivalent.

Figure 3-1 Chemical Structure, Chemical Name, Generic Name, and Two Brand Names of a Commonly Used Prescription Drug

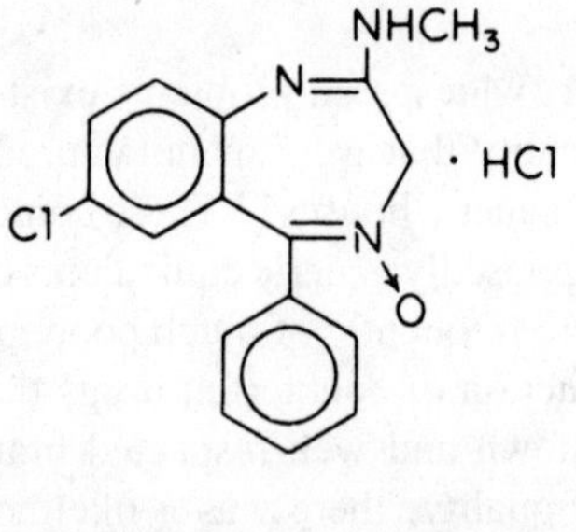

Chemical name: 7-chloro-2-methylamino-5-phenyl-3H-1,4-benzodiazepine-4-oxide hydrochloride
Generic name: chlordiazepoxide hydrochloride
Brand name: Librium® (Roche Laboratories) and A-Poxide® (Abbott Laboratories)

---

therapeutic equivalence. Two or more drugs that are chemically equivalent may produce the same therapeutic effect, at the same level of safety, in the same individual, under identical conditions.

generic equivalence. Two or more medications may be identical in regard to the type and amount of active ingredient(s) they contain. Generically equivalent medications are usually also therapeutically equivalent, but not always.

bioavailability. This is the degree to which a drug is absorbed into the bloodstream. Since most medications are taken by mouth, their bioavailability usually refers to the absorption that takes place in the stomach or the intestine.

multiple source product. A drug may be available for sale by more than one company. This term usually refers to multiple sources of sale and not necessarily to multiple sources of manufacture, because two or more pharmaceutical companies may sell their own form of the same product after purchasing it from a common source.

substitution. A drug may be dispensed that is a different brand than the one that was prescribed but is generically equivalent.

in vivo. This term means "in the living body" and is usually used in reference to the effect of a drug.

in vitro. This term means "in the test tube" and is usually used in reference to the properties of a drug, such as the time required for its disintegration or its degree of solubility, which can best be measured in a test tube or similar laboratory apparatus.

HISTORICAL PERSPECTIVE OF GENERIC DRUG USE

Past

In the 1950s and earlier, widespread problems existed with the production of medications of inferior quality that were manufactured by companies that were sometimes referred to as "generic houses." These companies primarily produced drug products that were supposedly generic equivalents of more well-known brand name drugs but in fact were frequently of much poorer quality. Another problem that existed was the production of counterfeit drugs that were illicitly manufactured to look like well-known and well-respected brand name medications. In addition to being of poor quality, there was a likelihood that these counterfeit products were manufactured under unsanitary conditions; therefore, their use represented a significant danger to the consumer.

Development of Antisubstitution Laws

In response to this problem of the production of inferior medications, laws were created requiring pharmacists to dispense only the brand of medication that was prescribed by the physician, thereby prohibiting them from dispensing a generic substitute for a brand name drug. These "antisubstitution laws" were passed as a direct effort to protect the consumer from receiving medications that were impure, unsafe, or ineffective.

Since then, the manufacturing standards that apply to pharmaceutical manufacturers have increased, as have the surveillance powers of the U.S. Food and Drug Administration (FDA) so that the counterfeiting of legitimate prescription medications is no longer considered to be a major problem, although it probably still occurs. Additionally, standards exist that govern the quality of medications produced so that the production of medication of poor quality generally occurs only in isolated instances, resulting from errors in manufacturing processes rather than reflecting an industry-wide problem.

Repeal of Antisubstitution Laws

In the 1970s a strong interest in the repeal of the antisubstitution laws developed. Consumer groups argued that the laws were no longer necessary because generic drugs were equal in quality to brand name drugs and thus there was no need to protect the consumer from these products. It was also argued that these laws were restrictive and unfair to consumers because once the physician wrote a prescription specifying that a particular brand of drug be dispensed, patients had no say as to which brand of drug they would receive in spite of the availability of a number of other brand name and generic products that were generically equivalent to the particular brand specified by the physician.

The basis for the main argument supporting the repeal of these laws was that prescriptions filled with the generic equivalent of brand name drugs were considerably less expensive than those filled with the brand name product. It was further believed that in many instances when brand name drugs were specified on prescriptions, a suitable generic product was available at a lower cost to the consumer.

Present

Nearly every state has repealed its antisubstitution laws in an effort to reduce the cost of prescription drugs to the consumer and in response to consumers' demands. In the states that now allow the pharmacist to substitute a drug product for the brand specified by the prescriber the procedure for this substitution varies somewhat. In some states the pharmacist is permitted to select and dispense any generically equivalent medication that is available, but other states only allow such substitution according to a state-approved formulary that lists drugs that can or cannot be substituted. Formularies for drug substitution may be considered to be "positive" or "negative," with positive formularies limiting product selection from an approved list of medications that have been judged to be suitable for substitution and negative formularies specifying a list of drugs for which substitution is prohibited.

Where generic substitution is allowed, the prescriber may specify particular instances in which the pharmacist must not dispense a generic equivalent but rather must dispense only the brand of drug prescribed. Depending on the individual state laws that apply, the prescriber can exercise this option by writing "dispense as written," "no substitution," or some similar instruction on the prescription. Some states also provide for this practice by allowing the prescriber to sign either one of two signature lines on the prescription, one allowing for substitution, the other prohibiting it. Prescription blanks may also have a small box that when checked disallows generic substitution. This option is used in less than five percent of prescriptions written (Goldberg, Aldridge, DeVito, Vidis, Moore, & Dickson, 1977; U.S. Bureau of Consumer Protection, 1979), indicating that although physicians usually write prescriptions for brand name medications they do not feel strongly that patients must actually receive that particular product.

In the institutional setting, different constraints exist governing the substitution of generic drugs. For financial and practical reasons, most hospitals and many nursing homes use a limited formulary that is designed by a committee, which usually consists of physicians and pharmacists and perhaps nurses or other health professionals. Formularies govern which drugs are to be used in that facility, and should a prescriber order a medication that is not on the formulary its equivalent may automatically be substituted.

Opportunities for Generic Drug Use

More than 85 percent of all new prescriptions are written for brand name products ("Top 200 Drugs," 1982). However, since more than half of the prescriptions filled in the United States are available as multiple source products (U.S. Bureau of Consumer Protection, 1979), it is obvious that many opportunities for generic substitution exist, especially considering the fact that almost 1.4 billion prescriptions were filled in the United States in 1981 ("Top 200 Drugs," 1982).

For example, the antibiotic tetracycline is a multiple source product. If a patient has a prescription for tetracycline filled with Achromycin V® capsules, the person is actually receiving the tetracycline hydrochloride that is being sold by Lederle Laboratories. However, tetracycline is available through other sources also. It is sold by E.R. Squibb & Sons, Inc. as Sumycin®, by The Upjohn Company as Panmycin®, and by other companies using their own brand names. Premo Pharmaceutical Laboratories, Inc., Purepac Pharmaceutical Laboratories, Inc., Comer Pharmaceuticals, Inc., and others sell tetracycline as a generically labeled "tetracycline hydrochloride," without assigning a brand name to the product. Some of the many sources of tetracycline hydrochloride are given in Table 3-1.

In recent years a trend toward the use of generic drugs has been significant. In Table 3-2 it is shown that in 1966, 6.4 percent of new prescriptions (not including refill prescriptions) in the United States were written for generic medications, while in 1980 and 1981 that percentage had climbed to 14.7 percent, with the actual number of generic prescriptions written increasing from 29,741,000 in 1966 to 105,362,000 in 1982. In 1980 a total of 174,762,000 generic prescriptions (including both new and refill prescriptions) were written in the United States, while in 1981 that number increased to 193,676,000, an increase of almost 11 percent and the biggest increase in the preceding seven years.

Further underscoring the trend toward the use of generic drugs is the fact that between 1966 and 1981 the total annual number of generically written prescriptions (both new and refill) increased by a factor of 178 percent, compared with a more modest 39 percent increase in the total number of prescriptions written, including both generic and brand name prescriptions ("Top 200 Drugs," 1982).

Table 3-1 Examples of Multiple Sources of Tetracycline Hydrochloride

Product name	Source
Achromycin V®	Lederle Laboratories
Sumycin®	E.R. Squibb & Sons, Inc.
Panmycin®	The Upjohn Company
Tetracycline hydrochloride	Premo Pharmaceutical Laboratories, Inc.
Tetracycline hydrochloride	Purepac Pharmaceutical Co.
Tetracycline hydrochloride	Comer Pharmaceuticals, Inc.

Table 3-2 Percentage and Number of New Prescriptions Written for Generic Drugs 1966-1982

Year	Number of new generic prescriptions	Percent of all new prescriptions
1966	29,741,000	6.4
1967	34,500,000	7.0
1968	43,293,000	8.2
1969	48,425,000	8.8
1970	53,605,000	9.0
1971	58,570,000	9.2
1972	66,675,000	9.7
1973	76,234,000	10.6
1974	79,196,000	10.7
1975	82,608,000	11.1
1976	86,473,000	11.7
1977	90,885,000	12.5
1978	101,540,000	13.7
1979	103,399,000	14.1
1980	110,404,000	14.7
1981	111,027,000	14.7
1982	105,362,000	13.8

Source: National Prescription Audit, IMS America Ltd., and Adapted from *Top 200 Drugs in 1981*, published by Romaine Pierson Publishers, Inc., by permission of *Pharmacy Times*.

Future

If these present trends continue, the use of generic drugs will continue to increase, thereby making them even more important to the elderly patient.

It is also felt by some that this continued increase in the use of generic drugs will be due in part to the expiration of patents for a number of commonly prescribed drugs, thus making it possible for competing drug companies to make available their own generic equivalents in an attempt to garner a portion of the market of these popular drugs. Prior to 1982 a decline in the introduction of new prescription drugs in the United States was observed. Some felt that this trend might result in a smaller percentage of the drugs on the U.S. market being under patent protection, thus increasing the potential availability of generic products. A reverse of this trend was seen, however, in 1982, during which 28 new chemical entities were approved by the FDA for use as prescription drugs. Whether or not this increase in new drugs becomes a new pattern or has any effect on the use of generic drugs remains to be seen.

One event that could significantly reduce the use of generic drugs is the proposal to extend a drug's patent protection period, thus increasing the length of time that a company has a monopoly on that product; during this period generic drugs could not be sold by competitors. Although pharmaceutical manufacturers would obviously favor such an extension, at present it appears that such an extension is not forthcoming.

It is possible that the prescription of generic drugs will change significantly as more health professionals, such as nurse practitioners, physicians' assistants, and pharmacists, obtain prescription-writing privileges. However at this time such a prediction, although interesting, is speculative.

WHY DO PHYSICIANS PRESCRIBE BRAND NAME DRUGS?

There are a number of reasons why physicians write the overwhelming majority of prescriptions for brand name drugs.

Familiarity with Brand Name

Physicians are frequently more familiar with a product's brand name than they are with its generic name. Because pharmaceutical companies are interested in selling their particular product, advertisements for those products that appear in professional journals and other professional publications understandably stress the product's brand name. Thus, each supplier of a brand name drug has a definite interest in selling their particular brand, since a company obviously receives no income when a competitor's product is purchased.

The emphasis on brand name drugs is also seen when sales representatives of pharmaceutical companies visit physicians in their offices or hospitals. This is a common practice in the pharmaceutical industry. Sales representatives present information about their company's drug products to the physician in order to familiarize him or her with the use of that particular product and to answer any questions about it. Again, as with advertisements in medical journals, the sales representative presents the product by its brand name, in an effort to encourage the physician to write prescriptions for that product.

Companies that primarily sell generically labeled drugs do not usually advertise heavily in professional journals and typically do not have large sales forces that visit prescribers. Their approach is based on the general assumption that prescribers are familiar with the pharmacological and physiological effects of the medications that these companies sell and that when allowed the choice, pharmacists will choose to dispense their particular generic product for certain reasons, primarily lower cost, compared with the more heavily promoted, and perhaps better known, brand name drugs. For these reasons the companies that sell generic drugs do not encourage *physicians* to specify the use of their particular generic product but rather try to encourage the *pharmacist* to dispense their product.

Since the brand names of medications are the ones that are most promoted to physicians, they generally tend to be unfamiliar with the drug's generic name. In addition, brand names are usually shorter and easier to remember than the longer, more complex generic names, and since the pharmacist is the health professional who most frequently decides which generic product is to be dispensed, it can be argued that it is not always necessary for the physician to know the drug's generic name.

Confidence in Brand Name Drugs

Another reason that physicians primarily prescribe by brand name is that they may have greater faith in brand name medications because they are produced and backed by pharmaceutical manufacturers with established reputations. By specifying a brand name medication, the prescriber may assume that the patient will receive the highest quality product, either because one particular brand has been demonstrated to be more effective or because it has been found to be less toxic than competing brands or generic equivalents.

Professional Liability

A prescriber may believe that his or her professional liability will increase if a prescription is written for a less expensive generic medication that might possibly be of lesser quality than the brand name product.

Generic Drug Not Available

One very obvious reason for a prescriber to specify one particular brand name medication is the possibility that it is the only product available because no competing brand name drugs or generically equivalent products exist. This is usually the case when one pharmaceutical manufacturer holds an exclusive patent on a particular drug product, as explained later in this chapter.

Nonphysician Prescribers

Now that additional health professionals including nurse practitioners, physicians' assistants, and pharmacists are able to write prescriptions in some states, it will be interesting to note if they, too, prescribe primarily by brand name or if they are more prone to prescribing drugs by their generic name.

PATENT PROTECTION FOR BRAND NAME DRUGS

Specific drug entities can be patented for a 17-year period during which no other companies may produce or sell that product without the permission of the patent holder. Since it may take 5 to 10 years from the time a drug is patented to the time that it is approved for human use, a large portion of the patent period protects the drug while it is in the research and development phase; however, the latter portion of the patent period protects the drug from competition after it has been approved for human use and is being marketed.

Pharmaceutical manufacturers feel that this period of sales under patent protection is very important because it is usually during this period that the company recoups the significant investment that was required to get the drug on the market. For example, the popular antiulcer medication cimetidine (Tagamet®) was patented in 1974 and was released for use in humans in the United States in 1977. Therefore, the manufacturer, and patent holder, Smith Kline & French Laboratories will be the sole source of cimetidine until 1991 when the patent expires. After the patent to cimetidine expires, other companies will be free to manufacture or sell cimetidine, either as a product with its own brand name assigned by the new suppliers of the product or as a generic drug.

ECONOMIC CONSIDERATIONS

The main advantage of generic drugs is the potential cost savings to the consumer that can result from their use. The financial aspect is an important one, especially for the elderly individual who may be receiving a minimal, fixed income. If generic drugs are able to save the elderly just one or two dollars per prescription the savings could be significant. There are also financial implications that involve the pharmaceutical manufacturer and the pharmacist with which the reader should be familiar in order to more fully appreciate this important ramification of generic drug use.

Consumers

The basic assumption that prescriptions filled with generic drugs are, on the average, less expensive than those filled with brand name drugs is true; however, the difference in price between the two is not the 200 or 300 percent difference that some people believe but rather is a more modest one to two dollars per prescription.

A 1978 study in New York demonstrated an average savings of two dollars with each generically filled prescription, but a significant variation in price was found to exist between different pharmacies (Francetic, Lasagna, Weintraub, & Karch, 1980). More recent information, determined by a comprehensive study of the 200 most commonly prescribed medications in the United States, showed that the average price of all prescriptions was $8.29, while the average price of generic prescriptions was $6.05 (DiNuzzo, 1982).

In 1977 a study from Wisconsin estimated a savings of between $1.00 and $1.50 per prescription when generic substitution took place (Herman, 1977). The data obtained were used to project a possible annual savings of $400 million nationally.

In 1974 the Federal Trade Commission estimated that the maximum potential savings in the United States resulting from the selection and substitution of generic drug products by the pharmacist to be between $283 and $469 million annually (U.S. Bureau of Consumer Protection, 1979). These figures were supported by a 1976 study sponsored by the Pharmaceutical Manufacturers Association that estimated that consumer savings would amount to $323 million annually if all brand name prescriptions had been written by the generic name (U.S. Bureau of Consumer Protection, 1979).

It is important to note that the above figures for annual savings are based on the situation in which generic drugs were substituted for brand name prescriptions *whenever* possible. This assumption is really the key to the issue of cost savings resulting from the use of generic drugs and is an important area to look at in order to determine what is the real financial impact of generic substitution. This is because it has been estimated that prescriptions are filled with the generic drug in only 20 percent of the instances in which it is legal to do so (Kolata, 1979), indicating that the *potential* maximum cost savings of generic drugs is much more than the actual savings that are being realized.

Now that all states except Indiana permit generic drug substitution it is unclear what the savings to the elderly patient really are. However, it is certain that these savings are nowhere near those that can potentially be realized. Numerous factors contribute to this underuse of generic drugs, but a large share of the blame must be placed on the elderly consumer. These factors and methods to encourage the rational use of generic drugs are discussed at the end of this chapter.

I find it interesting that consumer activists and other supporters of generic substitution emphasized this potentially huge consumer savings when efforts were being made to repeal the antisubstitution laws without underscoring the fact that actual savings may be less than expected. This seems to be somewhat analogous to the car salesperson who claims that a particular vehicle will get 35 miles per gallon without mentioning that it will only do so with properly inflated tires, while properly tuned, and traveling at a steady speed on level ground.

Manufacturers

Obviously pharmaceutical manufacturers have strong feelings concerning the use of generic drugs and the allowance for pharmacists to substitute a generic product for a brand name drug. Since the review process necessary for a drug to receive final approval for use in humans by the FDA may take 10 years or longer, the manufacturer may often be left with only a relatively short period of time that the drug can be marketed within the 17-year period of the drug's patent protection. Manufacturers feel that this limited time period barely allows the company the time that is needed to recoup their multimillion dollar investment. They argue that when generic substitution is allowed following the end of the period of patent protection, the generation of income that is necessary for companies to perform research into new drugs will be restricted.

Although this review process has recently been streamlined by the FDA to allow approval of new drugs ("New Drug Application Data Summaries," 1982), some manufacturers still feel that the process takes too long. This argument may be countered by the fact that while research is certainly expensive, some drug companies may devote four to five times as much money to advertising, promotion, and marketing than they do for research (Herman, 1977).

When the 17-year patent period for a brand name drug expires, competitors move to produce generically equivalent products that may either be sold under a brand name or as a generically labeled product, thus reducing the income of the company that originally held the patent. The fact remains, however, that when the patent expires, the price of the original brand of drug usually drops significantly because the monopoly on that drug no longer exists.

Pharmacists

Pharmacists may unfairly increase their profit margin by dispensing less expensive generic drugs while charging a price that is equivalent to that of the brand name product; however, this blatant form of consumer fraud is not a common practice. It has been found that pharmacists do pass the cost savings of generic drugs on to the consumer (Gumbhir & Rodowskas, 1974).

Another major financial consideration concerns the advantages that the use of generic drugs can afford pharmacists. The inventory expenses of pharmacists can be significantly reduced if they are not required to stock every brand of a medication that exists. For example, the antibiotic ampicillin is available under 224 different product labels, including both brand name products and generically labeled products, so if pharmacists only have to stock one or two brands of ampicillin instead of dozens they can save a considerable amount of money by reducing the inventory of drugs that it is necessary to stock. Also, the purchase of only one or two brands of ampicillin may enable the pharmacist to purchase large supplies of those products, thereby resulting in significant bulk purchase savings that can be shared by the pharmacist and the consumer. Also, the decreased space requirements resulting from the decreased inventory may allow the pharmacist to use this space profitably as increased storage space or for the sale of additional merchandise.

GENERIC EQUIVALENCE VERSUS THERAPEUTIC EQUIVALENCE

In order for the use of generic drugs to be acceptable, they must obviously be therapeutically equivalent to the products for which they are being substituted. While this is usually true, it unfortunately has not always been the case, since relatively minor alterations in the manufacturing process have been found to cause significant alterations in a drug's bioavailability, therapeutic effect, or toxicity.

For example, in the early 1970s an alteration in the manufacturing process of Lanoxin®, the brand of the cardiac medication digoxin produced by the Burroughs Wellcome Co., resulted in a twofold increase in the bioavailability of the product. It was found that although the altered tablets contained the same amount of digoxin that the original version did, a change in the manufacturing process of the tablet significantly increased the product's absorption into the bloodstream. Owing to this increase in bioavailability a number of patients experienced severe digoxin toxicity (Danon, Horowitz, Ben-Zvi, Kaplanski, & Glick, 1977).

Other instances of alterations in product bioavailability caused by changes in the manufacturing process have occurred. For example, in one instance in Australia the manufacturing process for the anticonvulsant medication phenytoin (Dilantin®) was altered by substituting one of the inactive ingredients in the capsule for another inactive ingredient. This alteration increased the product's bioavailability, resulting in toxicity in some patients, even though the capsules continued to contain the same amount of the active drug (American Pharmaceutical Association, 1978).

The two examples illustrated previously show that minor changes in a company's manufacturing process may result in clinically significant alterations in the therapeutic effect of its product. The fact that this problem can occur as the result of one company's alterations of its manufacturing process emphasizes the likelihood that it may occur when a generically equivalent drug is manufactured by a number of different companies.

Changes in the inactive ingredients of a product or differences in manufacturing procedures or technique may, for example, result in alterations in the speed at which a tablet disintegrates within the stomach or intestine or the extent or rate at which the product dissolves. Other alterations that might exist between drug products produced by different companies include the presence of dyes, flavoring agents, or other inactive ingredients to which a patient may be allergic.

These and other factors may alter the bioavailability or toxicity or both of a particular drug product, creating a situation in which two or more products may be generically but not therapeutically equivalent. Fortunately most medications that are generically equivalent are also therapeutically equivalent in spite of the numerous possible causes of inequivalence.

The FDA pays close attention to the subject of generic equivalence and requires generic drugs to undergo testing to identify potential problems with therapeutic inequivalence. As part of this effort, the FDA has also published lists of generic drugs that are therapeutically equivalent and of drugs that have either a potential for, or demonstration of, bioinequivalence ("Substitution Foes," 1977; U.S. Bureau of Consumer Protection, 1979; U.S. Department of Health and Human Services, 1980).

The FDA also requires in vitro and in vivo testing of drug products to identify such problems. However, although these tests are valuable in identifying such problem drugs, they are unable to identify all drug products that are not generically equivalent.

Information regarding the therapeutic inequivalence of medications is also published frequently in medical and pharmaceutical journals so physicians and pharmacists can work together and avoid the use of generic drugs that are not therapeutically equivalent.

Another interesting fact concerning the manufacture of generic drugs is that the same generic medication may be sold by numerous companies yet be manufactured by the same company! In fact, some generically labeled drugs are manufactured by the same company that produces the brand name product against which the generic drug is competing!

I do not mean to condemn this practice because it certainly is not unique to the pharmaceutical industry and occurs frequently with products ranging from potato chips and canned tuna fish to home appliances and automobile tires. The extent to which this practice exists is dramatically illustrated during a product recall, such as when the possibility of the distribution of a spoiled food product such as canned tuna fish, canned mushrooms, or some other product is discovered. When this occurs it is not uncommon to hear that four or five separate brands of the product may have been recalled because they were all processed and packaged by the same manufacturer, sold to other companies, and labeled with their own individual brands.

This practice is not uncommon within the pharmaceutical industry because many of the smaller companies that sell generic drugs do not have the resources, facilities, or expertise required for the large-scale manufacture of pharmaceuticals. An example of the extent to which this practice occurs may be demonstrated by the commonly used antibiotic ampicillin. This drug has been reported to be available from 224 different sources; yet it is manufactured by only 24 different companies (Hecht, 1979). This points out the fact that generic drugs may be of identical quality to the more well-known, and usually more costly, brand name drug, although in most states the laws do not require the name of the actual manufacturer to appear on the product label so that the consumer and even the pharmacist may not be aware of who actually is the manufacturer.

DISADVANTAGES OF GENERIC DRUG USE

As previously mentioned, the substitution of generic drugs for brand name drugs represents a potentially significant financial savings, especially for the elderly patient. However, the use of these drugs is not without disadvantage to the consumer, the physician, the pharmacist, and the nurse.

Consumers

One of the major disadvantages that generic drugs present to the consumer is the fact that they usually do not look like the brand name products with which they are equivalent. This may create an awkward situation if, when elderly patients receive a new prescription, they are told by the physician or nurse about the "little blue tablet" that they will be taking without realizing that the pharmacist may be able to dispense a generically equivalent drug that may not fit the same description of the brand name drug.

For example, a nurse may design a medication calendar that includes a description of the medication that is prescribed, perhaps even fastening a sample tablet or capsule to the calendar. If such medication aids are going to be used, it would probably be best for the nurse or other person preparing the calendar either to eliminate the descriptions of medications from the calendar if the medication is available in the generic form or at least to emphasize to the patient that generic equivalents may exist, which, while being identical in content and effect, may not have the same appearance as the brand name drug. The physician should also be alert to this fact and be careful not to describe the appearance of the medication to the patient without mentioning that generically equivalent drugs may have a different appearance.

If a patient is told what a drug will look like and on receiving it finds that it does not appear the way that it was described, severe credibility problems can occur in the relationship between the patient and the health professional. The patient may harbor some doubt concerning the competence of the physician or the nurse since it might appear to the patient that these professionals did not even know what the medicine looked like, or it may be concluded that the pharmacist has filled the prescription with the wrong drug.

In either case it is likely that a greater amount of time will have to be spent correcting the patient's misunderstanding than if the person had been informed of the situation prior to the receipt of the prescriptions.

Another disadvantage to the use of generic drugs by the elderly consumer is that the elderly individual may actually perceive a substantial risk in using generic drugs for a variety of reasons, including financial, social, psychological, and physical factors (Bearden, Mason, & Smith, 1979). In spite of the potential financial savings that the appropriate use of generic drugs represents, the persons that have been found to be the least likely to use generic drugs are the elderly poor, ironically those who could be helped most by these savings (Lambert, Doering, Goldstein, & McCormick, 1980).

Physicians

To many, the repeal of antisubstitution laws represents new freedom for both the pharmacist, who can now exercise an increase of professional judgment, and consumers, who now have a greater say regarding the medications they may be receiving. However, initial concern was voiced by some physicians, who believed that allowing pharmacists to substitute a brand of drug different from that prescribed by them represented an erosion of the authority of the physician that would result in a reduction of the quality of health care. Whether these concerns truly represented those of physicians in general or were simply the comments of a limited number of vocal physicians who were afraid of losing some of their authority over the patient is unclear, but in any case this attitude does not appear to exist widely today.

Physicians still have the authority to block generic substitution by indicating so on the prescriptions that they write. This option is not frequently exercised, however, indicating that physicians now support the concept of generic drug substitution.

Nurses

As mentioned earlier, the use of generic drugs may create problems with nursing staff in educating patients about their medications. Nurses may also experience difficulty when administering generic medications to the patient. This example is especially pertinent to nursing practice in the institutional setting where the nurse may have become familiar with the appearance of a particular brand of medication used in that facility. Problems might then arise if a different brand of generically equivalent medication is used, possibly causing some confusion or concern that the patient might not be receiving the proper medication. This problem can be overcome if the nurse pays close attention to package labeling, rather than the appearance of the product, especially in unit-dose drug distribution systems where the product labeling might be in small print. A familiarity with the generic names of commonly used medications will also lessen any possible confusion.

Pharmacists

Pharmacists may be required to spend more time with their patients who have questions regarding the availability, benefits, risks, or general use of generic drugs, and although some pharmacists may consider this additional communication to be a disadvantage, I believe it is an excellent opportunity for pharmacists to increase their contact with patients while gaining an increase in professional recognition.

Another area of generic drug substitution that concerns pharmacists is that of professional liability. If a pharmacist decides to substitute a generic drug for a brand name product that was specified by the physician, and the patient is subsequently injured or does not appropriately respond to this substituted drug product, then the possibility of legal action on behalf of the patient exists. One pharmacist has been indicted on a charge of involuntary manslaughter for dispensing a generic form of a diuretic, furosemide, to a 62-year-old woman who subsequently died of congestive heart failure. Although the particular generic drug that was substituted by the pharmacist for the common brand name drug Lasix® had not been approved by the FDA and was being used illegally, this tragic incident does demonstrate the type of problem that can occur with generic drugs that are in fact not equivalent to their brand name counterparts.

The problems caused by the use of a generic drug that has not received FDA approval are obviously different than if the drug had received such approval, but pharmacists may increasingly find themselves in the conflicting situation of receiving consumer pressure to dispense generic drugs, while on the other hand having to face the consequences, including legal action, resulting from the possibility that the generic drug dispensed does not possess equivalent therapeutic efficacy. These factors make it crucial for pharmacists to determine that all of the medications that they dispense have received the approval of the FDA and that all of the generic products that they choose to use have been shown to be therapeutically equivalent either by specific studies or through widespread use.

WHY AREN'T GENERIC DRUGS USED MORE?

Now that antisubstitution laws have been repealed in most states for at least a few years, it is possible to observe the results of this action. Two facts have become evident. First, financial savings usually do occur when generic medications are substituted for brand name products. These savings are modest and generally range between one and two dollars. With some drugs, however, the savings may be less or even nonexistent. I certainly do not mean to underestimate these potential savings, but rather I am attempting to put them in proper perspective. Indeed a two-dollar savings per prescription can be very significant to an elderly individual who is on a low, fixed income while receiving many prescriptions. Second, on a national level, savings to the consumer have been significantly less than predicted.

This failure to realize the full potential savings from generic drugs is due to a number of complex interacting factors pertaining to both consumers and health professionals.

Patients May Be Unaware of the Existence of Generic Drugs

In spite of the publicity that has surrounded the subject, I have seen instances in which elderly individuals were either completely naive to the existence of generic drugs or had heard about them but did not know enough to request them from their physician or pharmacist.

The blame for this lack of familiarization with the subject can be shared by health professionals and consumers alike. Prescribers must be alert to the fact that their patient may be unaware of the existence of generic drugs. Prescribers should also refrain from indicating on the prescription that the pharmacist is not allowed to substitute a generic drug unless a valid reason can be given. Nurses should be willing to explain to their patients what a generic drug is if such information is requested or if the consumer appears to be unaware of the potential cost savings of generic drugs. Pharmacists should be willing to provide information about generic drugs to the consumer and to answer questions concerning these drugs.

Some states require that signs be posted in all pharmacies to inform consumers that it may be possible for them to obtain a less expensive generic drug in place of the brand name drug that might have been prescribed. Exhibit 3-1 is an example of the announcement that must be posted in all licensed pharmacies in Oregon.

The Federal Government is also attempting to encourage generic drug use, as illustrated in Exhibit 3-2, the text of an advertisement supplied to newspapers and magazines by the Federal Trade Commission.

Lack of consumer knowledge is not entirely the fault of health professionals however, and consumers should take the initiative to adopt a responsible and

---

Exhibit 3-1 Example of Sign in Pharmacy Informing Consumers of Availability of Generic Drug Substitution

THIS PHARMACY MAY
BE ABLE TO SUBSTITUTE A
LESS EXPENSIVE DRUG THAT IS
THERAPEUTICALLY EQUIVALENT TO
THE ONE PRESCRIBED BY YOUR
DOCTOR, UNLESS YOU DO NOT
APPROVE

ORS 689.865
Effective September 14, 1975

Exhibit 3-2 Advertisement for Generic Drug Use

RX FOR CONSUMERS: ASK YOUR PHARMACIST ABOUT GENERICS

If you're looking for a way to cut your medical costs, the Federal Trade Commission suggests you ask your pharmacist about choices in filling prescriptions. These can often include generic drugs: low-cost, effective substitutes for brand name prescription medicines.

"Potential consumer savings for all multisource generic drugs could reach $400 million each year," says the FTC.

Forty-eight states allow pharmacists to substitute low-cost generics on brand-name prescriptions, the FTC notes. Generics are usually sold under shortened chemical names by competing manufacturers.

"About half of all brand-name drugs have a generic equivalent," says the FTC. "And generics can save the consumer up to 50 percent on some drugs."

The Federal Trade Commission, which wants to "inject a little old-fashioned choice" into the health care marketplace, has launched a campaign to encourage consumers to consider their choices knowing that generic drugs are available.

The theme of the FTC's campaign is "Generic drugs . . . get the facts from your pharmacist."

Source: Federal Trade Commission

informed attitude regarding their health and the medications that they may be taking.

Patients May Choose Not to Use Generic Drugs

Patients may be aware of the existence of generic drugs and the potential cost savings that they may represent, yet they may still choose to have their prescriptions filled with brand name drugs because of the concern that generic drugs may not be of as high a quality as brand name drugs or may not work as well. I have seen instances and have spoken to older consumers who have specifically requested that generic drugs not be used, based on their attitude that they want the best possible medications even if they may cost slightly more.

Savings May Not Be Passed on by the Pharmacist

In order for the consumer to save money, the savings that can result from the sale of generic drugs must be passed on to the consumer by the pharmacist. Pharmacists may unfairly increase their profits by charging the patient "brand name prices" for prescriptions that are filled with generic drugs. Since the pharmacist can save money through the purchase of generic drugs, a fair share of this savings should be passed on to the consumer.

CONCLUSIONS AND RECOMMENDATIONS

The negative aspects of generic drug use that were discussed in this chapter were included to familiarize the reader with the problems that may be associated with generic drug use and were not meant to discourage the consumer from using generic drugs. I wholeheartedly encourage the use of generic drugs by the elderly consumer, because through the rational use of generic drugs consumers may experience financial savings that in some instances may be quite significant.

Based on considerable experience with the use of generic drugs in the United States, it can also be concluded that, in most instances, they are as effective as brand name drugs from a therapeutic standpoint and do not usually represent a significantly increased risk of toxicity.

Because of their potential cost savings the use of generic drugs has risen considerably during the past decade and will most likely continue to rise as more consumers realize this potential financial benefit. It is apparent, however, that consumers currently underuse generic drugs and therefore are not capitalizing on the possible savings that the use of these products represents.

Health professionals should encourage the elderly consumer to consider the use of generic drugs. By adhering to the following recommendations the consumer will be able to use these products safely while receiving the benefits of their cost savings:

- *Trust generic drugs.* The consumer should have faith in generic drug products. Over a period of years generic drugs have been widely used and have been found to be both safe and therapeutically effective in the overwhelming majority of instances.
- *Trust the advice of health professionals.* The consumer should trust the recommendations of knowledgeable health professionals, especially the physician and pharmacist, concerning the use of generic drugs. If the physician has good reason to believe that the use of a generic drug is not wise in a particular instance, the patient should trust that decision. Likewise, the consumer should support the pharmacist's conclusions that a particular drug should only be used as the well-known brand name product or that the generic form of the drug would be both safe and effective.
- *Ask the physician if a generic drug is available.* When receiving a new prescription, the elderly consumer should ask the physician if a generic product is available and should seek his or her opinion as to whether the use of that product is recommended or if the brand name product should be used. One study has found that only 17 percent of the adult population asks physicians to prescribe a generic drug product ("Survey Puts Generic Drug Use," 1982).

- *Ask the pharmacist if a generic drug is available.* When receiving a prescription in a pharmacy, the consumer should ask the pharmacist whether a generic form of the medication prescribed is available and, if so, whether he or she recommends its use. Also the person may ask what the price differential is between the generic and brand name drug. A significant savings could convince the consumer to use the generic drug. It has been shown that generic drugs are used most frequently by those consumers who request generics; however, only 20 percent of consumers ask pharmacists to fill prescription orders with generic products ("Survey Puts Generic Drug Use," 1982).

REFERENCES

American Pharmaceutical Association. *The bioavailability of drug products.* Washington, D.C. : Author, 1978.

Bearden, W.O., Mason, J.B., & Smith, E.M. Perceived risk and elderly perceptions of generic drug prescribing. *The Gerontologist,* 1979, *19,* 191-195.

Danon, A., Horowitz, J., Ben-Zvi, Z., Kaplanski, J., & Glick, S. An outbreak of digoxin intoxication. *Clinical Pharmacology and Therapeutics,* 1977, *21,* 643-646.

DiNuzzo, R.V. The 26th Albany Rx survey. *Medical Marketing and Media,* 1982, *17,* 36, 38,40,42,44,46,48,50,55,56,58,60,62,64-66.

Francetic, I., Lasagna, L., Weintraub, M., & Karch, F.E. Prescription prices under the New York generic substitution law. *Annals of Internal Medicine,* 1980, *92,* 419-423.

Goldberg, T., Aldridge, G.W., DeVito, C.A., Vidis, J., Moore, W.E., & Dickson, W.M. Impact of drug substitution legislation: A report of the first year's experience. *Journal of the American Pharmaceutical Association,* 1977, *17,* 216-226.

Gumbhir, A.K., & Rodowskas, C.A. Consumer price differentials between generic and brand name prescriptions. *American Journal of Public Health,* October 1974, *64,*977-982.

Hecht, A. *Generic drugs: How good are they?* (DHEW Publication No. [FDA] 78-3068). Washington, D.C.: Department of Health, Education and Welfare, Public Health Service, Food and Drug Administration, Office of Public Affairs, 1979.

Herman, M.A. Generic drug substitution: Pro. *State Government,* 1977, *50,* 102-107.

Kolata, G.B. Large drug firms fight generic substitution. *Science,* 1979, *206,* 1054-1056.

Lambert, Z.V., Doering, P.L., Goldstein, E., & McCormick, W.C. Predispositions toward generic drug acceptance. *Journal of Consumer Research,* 1980, *7,* 14-23.

New drug application data summaries, to include foreign marketing experience, will become basic narrative document in all applications, FDA proposes in NDA re-write. *The Pink Sheet,* October 25, 1982, *44*(43), 13-14.

Substitution foes get bioavailability "club." *American Druggist,* 1977, *175*(3), 20, 69.

Survey puts generic drug use at 25 percent. *American Pharmacy,* 1982, *NS22*(2), 12.

Top 200 drugs in 1981. *Pharmacy Times,* April 1982, *48*(4), 23-32.

U.S. Bureau of Consumer Protection. *Drug product selection: Staff report to the Federal Trade Commission* (Publication No. 79-15070). Washington, D.C.: U.S. Government Printing Office, January 1979.

U.S. Department of Health and Human Services. *Approved prescription drug products with therapeutic equivalence evaluations.* Washington, D.C.: U.S. Government Printing Office, 1980.

Chapter 4

Compliance to Drug Therapy

A British physician once stated: "The failure of an elderly person to respond to an effective drug is nearly always due to failure of the patient to take the drug rather than to absorb it" (Hall, 1973, p. 582). This statement alludes to the fact that many elderly patients do not comply properly with their prescribed drug therapy; however, it should not be interpreted as an indication that the elderly are the only persons guilty of improper compliance. Poor compliance to drug therapy is a problem in all patients, young and old alike, but certain factors that influence or result in noncompliant behavior are somewhat different in the elderly than in the young.

The following discussion of patient compliance, or noncompliance, to prescribed drug therapy, generally applies to patients of all ages; however, a number of factors, including increased consumption of prescription and nonprescription medications, increased susceptibility to adverse drug reactions, and limited financial resources, may make the impact of poor compliance more significant in the elderly than in the young.

Persons who work with the elderly should be aware that their elderly patients or clients may not comply appropriately with their drug therapy and that this behavior may have a significant effect on the health of these individuals. With this understanding it may then be possible to identify noncompliant patients, intervening in an effort to encourage cooperation with their drug therapy.

TYPES OF NONCOMPLIANCE

Noncompliance can be broadly defined as the failure of patients to follow instructions provided regarding the use of medication (Hussar, 1975). With this definition it is easy to see that noncompliance is certainly more than just the failure

65

of patients to take their medication. While omission, or the failure to take a dose of medication, is a major type of noncompliance, other types of noncompliant behavior exist.

Failure to Take Medication

The most common type of noncompliant behavior is simply the failure of patients to take their medications, which accounts for 50 percent or more of the incidences of noncompliance (Cooper, Love, & Raffoul, 1982; Smith, C.R., 1979). Not all of the incidences of omission of medication doses are a result of the forgetfulness of the patient, but rather they may be the result of other pertinent factors, such as not being able to afford the purchase of the prescription drugs.

Additionally, the omission of one or more medications may be the result of an active decision on the part of the patients who have decided, for one reason or another, not to take their medication. This type of behavior has been called "intelligent noncompliance" (Weintraub, 1981) or "intentional prescription non-adherence" (Cooper et al., 1982) and may be a result of the patient's attempts to decrease the severity of an adverse reaction to the drug because of an excessive dosage ordered by the physician. Patients may also intentionally reduce or omit medication doses because of an exaggerated response to a dose of medication that would otherwise be appropriate. Although intentional noncompliance may sometimes be "intelligent," such as to avoid an adverse drug reaction, it may also be inappropriate. For example, patients may wrongly decide that they no longer need a particular medication and therefore discontinue taking that medication without informing their physician.

Taking Medication at the Wrong Time

Another common type of noncompliance occurs when patients do not take their medications at the appropriate time. This behavior may have little or no clinical significance, such as in the case of the patient who is instructed to take one digoxin (Lanoxin®) tablet in the morning but who takes the tablet every evening instead. Since this heart medication has a long duration of action, it really does not matter when during the day or night the drug is taken.

This behavior may become more significant as illustrated by the example of a patient with a prescription for the diuretic furosemide (Lasix®) who is supposed to take the tablet every morning but decides to take it in the evening instead. Since this drug significantly increases urine flow for a six- to eight-hour period, the patient improperly taking the drug in the evening may experience annoying or embarrassing urinary frequency or incontinence during the night.

Excessive Consumption

Excessive consumption could occur when the patient increases the frequency or the dose of medication that has been prescribed, either on purpose or inadvertently. Numerous reasons for this type of behavior may exist but include the improper belief that "if one pill is good, two will be twice as good."

Additionally, some elderly individuals may experience some difficulty remembering whether or not they took their medication. This doubt could lead to one or more additional and therefore excessive doses being taken, possibly resulting in drug toxicity. Patients who have difficulty remembering whether they took their medication as prescribed can frequently benefit from the use of certain compliance aids, such as those that are discussed later in this chapter.

Premature Discontinuation of Medication

Another fairly common form of noncompliance is the premature discontinuation of drug therapy, when the patient decides, for one of many possible reasons, to stop taking medications before the time indicated by the physician (Lamy, 1980; Sackett, 1979). This type of improper compliance occurs relatively commonly, such as in the case of antibiotics that have been prescribed to treat conditions such as a urinary tract infection. In spite of receiving a seven- or ten-day supply of the medication, it is not uncommon for patients to stop taking the drug after two or three days of therapy because they feel better and the symptoms of their infection have disappeared. This type of practice could result in a recurrence of the infection, perhaps even with bacteria that are more resistant to antibiotics than the original one.

Failure to Have Prescription Filled

One interesting, and often overlooked type of noncompliance is the patient's failure to have prescriptions filled (Smith, C.R., 1979). Health professionals usually assume that prescriptions are faithfully obtained by patients after being issued by a prescriber; however, studies have shown that approximately five percent of prescriptions that are written are not filled (Blackwell, 1973; Boyd, Covington, Stanaszek, & Coussons, 1974b). The reasons for this include the patient's inability to afford the medication or the decision that the medication is unnecessary or that its use represents too great a risk.

Consumption of Interfering Medications or Nutrients

It is also possible that patients who are taking their medications at the proper time, and in the proper dose, may still be noncompliant with the intention of their prescribed therapy if they concurrently ingest medications or nutrients that interfere with that therapy. As discussed in more detail in Chapter 8, concurrent administration of interfering drugs or nutrients may significantly alter the effect of some medications.

The medications that can interfere with therapy include both prescription and nonprescription drugs and also include the use of alcohol. A number of serious and even life-threatening interactions may be caused by the concurrent ingestion of alcoholic beverages.

Use of Medications Not Prescribed

The ingestion of medications that are not currently prescribed can also be considered to be improper compliance to drug therapy (Smith, C.R., 1979). Certainly the chance of drug interaction with other medications exists, as described above, but also the use of these additional medications may be therapeutically inappropriate. For example, individuals may take a previously discontinued prescription, such as antibiotic capsules left over after treatment of a past infection, because they think that they may need them, or they may take prescription medications such as analgesics or tranquilizers that they have obtained from a friend or relative without the approval of their physician.

INCIDENCE OF NONCOMPLIANCE

It has been difficult to determine the precise incidence of noncompliance in the elderly because noncompliance relates to many different factors. Also the types of studies that have been performed in an effort to estimate the incidence of noncompliance vary considerably, thus influencing the conclusions.

Some studies have assigned extremely rigid parameters to define noncompliance so that even a slight alteration in the drug regimen, such as taking a prescribed dose a little earlier or later than intended, was defined as noncompliance. On the other hand, some studies have been quite liberal in their definition of noncompliance so that patients would be labeled noncompliant only if they altered their therapy in a major way, such as by skipping a medication dose entirely.

Other study variations that contribute to this difficulty in determining the precise incidence of noncompliance include the use of extremely different populations, such as elderly patients taking cardiac medications as compared with young women taking oral contraceptives. Additionally, methods used to assess the noncompliant behavior of the patients being studied may vary from simply asking patients whether they have been taking their medication to the actual analysis of urine samples to detect the presence of drug, proving that the patients had indeed taken the medication.

Because of these differences and others, estimates of the incidence of non-compliance have ranged from 2 to 95 percent!

In my estimation, based on data derived from noncompliance studies (Brook, Appel, Avery, Orman, & Stevenson, 1971; Curtis, 1961; Davis, 1968; Johnson, 1979; Logan, Milne, Achber, Campbell, & Haynes, 1979; Maddock, 1967; Mazzullo, Lasagna, & Griner, 1974) and my personal observations, it is safe to say that somewhere between one fourth and one third of the elderly outpatient population exhibit some form of noncompliance to their drug therapy that may *potentially*, but not necessarily, result in compromise of their therapy in some clinically significant manner.

This estimation must be qualified in two ways. First, it is simply an average, and some patient populations may exhibit much higher or much lower incidences of noncompliance depending on many factors, which will be discussed later. Second, patients may be noncompliant with their drug therapy, yet not suffer any ill effects. This would be especially true if the prescribed drug or drugs were unnecessary in the first place!

FACTORS CONTRIBUTING TO NONCOMPLIANCE

It is important for health professionals to be aware that numerous factors may contribute to noncompliant behavior in all patients. Noncompliance is a major problem in both young and old; however, some of the factors that contribute to noncompliance assume a more important perspective in the elderly because of the potential severity of the problems that may arise and as a result of the particular health and disease-related problems that may occur more commonly in the elderly patient.

For the purpose of this discussion I have divided these factors into three major groups: (1) factors that are patient related, (2) those that are related to the individual's drugs or drug therapy, and (3) those that are related to the health professionals who may interact with the patient (Exhibit 4-1).

Patient-Related Factors

Not Understanding Drug Therapy

A relatively important cause of improper compliance is the patients' lack of understanding of their drug therapy (Fletcher, Fletcher, Thomas, & Hamann, 1979; Hussar, 1975; Lamy, 1980; Smith, D.L., 1976). Patients may either not appreciate the importance of their drug therapy in treating their particular health problems or they may not understand how to take their medications properly.

For example, individuals with high blood pressure who do not fully understand the disease and the importance of taking medication to control it may be more

Exhibit 4-1 Selected Factors Contributing to Noncompliance and Drug
Therapy in the Elderly

Patient related

- failure to understand importance of drug therapy
- failure to understand instructions concerning drug therapy
- concurrent self-administration of prescription medication, nonprescription medication, or alcohol
- lack of social supervision
- feeling too ill or too tired to take medication
- physical disabilities, including impaired vision or hearing and arthritis

Therapy related

- increased number of medications and frequency of doses
- increased rate of adverse drug reactions
- difficult dosage forms
- expensive drug therapy
- characteristics of illness

Health professional related

- poor relationship with patient
- expression of doubt concerning therapeutic potential
- unwillingness to educate patients

---

likely to miss an occasional dose or perhaps may take their medications only when they are not feeling well. Obviously this behavior could result in improper control of the blood pressure and consequently a patient could suffer from the long-term problems of untreated hypertension such as stroke, heart attack, and other serious consequences.

Patients who understand the importance of their drug therapy but either do not understand or misinterpret the medication instructions may also be noncompliant. For example, an elderly patient who is required to take five or six different medications may become confused as to the times that the medication should be taken or may even forget what one or more of the medications are for, possibly resulting in insufficient therapy or toxicity.

Insufficient understanding of both the disease process and the drug therapy can be prevented by making certain that patients have received the proper education about their disease and fully understand their drug therapy, including what effects their drug therapy will have and how their medications should be taken.

Self-Medication Practices

Another factor contributing to noncompliance may be the self-medication practices of the patient (Schwartz, 1962). If an individual is a user of nonprescription medications, a potential problem could result if a nonprescription medication either augmented or counteracted one or more prescription medications that the patient was taking. For example, a patient experiencing a great deal of pain may decide to use significant doses of aspirin in addition to an aspirin-containing prescription analgesic, such as Empirin® with Codeine. This potentially excessive use of aspirin could result in stomach irritation or ulcers. Although the prescription drug may be taken as the prescriber had wished, the patient could still be considered noncompliant because the prescribed therapy did not call for additional aspirin. Noncompliance resulting from the interference of nonprescription drugs may be a greater problem in the elderly than in the young since the elderly tend to consume more nonprescription medications than do younger individuals.

Such interference with prescribed therapy can also result from the concurrent use of alcohol, possibly causing a serious or even fatal drug interaction.

Lack of Social Supervision

Lack of social supervision is another factor contributing to noncompliance that may have special significance in the elderly (Blackwell, 1973; Hussar, 1975). It has been found that individuals who live alone are less likely to comply with prescribed drug therapy than those living with another person; therefore, elderly patients who live alone due to the loss of a spouse, for example, may be less compliant with their drug therapy than when living with someone who could provide support or assistance with their medication.

Too Ill or Too Tired to Take Medication

Another factor possibly resulting in noncompliance in the elderly is that some individuals may feel too ill or too tired to take their medication (Schwartz, 1962). This behavior is understandable because many of us can remember at least one occasion when we were sick in bed, knowing that the best thing to do would be to get up and take our medication, but finding it extremely difficult to do so. A decrease in the ability of some elderly to ambulate due to frailty, arthritis, dizziness or drowsiness resulting from the adverse effect of a medication, or some other condition could complicate this situation.

Sensory Losses

Additional disabilities that are experienced more commonly in the elderly population may also tend to cause noncompliance. Age-related or disease-related decreases in vision may make it very difficult for elderly patients to identify their prescriptions and to read the small print on the prescription labels (Dirckx, 1979; Jenkins, 1979). Hearing problems may make it difficult for the elderly patient to comprehend verbal instructions concerning the proper use of medications (Ebersole & Hess, 1981), and physical problems, such as arthritis, may make the safety closures that are required on most prescriptions "elderly proof" in addition to being "child proof" (Jenkins, 1979).

Numerous additional patient-related factors such as education, sex, and socioeconomic status have been attributed to noncompliance, but general agreement does not exist on the actual influence of these factors and they will not be discussed further. The reader who is interested in a more detailed discussion of these factors is referred to the book *Compliance in Health Care*, which is cited in the reference section of this chapter.

Therapy-Related Factors

Certain characteristics of a patient's drug therapy have also been found to result in noncompliance. Although these factors are not influenced by age alone, many of them may be significant in the elderly.

Complex Drug Therapy

Compliance has been found to decrease with an increase in the number of medications that an individual takes and the frequency with which the doses are to be administered. Apparently, patients find it difficult to manage the more complex scheduling and greater number of doses that accompany an increase in the number of prescriptions that they take. Since the elderly consume more prescription medications than younger patients, the potential for noncompliance is obviously increased (Blackwell, 1973; Haynes, Sackett, & Taylor, 1980; Hussar, 1975).

Adverse Drug Effects

Compliance to prescribed therapy may also decrease as the occurrence of adverse reactions increases (Haynes, 1979; Hussar, 1975). I have spoken to many elderly individuals who, when aware that a particular problem that they are experiencing is related to the medications that they are taking, discontinue taking one or more of their medications, or at least reduce the amount that they are taking, in order to avoid or reduce annoying side effects. Since the incidence of adverse drug reactions is greater in the elderly than in the general population this factor could be of significance in elderly individuals.

Dosage Form

Some medications are available in dosage forms that may be difficult for an elderly patient to use. For example, a person with arthritis may have problems removing a rectal suppository from its foil wrapper and inserting it, or a person with decreased visual acuity may have difficulty measuring out a specified amount of liquid medication (Hussar, 1975).

Some liquid medications are formulated as a thick suspension that requires brisk, forceful, and repeated shaking rather than simply inverting the bottle once or twice. Some individuals, especially the frail elderly or someone who is ill, may be unable to shake this type of medication adequately. If this occurs, the active ingredient may remain at the bottom of the bottle so the patients first use subpotent doses of liquid that are poured from the top of the bottle and as they get down to the medication near the bottom the concentration of active ingredient may be much greater.

Occasionally individuals will attempt to crush tablets that they have difficulty swallowing. The crushed tablet can then be mixed with applesauce or another food so that it may be taken more easily. This may make it easier for some individuals to take their medications, but it may also result in inappropriate use of a drug, since a number of medications are specially designed to release their active ingredient slowly over a period of hours. Other drugs may have a protective coating designed to prevent the tablet from dissolving in the stomach in order to prevent stomach upset. Before any medication is crushed, it is best to ask a pharmacist if it can be crushed and still be effective or, better yet, if the medication is available in an easy-to-take liquid form.

The dosage form of some medications may also cause problems because of its bad taste. An example of a medication that does not taste good is potassium chloride solution. Some persons find the taste of this drug to be so objectionable that they refuse to take it. In this case it may be possible to mask the taste by mixing it in juice, or the physician may be able to prescribe a brand with a taste that a patient finds less objectionable.

Financial Considerations

The financial aspects of drug therapy may also be a significant deterrent to proper compliance (Brand, Smith, & Brand, 1977; Rodstein, 1966; Smith, C.R. 1979) especially in the many elderly persons who are on a minimal, fixed income. Although prescription prices have risen much more slowly than other components of health care, they may still represent a significant financial outlay. Elderly patients may decide that they either cannot afford to obtain medication that was prescribed for them or that they will take fewer doses than prescribed in order to make their prescription last longer.

Characteristics of Illness

The characteristics of various types of illness may also influence compliance to drug therapy (Blackwell, 1972; Boyd et al., 1974a; Hussar, 1975). Diseases, such as adult-onset diabetes and hypertension, whose presentation is mild or without symptoms, may result in some degree of noncompliance owing to the patients' perception that the lack of severe symptoms means that it is not necessary to take their medication all the time.

Treatment of diseases such as tuberculosis or hypertension, which require long-term therapy, may also be accompanied by noncompliance because compliance tends to decrease as the duration of therapy increases. Also, diseases of a psychological nature, such as confusion, agitation, or depression, may create obvious problems with compliance.

Factors Related to Health Professionals

Attitude toward Therapy

Health professionals themselves may have a significant impact on patient compliance (Francis, Korsch, & Morris, 1969; Hulka, 1979). It is important that the prescriber develop a positive relationship with the patient, encouraging loyalty and trust. While not promising unrealistic results, he or she should express a confident attitude to the patient when prescribing a particular medication, rather than indicating that there is little or no hope for improvement in the individual's condition.

Patient Education

If health professionals, including physicians, pharmacists, and nurses, do not properly educate their patients concerning the medications that they are taking, noncompliance will likely result. Patients should be educated concerning why the medication is being ordered, what is to be expected from the medication, and how the medication should be used. Patient education is described in further detail in Chapter 5.

CONSEQUENCES OF NONCOMPLIANCE

The consequences of noncompliance can be numerous and can place the patient in significant jeopardy.

Insufficient Treatment of Patient's Condition

One of the most serious consequences of noncompliance to prescribed therapy is the fact that the patient's disease-related condition, for which the medication(s) was originally prescribed, may not improve or may in fact worsen, resulting from insufficient therapy (Hussar, 1975). This is of course with the assumption that the medication(s) prescribed was necessary in the first place, an assumption that may not always be true.

Need for Additional Medication

If the prescriber is unaware of the patient's noncompliance, additional medication or increased dosage of the original medication may be prescribed with the belief that the original medication was ineffective, at least at the dosage prescribed. In some cases the patient may then decide to take their original medications at the correct dosage, which, when combined with their modified drug therapy, could result in toxicity. Of course one of the major concerns with increased medication use in the elderly, especially unnecessary medication, is that the risk of adverse reactions increases significantly with each additional medication.

The use of additional medication may also increase the chances of the patient experiencing an interaction with other prescription or nonprescription drugs that the patient might be using or with alcohol or nutrients, possibly resulting in a number of serious outcomes, including a negation of the therapeutic effects of one or more of the medications or the potential for an adverse drug reaction.

Economic Consequences

The economic consequences of noncompliance must also be considered in light of the fact that many elderly are on limited fixed incomes. If medication is purchased and not used as a result of noncompliance, it may represent a significant expenditure. Perhaps the greatest financial consideration of noncompliance, however, is that noncompliance to drug therapy may result in inappropriate or insufficient therapeutic response or adverse drug reactions, requiring additional visits to the physician, additional prescription medications, or even hospitalization if the patient's condition warrants (Blackwell, 1973). Obviously these financial consequences could amount to a significantly greater expenditure than that necessary to purchase the original prescription.

Accumulation of Leftover Medication

A significant danger exists when medication that has not been consumed accumulates in the medicine cabinet, refrigerator, or other location. Such medication may be used inappropriately at a later time either by the person for whom the medication was originally intended or by a friend or relative for whom the medication was not prescribed. A real danger also exists if the unconsumed medication is accessible to youngsters, such as curious grandchildren who may be visiting their grandparents, with the possibility of a tragic outcome resulting.

DETECTION OF NONCOMPLIANT PATIENTS

Although many health professionals believe that they are able to tell which of their patients are noncompliers, it has been found that the patient's degree of compliance cannot be reliably predicted (Haynes et al., 1980; Roth & Caron, 1978; Sackett, 1979; Weintraub, 1981). This fact was recently reemphasized to me by a 36-year-old woman whom I saw in a local hospital. The patient had severe asthma for which oral theophylline and prednisone had been prescribed. The theophylline was being used to reverse the bronchoconstriction that she was experiencing and therefore relax and dilate her bronchial tubes. The prednisone was being used to decrease the inflammatory process with which asthma is associated. Since the patient had expressed what had appeared to be a sincere desire to get well, and because the medication was administered to the patient by nurses in the hospital, no one expected compliance to be a problem. However, after we repeatedly measured the amount of theophylline in her blood in an effort to adjust her medication dosage a series of unexplicably low serum theophylline concentrations were found. The patient was confronted and tearfully admitted that she was purposely inducing vomiting shortly after the medication was administered.

The difficulty in being able to predict which patients do not comply well with their drug therapy was again emphasized when I had the opportunity to interview an elderly gentleman who was taking ten medications for a number of different disease conditions. My initial (and unfair) judgment as I started speaking with this individual was that he most likely frequently confused his medications and exhibited noncompliant behavior. However, much to my surprise I discovered that he indeed was remarkably compliant and knew a great deal about each of his medications, including how to take them properly and when to take them. He had even devised a clever system that he used with the assistance of his wife to guarantee that he would take all of his medications at the correct time.

TRAITS OF NONCOMPLIANT INDIVIDUALS

Although, as mentioned, it is not possible to predict reliably a patient's compliance to drug therapy, it is possible to identify certain factors or traits that tend to be present in noncompliant patients. Although it must be realized that these traits are certainly not absolute indicators, they can be looked for by health professionals who suspect that noncompliance may be a problem (Haynes, 1979; Haynes et al., 1980).

- Illness fails to respond to therapy.
- Patient is socially isolated.

- Patient is forgetful or confused.
- Sensory deficits are present.
- Drug therapy is complex.
- Patient fails to keep appointments.
- Drug therapy is expensive.
- Patient fails to obtain timely prescription refills.

Although these factors may pertain to all patients of all ages, it is obvious that some of them may have considerable significance in the elderly. These factors should not be used as indicting evidence that a patient is not complying with therapy but rather could be used as a rough guideline that could enable health professionals to identify patients in whom noncompliance could be a problem.

Perhaps the simplest and most obvious method of determining whether a patient is complying with a drug therapy regimen is by simply asking the patient whether the medication is being taken. Approximately one half of patients who are noncompliant will admit to being so when asked; however, it may be difficult to assess the precise extent of noncompliance by using this technique.

ENCOURAGING PROPER COMPLIANCE

Health professionals can encourage their patients to comply properly with their drug therapy or assist them in this effort in a number of ways (Exhibit 4-2):

- *Simplify drug therapy.* By making a patient's drug therapy as simple as possible health professionals can improve the patient's compliance to that therapy. This can be accomplished through the use of the least possible number of medications and drug therapy regimens that are compatible with daily habits such as meals, bedtime, or after arising. For example, if an individual is to take a medication once daily, suggest that the patient associate that dose with a routine daily event, such as setting the breakfast table or watching a favorite television show.
- *Provide proper patient education.* Patients who understand their disease conditions and their drug therapy will exhibit better compliance toward their drug therapy (Norell, 1979). The role of the health professional in patient education is discussed in more detail in Chapter 5.
- *Use special medication packaging and labeling techniques.* In an effort to assist elderly patients with their medication compliance, special packaging and labeling techniques can be used. These include the use of typewriters that have large print to make prescription labels easily legible by persons with vision disturbances; the routine use of auxiliary prescription labels that attach

Exhibit 4-2 How Health Professionals Can Encourage Proper Medication
Compliance

Simplify drug therapy:

- minimal number of medications
- simple regimens that are compatible with daily activities

Educate patients concerning the important aspects of the following:

- disease state
- medications and their use

Use special labeling and packaging:

- large print typewriters
- auxiliary labels
- proper positioning of prescription labels

Use compliance aids:

- medication reminders
- medication calendars
- household items

---

specific instructions to the prescription vial, such as "take with meals" or
"do not drink alcohol while taking this medication" (Fedder, Goldstein,
Manes, Benko, & Shangraw, 1979); and affixing prescription labels parallel
to the central axis of small prescription vials so that the patient need not rotate
the vial repeatedly to read the directions (Dirckx, 1979).

- *Use compliance aids.* Specially designed memory aids can also be used by
  elderly patients to increase their compliance to drug therapy (Kramer, 1977;
  Linkewich, Catalano, & Flack, 1974; Rehder, McCoy, Blackwell, Whitehead, & Robinson, 1980). These aids include various commercially prepared
  "pill boxes" and medication containers that are available for sale at most
  pharmacies. Commercially available or homemade medication calendars can
  also be used, as well as common household items such as empty egg cartons
  and muffin tins. These types of containers may be able to provide assistance
  to an individual, but they must be used with extreme care. The greatest
  drawback to the use of medication containers other than the original prescrip-

tion vial is that when the drug is transferred from the prescription vial to the compliance aid, it loses its identifying labeling and instructions. Consequently the patient may make errors with both the medications to be taken and the time of administration. In some cases it may be necessary for a health professional or responsible family member to place the medications in the compliance aid in order to prevent such confusion. In spite of the potential problems associated with the use of such compliance aids they can significantly reduce the incidence of noncompliance. One study (Martin, 1982) demonstrated that the use of color-coded pill bottles that were matched to a color-coded weekly pill tray was the most effective method to decrease medication errors and to increase proper compliance to drug therapy in a population of elderly outpatients.

THE USE OF "CHILD-PROOF" CONTAINERS

As mentioned earlier, the use of "child-proof" closures (safety caps) on prescription vials can present a significant problem to the elderly. Many of these closures are extremely difficult to open by persons with good eyesight and a strong grip, so one can understand the problems that a frail elderly patient with cataracts and arthritis may have. Although these closures have been the subject of much derision, they save the lives of many children each year by preventing accidental poisoning. They are required for most prescription medications, although a number of prescription medications that are considered to possess relatively little danger of causing acute poisoning have been exempted from the safety closure requirement. Actually, the biggest problem created by these hard-to-open closures is not the fact that they are difficult to open, but rather once they are opened the safety closure is frequently left off. This exposes the medication to the atmosphere and moisture, which can cause the medication to lose potency, or it could become contaminated with dirt, bacteria, or other foreign material. Sometimes the patient may transfer the contents of the prescription vial to another container, which could be unmarked or improperly marked. The danger of this practice is illustrated by two patients about whom I was informed. The first patient was admitted to the emergency room of a local hospital with a small bottle that had a handwritten label on it that read "Demerol®, 50 mg," which is a narcotic analgesic. After examining the contents of the vial it was found to contain digoxin, 0.25-mg tablets, which is a heart drug, and no Demerol® tablets at all! The second patient, an elderly woman who was being visited by a home health nurse and a pharmacy student, had emptied her digoxin (Lanoxin®) and furosemide (Lasix®) prescriptions into the same ashtray to eliminate the need to open the prescription containers each time she needed the medication. Since both of these tablets look somewhat similar, she would obviously have experienced difficulty selecting the proper tablet.

If safety closures are creating a problem for the patient, there are a number of ways in which an easy-to-open "nonsafety" prescription closure can be substituted.

First, the physician may request that the substitute closure be used. Second, the patient can also request that a nonsafety closure be used; or, third, the pharmacist may ask the patient if he or she desires a nonsafety closure. It is recommended that the pharmacist obtain the patient's signature when substituting an easy-to-open closure for a safety closure to document that the patient truly desired to have the easy-to-open closure and that a choice of closures was actually available to the patient.

In addition, in what may be the easiest solution to the problem, the pharmacist can dispense medication in vials or bottles that have a "two-way cap," one side of which is "child proof" and the other a "standard" cap. With the two-way cap the consumer can then decide whether to use the standard cap for ease of opening or the safety cap to protect children, or perhaps a confused elderly individual, from poisoning.

Health professionals should be alert for problems that their patients may be experiencing with safety prescription closures and inform them that they can get their prescriptions filled in easy-to-open containers. However, it is important for health professionals to assess each individual situation carefully because of the possibility of small children gaining access to the medication. It would indeed be tragic if an effort to make the use of medication easier for an elderly patient resulted in the poisoning of a child.

REFERENCES

Blackwell, B. The drug defaulter, *Clinical Pharmacology and Therapeutics.* 1972, *13*, 841-848.

Blackwell, B. Drug therapy: Patient compliance. *New England Journal of Medicine*, 1973, *289*, 249-252.

Boyd, J.R., Covington, T.R., Stanaszek, W.F., & Coussons, R.T. Drug defaulting: Part i: Determinants of compliance. *American Journal of Hospital Pharmacy*, 1974, *31*, 362-367. (a)

Boyd, J.R., Covington, T.R., Stanaszek, W.F., & Coussons, R.T. Drug defaulting: Part ii: Analysis of noncompliance patterns. *American Journal of Hospital Pharmacy*, 1974, *31*, 485-491. (b)

Brand, F.N., Smith, R.T., & Brand, P.A. Effect of economic barriers to medical care on patients' noncompliance. *Public Health Reports*, 1977, *92*, 72-78.

Brook, R.H. Appel, F.A., Avery, C., Orman, M., & Stevenson, R.L. Effectiveness of inpatient follow-up care. *New England Journal of Medicine*, 1971, *285*, 1509-1514.

Cooper, J.K., Love, D.W., & Raffoul, P.R. Intentional prescription nonadherence (noncompliance) by the elderly. *Journal of the American Geriatrics Society*, 1982, *30*, 329-333.

Curtis, E.B. Medication errors made by patients. *Nursing Outlook*, 1961, *9*, 290-291.

Davis, M.S. Variations in patients' compliance with doctors' advice: An empirical analysis of patterns of communication. *American Journal of Public Health*, 1968, *58*, 274-288.

Dirckx, J.H. Labels for prescribed drugs (letter). *Journal of the American Medical Association*, 1979, *242*, 413-414.

Ebersole, P., & Hess, P. Drug use and abuse. In *Toward healthy aging*. St. Louis: C.V. Mosby, 1981.

Fedder, D.O., Goldstein, M., Manes, T., Benko, J.E., & Shangraw, R. Use of auxiliary labels to improve patient compliance. *Contemporary Pharmacy Practice, 1979, 2*(2), 51-55.

Fletcher, S.W., Fletcher, R.H., Thomas, D.C., & Hamann, C. Patients' understanding of prescribed drugs. *Journal of Community Health*, 1979, *4*, 183-189.

Francis, V., Korsch, B.M., & Morris, M.J. Gaps in doctor-patient communication. *New England Journal of Medicine*, 1969, *280*, 535-540.

Hall, M.R.P. Drug therapy in the elderly. *British Medical Journal*, 1973, *3*, 582-584.

Haynes, R.B. Determinants of compliance: The disease and the mechanics of treatment. In R.B. Haynes, D.W. Taylor, & D.L. Sackett (Eds.), *Compliance in health care*. Baltimore: Johns Hopkins University Press, 1979.

Haynes, R.B., Sackett, D.L., & Taylor, D.W. How to detect and manage low patient compliance in chronic illness. *Geriatrics*, 1980, *35*, 91-97.

Hulka, B.S. Patient-clinician interactions and compliance. In R.B. Haynes et al. (Eds.), *Compliance in health care*. Baltimore: Johns Hopkins University Press, 1979.

Hussar, D.A. Patient noncompliance. *Journal of the American Pharmaceutical Association*, 1975, *15*, 183-190, 201.

Jenkins, G.H.C. Drug compliance and the elderly patient (letter). *British Medical Journal*, 1979, *1*, 124.

Johnson, S.S. Health beliefs of hypertensive patients in a family medicine residency program. *Journal of Family Practice*, 1979, *9*, 877-883.

Kramer, J. Compliance packaging: Developing an idea whose time has come. *Medical Marketing and Media*, 1977, *12*, 17-19.

Lamy, P.P. Patient counseling and compliance. In *Prescribing for the elderly*. Littleton, Mass.: Publishing Sciences Group, 1980.

Linkewich, J.A., Catalano, R.B., & Flack, H.L. The effect of packaging and instruction on outpatient compliance with medication regimens. *Drug Intelligence and Clinical Pharmacy*, 1974, *8*, 10-15.

Logan, A.G., Milne, B.J., Achber, C., Campbell, W.P., & Haynes, R.B. Work-site treatment of hypertension by specially trained nurses: A controlled trial. *Lancet*, 1979, *2*, 1175-1178.

Maddock, R.K. Patient cooperation in taking medicines: A study involving isoniazid and aminosalicylic acid. *Journal of the American Medical Association*, 1967, *199*, 137-140.

Martin, D.C., & Mead, K. Reducing medication errors in a geriatric population. *Journal of the American Geriatrics Society*, 1982, *30*, 258-260.

Mazzullo, J.M., Lasagna, L., & Griner, P.F. Variations in interpretation of prescription instructions: The need for improved prescribing habits. *Journal of the American Medical Association*, 1974, *227*, 929-931.

Norell, S.E. Improving medication compliance: A randomized clinical trial. *British Medical Journal*, 1979, *2*, 1031-1033.

Rehder, T.L., McCoy, L.K., Blackwell, B., Whitehead, W., & Robinson, A. Improving medication compliance by counseling and special prescription container. *American Journal of Hospital Pharmacy*, 1980, *37*, 379-384.

Rodstein, M. The prevention of disability in the aged. *Geriatrics*, 1966, *21*, 193-196.

Roth, H.P., & Caron, H.S. Accuracy of doctors' estimates and patients' statements on adherence to a drug regimen. *Clinical Pharmacology and Therapeutics*, 1978, *23*, 361-370.

Sackett, D.L. A compliance practicum for the busy practitioner. In R.B. Haynes et al., (Eds.), *Compliance in health care*. Baltimore: Johns Hopkins University Press, 1979.

Schwartz, D., Wang, M., Zeitz, L., & Goss, M. E. W. Medication errors made by elderly, chronically ill patients. *American Journal of Public Health*, 1962, *52*, 2018-2029.

Smith, C.R. Use of drugs in the aged. *Johns Hopkins Medical Journal*, 1979, *145*, 61-64.

Smith, D.L. Patient compliance with medication regimens. *Drug Intelligence and Clinical Pharmacy*, 1976, *10*, 386-393.

Weintraub, M. Intelligent noncompliance with special emphasis on the elderly. *Contemporary Pharmacy Practice*, 1981, *4*, 8-11.

Chapter 5

Medication Education and the Elderly Patient

The aspect of drug therapy that has changed most drastically in the past ten years is that of patient participation in drug therapy. It seems difficult for me to believe it now, but when I was a pharmacy student in the late 1960s, my classmates and I were instructed to "never let the customers know what medications they are taking!" The prevailing attitude at that time was that persons had no right to know the names of, or anything about, the medicines that were prescribed for them, and that the "secret collusion" that existed between the physician and the pharmacist was for the patient's benefit. Fortunately, for everyone involved, especially the patient, that attitude has changed drastically.

In the early and middle 1970s, when the United States went through a period of political and social unrest, consumerism became a common philosophy in many areas, including health care and drug therapy. Persons realized that they had the right, and the responsibility, to become partners in their own health care with physicians, pharmacists, nurses, and other health professionals and that they had a right and a responsibility to understand their health status and their medication regimen, including its rationale, expected therapeutic benefits, and side effects.

This rather significant change in philosophy is most evident to pharmacists who formerly practiced their profession under the understanding to "*never* let the *customer* know what drugs they are taking," the dominant philosophy prior to the late 1960s, and now practice under the philosophy that "the pharmacist *must* tell the *patient* about their medications." In fact, the pendulum has swung so far that there have been some recent court decisions finding both physicians and pharmacists guilty of malpractice for not providing patients with sufficient information concerning their drug therapy!

Certainly proper medication education is important for all age-groups; however, as with patient compliance, particular aspects of medication education are unique to the elderly population. In this chapter I will first discuss some of the important general aspects of medication education and then the aspects of medication education that are most pertinent to the elderly.

GOALS OF PATIENT MEDICATION EDUCATION

Obviously one of the most important goals of proper medication education is to increase patients' understanding of their drug therapy. Through an understanding of the medication's purpose and how it should be taken, the number of medication errors that a patient commits will be reduced (MacDonald, MacDonald, & Phoenix, 1977). For example the following errors may be avoided: inappropriately skipping one or more doses, discontinuing the medication too soon, taking the medication at the wrong time, taking too little or too much medication, or ingesting other medications not currently prescribed. Additionally, a patient informed of common or potentially significant drug interactions can avoid the alcoholic beverages, prescription or nonprescription medications, or foods that might interact with the prescribed therapy.

Through proper medication education, the patient's general understanding of additional aspects of the prescribed drug therapy will also be enhanced. For example, a person informed of the early signs of drug toxicity would be able to notify the physician at their onset, thus preventing further, and potentially more harmful complications.

Proper medication education will also help to satisfy the very real consumer demand that exists for this education and, ideally, through the reduction of medication errors and the increase in compliance to drug therapy, will improve the patient's therapeutic outcome.

WHAT THE PATIENT SHOULD KNOW

The information that a patient should understand regarding a specific drug therapy will vary depending on a wide variety of individual situations or patient needs (McKenny, 1979; Statement on Pharmacist, 1976; Weibert & Dee, 1976) (Exhibit 5-1).

Name of Medication

It may seem obvious that patients should know the names of their medications, but I am amazed by the frequency that patients refer to their medications in terms such as "the little white pill." Normally patients should only be expected to know the brand names of their medications since pharmaceutical nomenclature is very

Exhibit 5-1 Information That Patients Should Know about Their Drug
             Therapy

- name of drug
- dose
- appearance
- reason for use
- expected action
- quantity to be taken
- frequency of administration
- duration of therapy
- adverse effects
- precautions
- special instructions
- what to do if a dose is missed
- refill information
- storage requirements

tricky for most lay persons to master. Brand names tend to be short, "catchy" words that are relatively easy to learn compared with the drugs' more complex generic names. Since patients are more likely to use a drug's brand name than they are its generic name, health professionals who have a responsibility for managing the patient's medications, including physicians, pharmacists, and nurses, should be able to identify any drug from its brand name and its generic name, even though a single dose may be sold under a variety of different brand names. This information can be obtained from a number of different references, including the *American Hospital Formulary Service,* the *Physicians' Desk Reference* (P.D.R.), the *United States Pharmacopeia Dispensing Information* (U.S.P.D.I.), and *Facts and Comparisons.*

Dose of Medication

Since many medications are manufactured in more than one strength, or potency, it is important for the patient to know what dosage is being taken. This is particularly important in instances in which it may be necessary for the patient to adjust frequently the dosage of the medication according to the prescriber's instructions. For example, a patient taking the anticoagulant warfarin (Coumadin®) may have a prescription for 5-mg tablets, and, based on the results of a prothrombin test performed on the individual's blood, be instructed to reduce the dose to 2.5 mg, which of course would be one-half of a 5-mg tablet. Knowledge of the strength of a medication is also especially valuable when the patient is taking medications that are available in many strengths, such as chlorpromazine (Thorazine®), which is available in 10-, 25-, 50-, 100-, and 200-mg tablets; 30-, 75-, 150-, 200-, and 300-mg capsules; and oral liquid, rectal suppository, and injectable dosage forms.

Appearance of Medications

Brand Name Drugs

Although there are a distressingly large number of medications that could be accurately described as "little white pills," many medications can be identified by their characteristic size, shape, color, identification code, or other remarkable features that may be characteristic of a particular brand of medication. If patients are aware of the appearance of their medications, they will be less likely to experience confusion between their different medications by taking them at the wrong time or inadvertently switching one prescription with another. Knowing the appearance will help the patient to make a "final check" before taking the medication.

Generic Drugs

With the increase in the popularity and use of generic drugs, it may be more difficult for individuals to identify medications by their appearance. Problems could arise when a pharmacist decides or is instructed by the prescriber or the patient to dispense one generic drug product in place of a generic or a brand name drug that the patient may already be familiar with (see Chapter 3 for more on generic drugs). Although the newly substituted medications may be chemically and therapeutically identical to the formerly used drug, their appearances may be radically different. If such a switch is made, it is imperative that the patients be informed of this change and told that they are receiving the correct medication. Failure to do so may seriously damage the credibility of the prescriber or the pharmacist in the eyes of a patient, who may understandably feel that a mistake has been made. Also, the patient may experience a great deal of unnecessary apprehension about the possibility of having received the wrong medication.

An additional problem with medications may also exist when patients are discharged from hospitals or nursing homes. I have seen numerous instances in which nurses, pharmacists, or someone else involved in patient education have prepared elaborate medication calendars designed to help patients to take their medications properly at home. Frequently these calendars have a sample tablet or capsule attached to them so that the patient can become familiar with the dosage form. This approach to patient medication education has obvious shortcomings, especially when the patient becomes familiar with a medication in one dosage form, such as a large yellow tablet, and the pharmacist dispenses a generic equivalent that may be in the form of a small green gelatin capsule.

Intended Use and Expected Action of Medication

Although patients should not be expected to comprehend the precise pharmacologic activity of the drugs that are being taken, they should know why they were prescribed and what the expected action of the drugs will be. The use of lay terms may be appropriate in some instances. For example, if the diuretic furosemide (Lasix®) is prescribed for a patient because of excessive amounts of body fluid, the drug can be referred to as either a diuretic or the more commonly used lay term *water pill*. The patient should be informed that since the drug is being used to eliminate excess body water, the expected action of the drug is to increase urine output.

Quantity to Be Taken

Normally patients take one dose, such as one tablet or one capsule, of a drug at a time, but it is important to know whether that quantity may vary, such as when a patient receives a prescription for an antibiotic and is required to take two tablets as the initial dose in order to achieve sufficient blood concentrations rapidly, followed by one tablet at specific intervals. Quantity may also be an important consideration when a patient is to take additional doses, such as with a prescription for the drug nitroglycerin, which is used to relieve chest pain (angina). With this drug the patient may be instructed to take additional doses if the initial dose is ineffective.

Dosing Frequency

Patients should be aware of how often they should take their medication. They should also know whether the doses should be spaced throughout the 24-hour period at equal intervals or whether it is appropriate to take all of the doses during the normal waking hours. For example, it might be best to take antibiotics such as penicillin at equally spaced time intervals throughout the day and night while it would be best to take the entire day's dosage of diuretics by the middle of the afternoon in order to prevent annoying and embarrassing urinary frequency or incontinence during the night.

Duration of Therapy

When drug therapy is begun, patients should be told how long the therapy will most likely continue. This will both encourage patients to take their short-term therapy for the full duration and will also help them to prepare themselves and accept the fact that they may have to take their medications for a long period of time, perhaps even for the rest of their lives.

Special Precautions

The use of some medications is associated with special precautions, such as not driving when taking medication that may cause dizziness or drowsiness.

Special Instructions

Numerous different special instructions may also be associated with the use of certain prescription medications. Some dosage forms, such as certain liquid medications like potassium chloride solution, may have to be diluted before being taken. Some less common dosage forms, such as rectal suppositories, may require thorough explanation before the patient can use them properly. In some instances certain foods or medications should be avoided when patients are concurrently taking various other medications or nutrients because of potential inactivation or toxicity. (Incompatibilities between medications and foods are discussed further in Chapter 8.)

Occasionally, patients will be able to assist the prescriber by participating in the self-monitoring of their therapy. One example of self-monitoring would be a patient on the cardiac drug propranolol who was instructed to periodically take his or her own pulse in an effort to detect a slow pulse, which could be a side effect of that drug.

What to Do If a Dose Is Missed

Proper compliance to drug therapy is desired; however, health professionals must understand that patients may frequently miss one or more doses of their medications. It is desirable for patients to know how to allow for these missed doses. Sometimes it is best for patients to take a double dose of medication after missing a dose, and sometimes it is better for patients to simply resume their normal schedule without making up the missed dose. This depends entirely on the individual, the condition, and the drug(s) that is being taken.

Prescription Refill Information

After receiving their prescriptions, patients should be informed of the refill status of those prescriptions. The patient should know whether prescription refills can be obtained and, if so, how many refills are allowed. If no refills are allowed, it is important that the patients be aware of that fact in order that they might plan to obtain a prescription renewal if necessary.

Storage Requirements

Although most medications simply need to be stored in environments that avoid sunlight, excess moisture, and heat, some medications have specific storage requirements, such as refrigeration, and the patient should be so informed.

Knowledge of Adverse Effects

All medications are capable of causing some type of adverse response, especially in the elderly (see Chapter 7 for more information about adverse drug reactions). Most of these problems are self-limiting and of little consequence, but some are serious and potentially life threatening. Patients should be aware of the serious side effects that could result from the use of a particular medication. In addition, they should be familiarized with the early signs and symptoms that are associated with this toxicity and should be aware of what they should do if such problems are noticed.

For example, a patient taking the anticoagulant warfarin (Coumadin®) should be aware that one of the major possible side effects of this drug is a potentially serious bleeding episode. The individual should be told that early signs of this problem include bleeding gums, which may be noticed during oral hygiene, or a darkening of the urine, which may indicate the presence of blood. The patient should also be instructed to contact the prescriber or the pharmacist if these or any similar problems are noticed.

Informing the patient of potential drug side effects is one of the most delicate aspects of medication education. All patients have the right to be informed of the serious life-threatening side effects such as liver damage, internal bleeding, or kidney failure that may rarely be caused by their medications as well as the more annoying side effects such as nausea, constipation, or diarrhea that may occur more frequently. On one hand patients have a right to know what the medication may do to their body because through this understanding they may be able to detect or prevent serious side effects. On the other hand, if patients become overly concerned, they may not take the medication and may suffer the consequences of the original problem, which may be far more serious than any potential adverse response to drug therapy. It is absolutely imperative for health professionals to educate patients about the potential problems of their medications, while emphasizing the fact that most of the drug's side effects can be minimized or eliminated through the cooperation of the patient and that the chance of experiencing these potential side effects is worth the benefits that can be achieved through the use of the medication.

THE TEAM APPROACH TO PATIENT MEDICATION EDUCATION

Obviously a proper program of patient medication education requires the transfer of a considerable amount of information to the patient, a task that may seem overwhelming to some. However it must be remembered that patient medication education should be an effort that is to be shared by different members

Exhibit 5-2 Examples of Information on Auxiliary Prescription Labels

- Take on an empty stomach.
- Take with food or milk.
- May cause drowsiness.
- Do not take with milk.
- Avoid aspirin while taking this medicine.
- This prescription may not be refilled.
- Keep in refrigerator.

of the health care team. It is also comforting to realize that it is possible to provide a great deal of this information to the patient through the complete and proper labeling of prescriptions, including the use of auxiliary prescription labels (Exhibit 5-2). Medication education can also be supplemented in writing with the use of the wide variety of patient-related medication information available, such as individual patient handouts describing either a disease state or a particular aspect of drug therapy or with the use of a consumer-oriented drug reference. (See Appendix 5-1 for a description of some of these references.)

Although the team approach to patient medication education is important, it is obvious that certain health professionals will have a greater opportunity to provide this education to the elderly than others. For example, a pharmacist practicing in a small prescription-oriented pharmacy located in the vicinity of a senior citizen housing complex will have a greater opportunity than a pharmacist who specializes in the preparation of intravenous admixtures in a hospital pharmacy; a geriatric nurse practitioner will probably have a greater opportunity than a nursing supervisor at an acute care hospital, and a family practice physician will have a greater opportunity than a radiologist.

Despite the variety of practice settings and opportunities in which to provide medication education it is possible to summarize the general responsibilities of physicians, nurses, pharmacists, and other health professionals.

Physicians

Physicians should inform each patient of the reasons for using (or not using) drug therapy. They should inform the patient of the desired effect(s) of the drug therapy, such as, "this medication will lower your blood pressure," or "this medication will strengthen your heart beat." They should also inform the patient of the major risks and benefits associated with the use of the prescribed medication(s), such as telling the patient that an antihypertensive medication may cause some drowsiness for a few weeks; however, control of the patient's high blood pressure will reduce the major long-term complications of untreated hypertension (Hulka, 1979).

Generally physicians will also tell the patient how often and how long the medication should be taken. For example, when a physician prescribes digoxin (Lanoxin®) for congestive heart failure, the patient might be informed that one tablet should be taken daily and that the medication will probably have to be taken for the rest of the individual's life.

Nurses

Nurses' responsibilities in patient medication education will vary considerably depending on their practice environments. A nurse practicing in cooperation with a physician, such as an office staff nurse or a nurse practitioner in an office or clinic environment, may take responsibility for much of the education that was previously mentioned as the responsibility of the physician, or the nurse may work in concert with the physician, reinforcing or supplementing points made by the physician or answering patients' questions. For nurses not working under the direct supervision of a physician, such as a nurse practitioner working in a satellite health clinic, the medication education responsibilities are essentially those of the physician, including making sure that the patient knows why the drug is being used, what are its risks and benefits, how often it should be taken, and for how long (Hogue, 1979).

Nurses may also be responsible for helping to assess the patients' understanding of their health status and knowledge of medications and ability to comply with their prescribed therapy (Alfano, 1982). With this assessment nurses can assist in the planning of acceptable treatment programs and may also be responsible for disseminating or clarifying drug information through direct patient counseling or the use of drug information sheets (Pavkov & Stephens, 1981). Through the provision of drug information nurses may be able to help elderly patients manage their medications more safely (Burk, 1982; Plant, 1977).

Pharmacists

In recent years, the role of the pharmacist as a patient educator has become more formalized, and in fact some states have mandated pharmacist medication counseling of patients receiving new prescriptions. However, the pharmacist has traditionally been the provider of such information, especially with nonprescription drugs and in instances in which the patient did not have ready access to a physician.

Pharmacists should be aware that many patients will already have some idea of the prescriptions that they are to take. The pharmacist should attempt to assess the amount of information that the patient has received and use that as a basis for supplementary education, although it may be effective for the pharmacist to repeat certain information that the patient has already received in an effort to reinforce what the patient should know.

The pharmacist should be extremely careful in responding to the patient's inquiry concerning what a particular medication is for, especially in the case of medications that have multiple uses. For example, a patient who receives a prescription for prednisone (Deltasone®) for an acute inflammatory condition should not be told that prednisone is used to treat some types of cancer. Although it is true that prednisone is a part of a number of different cancer treatments, the mere mention of that fact could generate a great deal of immediate anxiety on the part of the patient, thus rendering any other educational attempts futile.

The pharmacist can be especially effective in instructing the patient on how to take the medication properly and on how to store the medication. The pharmacist should also inform the patient of any major side effects that could occur with the medication. The patient should be made aware not only of the potentially serious side effects that may occur but should also be informed of the signs or symptoms that should be watched for in order to detect these side effects. This will allow the detection of a medication's side effects before they become serious, enabling the patient to consult with the physician for the necessary alterations in drug therapy.

One area of patient education in which pharmacists are highly qualified is that of drug interaction consultation. They should warn patients of major potential interactions between their prescribed drug therapy, nonprescription drugs, and nutrients.

Pharmacists may also hold a key role in educating family members or friends who may assist with or supervise the patient's medications. Frequently, primary contact with the patient is through these other individuals, especially in the case of elderly patients who have difficulty ambulating.

Other Health Professionals

Certainly other health professionals such as respiratory therapists, physician's assistants, and health educators may be involved in providing patient medication education. Since the academic training of these persons may vary significantly, it is absolutely imperative that these persons, and any others involved with patient medication education, be aware that the information that they provide is crucial to the patient's well-being and may actually determine whether the patient will live or die! All persons involved in patient medication education must be aware of their limitations and responsibilities.

THE EFFECTIVE PATIENT EDUCATOR

It is my belief that health professionals should meet three separate criteria before they can be effective and qualified to provide medication education. First, the individual should have had some classroom training regarding the pharmacology and toxicity of medications. This classroom study could be obtained through their formal training or through lectures or seminars given through universities, community colleges, or professional associations.

Second, the person should have some clinical training or experience in the use of medications. Knowing what "the book" says about a medication is certainly important; however, it is impressive to see the number of times that patients do not respond as predicted, which is especially true in elderly patients. A person who has not had the opportunity to see the clinical effects of drugs, either through formal training or employment, cannot truly appreciate the fact that each patient is different and that the response of patients to drug therapy may be different from what "the book" would lead one to expect.

The third criterion requires that the individual keep current on new drugs as they are approved by the U.S. Food and Drug Administration and also keep current on newly discovered uses, side effects, administration techniques, or drug interactions involving medication that has already been on the market for some time.

Another very important aspect of patient medication education is that health professionals should not assume that patients know too much about their drug therapy. For example, numerous cases of patients inserting suppositories without removing the wrapper have been reported, probably because no one told them that the wrapper had to be removed and the patients were unfamiliar with the dosage form. In spite of its almost humorous nature, the patient in that situation could experience rectal or vaginal lesions in addition to being humiliated if the error was ever uncovered by a health professional.

RESPONSIBILITIES OF THE PATIENT

The responsibility for educating the patient concerning medications must not fall entirely on the shoulders of health professionals but must also be a responsibility that is at least partially assumed by patients themselves. The patient can contribute to this effort by providing health professionals with accurate information when visiting both the physician and the pharmacist. This information could include the following (Responding to Problems, 1979):

- *all medications that are currently being taken, including nonprescription drugs.* With this information the prescriber will be able to avoid prescribing additional medications that will either duplicate or interact with existing therapy. This information will also aid the pharmacist in detecting potential drug interactions, including those that may occur between prescription and nonprescription drugs.

- *suspected or documented allergic reactions or other adverse responses to drug therapy that have previously occurred.* Knowing this the prescriber will be able to avoid the use of medications to which the patient may be allergic or intolerant. Also, pharmacists will be able to discourage the use of non-prescription medications that would be likely to have similar detrimental effects.

Patients should also be encouraged to be inquisitive about their drug therapy by asking health professionals for clarification or explanation of any aspect of their drug therapy, by reading the labels on nonprescription medications before taking them, and by asking the pharmacist for clarification, if necessary.

Patients can also take part in their medication education by understanding what they should know about their drug therapy and by making certain that after speaking with the physician, nurse, or pharmacist they have the answers to the following questions concerning their medication(s) (Responding to Problems, 1979, p. 62):

- What is the name of the drug?
- For what is it being used?
- How often should I take it?
- When should it be taken?
- Are there foods or other medicines that I should avoid while taking this medication?
- What side effects should I expect and watch for?
- What should I do if I miss one or more doses?
- Are there any special instructions about the use or storage of this drug?
- What should I do if an unexpected problem occurs?

RESPONSIBILITIES OF FAMILY AND FRIENDS

Occasionally patients may be unwilling or unable to be educated about their drug therapy and disease state, such as might be the case with debilitated or depressed elderly patients or individuals who are deaf or blind. In this situation, it may be necessary for family members or friends to assume some of the responsibilities for a patient's care. In this case, those individuals responsible for providing this care should be willing to provide the following assistance that would either aid the patients in the understanding of their diseases or drug therapy or would help to identify those individuals who are unable to do so (McKenny, 1979):

- *Understand the patient's medical problem and its therapy.* For example, in the case of a depressed patient, the individual should understand the importance of continued administration of antidepressant medication.
- *Supervise or assist the administration of medication to the patient when necessary.* For example, an elderly individual may understand the importance of the routine use of eye drops to treat glaucoma but may not be able to administer them. In this case assistance might be necessary.
- *Have a family member or friend provide encouragement to the patient to seek assistance or answers to any drug-related questions from the physician, nurse, or pharmacist.* In cases in which the patient exhibits noticeably poor medication-taking behavior it may be necessary to notify the prescriber or the pharmacist so that the patient or family member assisting the patient could receive further instruction and medication education.

SPECIAL CONCERNS IN MEDICATION EDUCATION FOR THE ELDERLY

To this point the discussion of the principles and content of patient medication education has been applicable to patients of all ages including the elderly, but now I would like to concentrate on the aspects that relate primarily to the elderly.

The greatest obstacles to patient medication education for the elderly include difficulties in communication and attitudes of both the elderly patient and health professionals. When understood, communication problems can be compensated for, and attitudes, especially unfair ones, can be corrected.

Not every elderly patient will develop communication problems; however, certain problems do occur with increasing frequency with age. The most obvious communication problems that occur with aging are deficits in vision and hearing. These changes occur at varying rates and to different degrees but obviously can create significant barriers to communication and, therefore, education.

Auditory Deficits

Patients suffering from auditory (hearing) loss may not fully comprehend what they are being told by the health professional. Since the primary hearing loss experienced by elderly individuals is a loss of high frequency tones, speaking louder is generally not helpful, and indeed the patients may sense that they are being shouted at. Measures that can be taken to compensate for the auditory deficits in the elderly include the following (Chermak, 1981; Ernst & Shore, 1976; Schmall, 1980):

- Be sure you have the individual's attention before you talk.
- Face the person with your face in good light; avoid moving around.

- Consider the use of visual aids or written material to reinforce instructions concerning drug therapy.
- Do not shout.
- Speak distinctly and allow slightly longer intervals between sentences.
- Remove objects (e.g., gum, hands) from your mouth.
- Eliminate distractions and background noise (e.g., cash registers, loud music, or computer terminals).
- Avoid complex terminology such as complicated drug or disease nomenclature.
- Repeat and rephrase sentences, if necessary.

Visual Deficits

Vision may decrease in the elderly as a result of cataracts, untreated glaucoma, discoloration of the ocular lens, or other problems. This commonly makes it difficult for the patient to see darker colors, such as amber, and for the elderly individual to distinguish fine print. Measures that can be taken to compensate for visual deficits in the elderly include the following:

- Use large print with contrasting background for display materials or patient handouts.
- Use large upper case type for prescription labels.
- Color code, or texture code, medication containers, such as attaching a piece of colored tape or a small piece of sandpaper.
- Increase illumination in areas where patient education takes place.
- Request that the pharmacist fasten prescription labels on the outside rather than on the inside of amber prescription vials. (This may be required by law in some states.)

Other Communication Obstacles

The elderly individual's ability to communicate effectively may be impaired by the increased stress and anxiety of a novel situation, such as a visit to a physician for diagnosis or treatment. In a foreign environment, accompanied by the concern and anxiety that is frequently associated with health-related problems, the patient may forget to ask certain key questions about the prescribed drugs or diagnosed diseases and, owing to preoccupation with other matters, may easily forget any verbal information about the medications that was provided. Although anxiety of this type may present as a communication barrier in elderly patients, it may affect communication with patients of all ages.

Elderly patients may also transfer an unrealistic perception to their health professionals based on previous experiences. For example, a person may think that the physician is incapable of error or, conversely, is incapable of doing anything right, with both situations obviously presenting some obstacles to patient medication education and therapy. Younger patients may also hold such biases.

Health professionals may also note that communication with elderly patients is dominated by their concentration on persistent themes, such as the frequent verbalization of various aches, pains, and other physical complaints. Conversations may also be dominated by reflection and reminiscence, an emphasis on the losses that patient has suffered in later life, the fear of losing physical or mental functions, and the fear of being alone at the end of life (Blazer, 1978). Not every conversation will be dominated by these themes; however, if they are found to be interfering with proper communication, the patient must be treated with sensitivity and respect and reminded that now is the time to learn about the medications that are needed.

As mentioned earlier, it is extremely important to realize that the losses and changes discussed above are simply generalizations. These changes occur at greatly varying rates and to greatly differing degrees and must not be looked at as a universal stereotype of old age.

The attitudes of health professionals involved in educating the elderly must be developed so that we do not harbor any unfair stereotypes of the elderly patient, but rather we must realize that all persons, including the elderly, are individuals. We must recognize society's and indeed our own common fears of aging and death in order to establish effective communication with the elderly regarding their drug therapy and we must not let our own negative attitudes or fears of aging interfere with our educational efforts. This common negative attitude, often stemming from our own fears, is illustrated by a former pharmacy student of mine who, when asked why he did not enroll in a nursing home clinical elective course responded, "I don't want to work with those old prunes." Health professionals must also be careful to separate myths from reality and must avoid stereotyping and labeling the elderly.

TECHNIQUES FOR FACILITATING COMMUNICATION WITH THE ELDERLY

Communication with the elderly can be facilitated by adopting the following techniques (Ascione, James, Austin, & Shimp, 1980; Blazer, 1978; Gossel, 1980; Longe & Taylor, 1980; Pfeiffer, 1979; Smith, 1970; Wandless & Davie, 1977):

- *Show respect.* Use the patient's surname unless told otherwise by the patient. It can be very disturbing for persons who commanded respect and title or propriety during their adult years to be relegated to being addressed as "Johnny" or "Susie" by total strangers who are much younger than themselves.

- *Remain near the patient.* In general, the elderly are less inhibited than younger persons about touch. Resting a hand on a patient's arm while teaching about their medications can promote relaxation and reassurance. However, as always, it is extremely important to be sensitive to the individual patient's needs and response. If the patient does not appear comfortable with being touched or indicates that it is inappropriate, refrain from unnecessary physical contact.

- *Speak slowly and clearly.* Speaking slowly and in a clear manner will make it easier for the patient to comprehend what is being said.

- *Be at eye level with the patient.* Equality and respect is inferred when the health professional is at the same level as the patient. Standing near a sitting or lying patient can be rather intimidating and may interfere with effective communication.

- *Be aware of nonverbal communication.* Changes in the patient's gestures, postures, and facial expressions can provide considerable information concerning their emotional state or ability to comprehend. Nonverbal communication of the health professional may indicate willingness, or lack thereof, to communicate.

- *Speak realistically.* Avoid making statements like "This medication will take care of all of your problems." Patients' hopes should not be artificially inflated.

- *Use understandable language.* Medical jargon and complex terminology must be avoided when communicating with the patient. Care must be exercised not to use even the simple medical slang that health professionals frequently use. I am reminded of an incident in which a physician, in a sincere attempt to help educate his patient on how to take a prescription properly, provided the patient with a sheet of paper on which was a reminder that his medication should be taken three times a day, except the well-intentioned physician gave the patient the instructions written in the Latin abbreviation *t.i.d!*

  Since the elderly may be sensitive to what they perceive to be a condescending tone or attitude, instructions should be as simple and as clear as possible, but not childish. If unsure about an individual's level of comprehension I feel that it is best initially to assume that the patient cannot comprehend sophisticated instructions. If this is inappropriate, the proper adjustments in terminology and approach can then be made.

- *Use professional demeanor and attire.* Elderly patients may be more sensitive to professional appearance than younger patients. While proper attire does not guarantee effective medication education it can lend credibility to the health professional in the eyes of many elderly patients.

- *Designate an area for medication counseling.* In an office environment it is usually easy to provide medication education to patients in an area free of distraction that can allow for confidential communication. In a more public environment, it is sometimes difficult to find such an area. Some pharmacists now provide a confidential area such as a small booth, office, or partitioned area to provide the privacy that is necessary to discuss the personal aspects of one's drug therapy.

- *Inform the patient of the availability of medication education.* Health professionals, especially pharmacists, should publicize the fact that they are able to provide the patient with medication information. While working as a pharmacist in a community pharmacy, I frequently encountered elderly patients who were either unaware that pharmacists were willing to answer such questions or who simply did not want to bother the pharmacist. In some instances the availability of pharmacists for such consultation is publicized through the posting of specially prepared signs (Exhibit 5-3).

- *Provide verbal and visual information.* Studies have shown that a combination of verbal and visual instructions, such as small patient-oriented brochures or pamphlets, educate a patient more effectively than either method

---

Exhibit 5-3 Examples of Pharmacy Displays to Encourage Patient Use of the Pharmacist as an Informational Resource

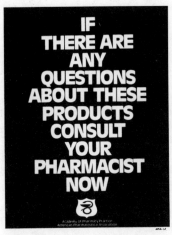

Source: Copyright by the American Pharmaceutical Association. Reprinted with permission of the American Pharmaceutical Association.

alone. In addition, it is helpful to provide the patient with your name and telephone number so that he or she will feel that it is appropriate to call to have any questions answered following the counseling session.

REFERENCES

Alfano, G. Meaning of the medication: Clue to acceptance or rejection. *Geriatric Nursing*, 1982, *3*, 28-30.

Ascione, F.J., James, M., Austin, S.J., & Shimp, L.A. Seniors and pharmacists: Improving the dialogue. *American Pharmacy*, 1980, *20*(5), 30-32.

Blazer, D. Techniques for communicating with your elderly patient. *Geriatrics*, 1978, *33*(1), 79-84.

Burk, J. Simon Farber, A man on a complex regimen. *Geriatric Nursing*, 1982, *3*, 41-43.

Chermak, G. Counseling the hearing-impaired older adult. *Drug Intelligence and Clinical Pharmacy*, 1981, *15*, 377-382.

Ernst, M., & Shore, H. Sensitizing people to the process of aging. Denton: Center for Studies in Aging, North Texas State University, 1976.

Gossel, T.A. A pharmacist's perspective on: Improving patient communications. *Guidelines to Professional Pharmacy*, 1980, *7*(3), 1, 3-4.

Hogue, C.C. Nursing and compliance. In R.B. Haynes et al. (Eds.), *Compliance in health care*. Baltimore: Johns Hopkins University Press, 1979.

Hulka, B.S. Patient-clinician interactions and compliance. In R.B. Haynes, D.W. Taylor, & D.L. Sackett (Eds.), *Compliance in health care*. Baltimore: Johns Hopkins University Press, 1979.

Longe, R.L., & Taylor, A.T. Basics of patient counseling. *American Pharmacy*, 1980, *NS20*(6), 19-20.

MacDonald, E.J., MacDonald, J.B., & Phoenix, M. Improving drug compliance after hospital discharge. *British Medical Journal*, 1977, *2*, 618-621.

McKenny, J.M. The clinical pharmacy and compliance. In R.B. Haynes, D.W. Taylor, & D.L. Sackett (Eds.), *Compliance in health care*. Baltimore: Johns Hopkins University Press, 1979.

Pavkov, J., & Stephens, B. Special considerations for the community-based elderly. *Geriatric Nursing*, 1981, *2*, 422-428.

Pfeiffer, E. Handling the distressed older patient. *Geriatrics*, 1979, *54*(2), 24-29.

Plant, J. Educating the elderly in safe medication use. *Journal of the American Hospital Association*, 1977, *51*(8), 97-102.

Responding to the problems of drugs and the aging. In F.T. Sherman & P. Lamy (Eds.), *Wise drug use for the elderly: Role of the service provider*. Washington, D.C.: Administration on Aging, 1979.

Schmall, V.L. Growing older: Sensory changes (Pacific Northwest Extension Publication [PNW-196]). Corvallis: Oregon State University, March 1980.

Smith, D.L. Pharmaceutical communications in the clinical environment. *Canadian Journal of Hospital Pharmacy*, 1970, *23*, 191-195, 197.

Statement on pharmacist conducted patient counseling. *American Journal of Hospital Pharmacy*, 1976, *33*, 644-645.

Wandless, I., & Davie, J.W. Can drug compliance in the elderly be improved? *British Medical Journal*, 1977, *1*, 359-361.

Weibert, R.T., & Dee, D.A. Experience in an organized patient education program. *Journal of the American Pharmaceutical Association*, 1976, *NS16*, 450-452.

Appendix 5-1

Consumer-Oriented References on Medications

A number of consumer-oriented references on medications are now available. Each has its own strengths and weaknesses. This appendix is not an attempt to list all, or even most of those references, but rather to give the reader an overview of the consumer-oriented references that I perceive to be some of the better ones that are available.

The reference books that I have cited have all been prepared by professional organizations and have the advantage of being reviewed by panels of experts for both accuracy and appropriateness.

Other material listed here, such as handout material from the U.S. government, professional organizations, or pharmaceutical manufacturers, is included because of its appropriateness to the elderly patient, although it must be realized that hundreds of such handouts are available to the consumer.

REFERENCE BOOKS

USP DISPENSING INFORMATION: *Advice for the Patient (Vol II)*
1983 edition, 793 pages, $17.95.
Ordering Information: USP DI, Publications Department, 12601 Twinbrook Parkway, Rockville, MD 20852

This reference is the product of the United States Pharmacopeial Convention, Inc., which is the organization that establishes the official standards of strength, quality, and purity for drugs sold in the United States. It has been prepared with the efforts of an expert panel comprised of hundreds of representatives from the profession of pharmacy and medicine.

Information on over 4,000 drug products is presented in monographs, which include brand name information, general precautions, important considerations to be evaluated before using the medication, instructions concerning the proper use of the medication, precautions to consider while using the medication, and side effects, with the most important information shaded for emphasis.

This particular book is written in lay terms and is the complete reference edition which, according to the U.S.P., is suitable for use as a reference in pharmacies, physicians' offices, and hospital wards.

USP DISPENSING INFORMATION: *About Your Medicines*
(abridged consumer edition), 1983 edition, 416 pages, $4.95
Ordering Information: USP DI, Publications Department, 12601 Twinbrook Parkway, Rockville, MD 20852

This reference, also produced by the U.S.P., is an abridged consumer edition containing selected monographs of the most frequently prescribed medications. In addition to a page summarizing important general information about the use of medicines, individual drug monographs contain information on brand names, important points to be considered before using the medicine; how to use the medicine properly, precautions to consider while using the medicine, and side effects. The monographs are listed by their generic names; however, a cross index is included so that patients can identify the drug's generic name by knowing only its brand name.

CONSUMER DRUG DIGEST
1982 edition, 477 pages, $9.95 soft cover
Ordering Information: American Society of Hospital Pharmacists, 4630 Montgomery Avenue, Bethesda, MD 20814 *or*
Facts on File, Inc., 460 Park Avenue South, New York, NY 10016

This reference has been abstracted from the American Hospital Formulary Service, a well-respected, detailed drug reference commonly used in many hospitals and nursing homes. It is written for a lay audience and contains monographs on over 200 prescription drugs and selected nonprescription drugs. The reference provides the reader with interesting information on topics such as how drugs act, dosage forms and routes of administration, toxicity, how drugs get to market, understanding how prescriptions are written, generic versus brand name drugs, and some of the financial aspects of drug therapy. The drug monographs are listed by generic name and are grouped according to the problem for which they are used, such as skin problems, arthritis, and sleep disturbances. In the beginning of each section is a brief description of the disease state(s) for which the medicines are frequently used. Information included in the monographs includes a listing of brand name information, a description of how the drug works, possible side effects, special precautions, how to take the drug and what to do if a dose is missed, and advice on storage.

This reference also includes an index that lists brand names of drugs so patients can look up their medications if they do not know the generic name. A listing of brand names that are used in Canada is also included.

PERIODICALS

ABOUT YOUR MEDICINES NEWSLETTER, $5.00/yr (6 issues)
Ordering Information: USP DI, Publications Department, 12601 Twinbrook Parkway, Rockville, MD 20852

This consumer-oriented newsletter is written about medicines and their use. Subjects covered include updated information on selected drug information monographs as well as information on current issues concerning drug use.

GOVERNMENT PUBLICATIONS

Elder—Ed
Ordering Information: National Institute on Drug Abuse, Bethesda, MD 20205

This packet contains brochures that address subjects pertinent to the use and misuse of medicine by the elderly. Topics include the following: Using Your Medications Wisely—A Guide for the Elderly; Saving Money with Generic Medicines—Can You?—Should You?; Do's and Don't's of Wise Drug Use; Keeping Track of Your Medicine.

PROFESSIONAL ORGANIZATIONS

Tips on Taking Medicine—The Right Way
Ordering Information: National Association of Retail Druggists, 205 Daingerfield Road, Alexandria, VA 22314

This handout provides basic information on medication storage and pharmacy consultation.

PHARMACEUTICAL MANUFACTURERS

Living With Your Arthritis
Ordering Information: William H. Rorer Inc., Fort Washington, PA 19034

This 23-page pocket-sized booklet discusses both rheumatoid arthritis and osteoarthritis and emphasizes proper management, including physical therapy and drug therapy.

The What If Book
Ordering Information: Hoffman-LaRoche Inc., Nutley, NJ 07110

This 10-page pocket-sized booklet is part of LaRoche's medication education program for the elderly and includes nine questions that are commonly asked by older individuals about the use of their medicines. Common sense answers are provided to these questions, advising the individual how to handle the hypothetical situation described by each question.

Chapter 6

The Effect of Aging on Medication Dosage

In order to explain why the elderly frequently require reduced medication doses it is necessary to discuss the science of pharmacokinetics, and in order to do that the scientific principles and nomenclature that are pertinent to the subject must be reviewed.

For those readers who experience some degree of difficulty understanding this information, take heart! My graduate students also find the subject confusing even after studying the topic for four or five years! There are even scientists who study pharmacokinetics for a number of years after receiving their doctorate, and I suspect that some of them also find the subject confusing. It is not my intention to make pharmacokinetic experts of my readers but rather to illustrate that there is a scientific basis for the changes in the drug dosage requirements of the elderly patient.

I suspect that most of the readers will not have an opportunity to use the principles of pharmacokinetics in their work with the elderly; however, it is still important to have an understanding that certain age-related alterations in physiology occur that may have a significant effect on the elderly individual's response to drug therapy.

It is important for everyone working with the elderly to understand that these changes exist and that they may affect drug therapy, because with this understanding we can better appreciate the fact that the requirements for medications in the elderly may at times be significantly different from those of the young.

As described elsewhere in this book, the effects of medications are frequently altered in the elderly patient. There is an increase in the rate of occurrence of adverse reactions to medications, significant drug interactions may occur, and the response to drug therapy may be altered in the elderly. From these discussions and from observing these effects in the elderly it is apparent that medication dosage requirements in the elderly may be significantly altered. Unfortunately, a simple formula for deciding proper medication dosages in the elderly does not exist and only a relatively few dosage recommendations that are specifically for the geriatric patient have been determined. However, progress is being made in this area. Some physicians reduce medication doses by a factor of one third to one half in their elderly patients, and, while this is a positive step, it is still rather imprecise.

Toward the end of this chapter, I have included some specific examples of methods that can be used to estimate proper medication dosage in elderly patients. These are included for purposes of demonstration only and should be used only by someone who is fully trained in the area of clinical pharmacokinetics.

As more is learned regarding the effect of aging on drug dosage requirements, we will be better able to take these changes into account and apply these principles to elderly patients in nursing homes, hospitals, and other health care environments.

DEFINITIONS

Since this discussion will most likely include pharmacokinetic terminology that the reader may not be totally familiar with, an introduction to certain important terms is necessary.

bioavailability—a measurement of the amount of drug that is available for absorption into the bloodstream. In essence this term is usually used to describe the amount of drug that is available for absorption into the bloodstream after a drug is given by mouth, but it may also refer to other routes of administration. For example, a medication is said to have a high degree of bioavailability if all or most of the drug can be effectively absorbed into the patient's bloodstream. It is said to have poor bioavailability if it cannot be sufficiently absorbed. Some medications possess poor bioavailability owing to various factors relating to the drug itself, such as poor solubility, and some do not have good bioavailability as a result of the way they are administered (e.g., by mouth versus intravenously) or resulting from different dosage forms (e.g., tablet versus liquid).

absorption—the passage of drug molecules into the blood. This term is usually used in reference to the passage of drug molecules into the bloodstream from the stomach or the intestine since the overwhelming majority of medications used by the elderly, and other age-groups, are given by mouth, either in a solid dosage form such as tablets or capsules or as a liquid.

volume of distribution—the volume of the compartment(s) of the body that a drug is distributed to. The volume of distribution is a concept that describes the distribution of a drug within the body by attempting to identify where in the body the drug actually goes. This value is determined by the relationship between a dose of drug administered to a patient and the concentration of drug found in the blood. For example, if a patient is given 10,000 mg of a particular drug, and the concentration of that drug in the blood was found to be 1 mg/ml shortly after the drug was given, it could be stated that the drug was distributed to a volume equivalent to 10,000 ml to achieve the final concentration of 1 mg/ml. Likewise, if after 10,000 mg of a drug was given to a patient and the concentration in the blood was found to be only 0.1 mg/ml, it could then be stated that the drug was distributed to a volume equivalent to 100,000 ml.

Rather than getting too involved with examples attempting to illustrate the concept of volume of distribution, it should be sufficient for the reader to understand that drugs with a large volume of distribution are usually considered to be widely distributed throughout the body, whereas the distribution of drugs having a small volume of distribution is considered to be to a limited area of the body. This concept becomes especially important in the elderly because of physiological changes that occur that may significantly influence the volume of distribution of a medication, affecting the concentration of drug in the blood and its therapeutic and toxic effect.

metabolism or biotransformation—the chemical alteration of a drug by the body. These terms usually refer to a process that takes place in the liver where the chemical structures of drug molecules may be altered so that they no longer possess any pharmacological activity. It is frequently necessary for a drug to be metabolized before it can be eliminated from the body by way of the liver, the kidney, or some other means.

excretion—removal of intact drug or drug metabolites from the body by the kidneys. Being one of the major organs of drug elimination the kidneys are frequently responsible for removing drugs from the body.

clearance—the intrinsic ability of the body or its organs of elimination to remove a drug from the body. *Clearance* is a general term indicating the body's ability to eliminate a drug. It is used as a collective term indicating the elimination by all mechanisms including the major routes of hepatic (liver) metabolism and renal (kidney) excretion and, in addition, the mechanisms of lesser importance such as excretion through the bile and elimination by the lungs.

half-life—the time required to reduce the amount of a particular medication in the body or the plasma drug concentration to one half of its original amount. The term *half-life* has a number of applications in various scientific areas, perhaps most commonly being used to describe the period of time necessary for a radioactive compound to lose one half of its radioactivity. When used to describe the length of time that a medication remains in the body, *half-life* is an indication of how long the effect of the medication will last. The longer the half-life, the longer the effect of the drug. It is interesting to note that most medications have half-lives of only a few hours; however, some, such as the digitalis glycoside digitoxin, may have a half-life of as long as one week!

loading dose—a priming, or initial drug dose that is usually larger than subsequent doses. It usually takes some period of time and a number of doses between the time that a medication is first started to the time that its therapeutic effect is seen. This is frequently because "tissue storage sites" in the body must first be saturated with drug and a therapeutic concentration of drug in the blood must be reached before it will be effective. A loading dose may therefore be given in order to reach effective concentrations, and therapeutic results, more quickly than if a loading dose were not given.

maintenance dose—a dose of medication that is administered routinely to maintain the therapeutic effect of a medication. This dose may be started following the administration of a loading dose, or the patient may be started on a maintenance dose of a medication without a loading dose. Maintenance doses of some medications used for chronic disease conditions may be routinely administered for many years.

THE SCIENCE OF PHARMACOKINETICS

Pharmacokinetics is a new area of science bridging the disciplines of pharmacy and medicine. It is essentially the study of what happens to a medication after it enters the body. Pharmacokinetics is the study of the absorption, distribution throughout the body, and elimination of medications through the processes of metabolism and excretion.

As a science, pharmacokinetics has evolved only recently, largely as a result of the development of the powerful computers that are necessary to develop and solve the complex calculations that are an integral part of theoretical pharmacokinetics and also as a result of recently developed assay procedures that can measure the concentrations of drugs that are too small to be imaginable. With sensitive assays that can measure quantities of drug in the range of a billionth of a gram, it is possible to measure the concentration of specific drug molecules in various tissues and fluids of the body with uncanny accuracy, enabling scientists to measure the rate and amount of drug that passes from one tissue to another.

The Compartmental Concept

The science of pharmacokinetics is based on the interesting theoretical concept that the body can be represented as a system of "compartments," such as the intravascular fluid, which consists of the blood and plasma that fill our circulatory system, the muscular tissue of the body, and the adipose, or fatty, tissue of the

Figure 6-1 Two-Compartment Pharmacokinetic Model

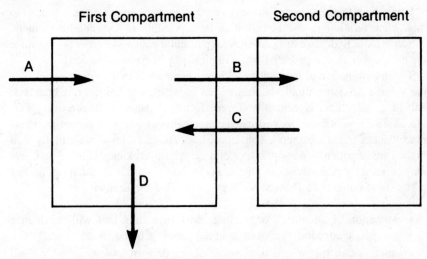

Arrow A identifies the drug as it enters the body, perhaps by the administration of a tablet by mouth or by injection. Arrow D identifies the elimination of the drug from the body, which is usually a result of the drug's metabolism by the liver or its excretion by the kidneys. The other arrows represent the passage of drug molecules from one compartment, the intravascular space, for example, to another, such as the skeletal muscle. Arrow B represents the passage of drug from the "main" compartment to the other compartment, and arrow C represents its return to the main compartment.

---

body. In addition to those mentioned, over 50 different tissue compartments have been identified that drug molecules have the potential of passing into.

The type of model shown in Figure 6-1 might be used by a pharmacokineticist (the scientist who studies pharmacokinetics) to study and describe the relationship between the absorption of a medication into the body, its distribution throughout the body, and, ultimately, its elimination from the body.

By measuring the rates of a drug's absorption, distribution, and elimination, it is then possible to assign mathematical constants thus making it possible for scientists to develop methods of drug dosing that can be individualized to suit the needs of each patient based on various factors, including age, weight, height, and kidney function. Actually, the body is a dynamic system that does not really behave in the fashion of a true "compartmental model"; however, this concept has been proven effective in the application of pharmacokinetic concepts to derive dosing methods that can accurately predict the concentration of certain drugs in the bloodstream.

Pharmacokinetic Applications

Since the effectiveness and toxicity of many medications is closely related to their concentration in the blood, it is then possible to use pharmacokinetic concepts to individualize drug dosages for particular patients in order to maximize the drug's therapeutic potential while minimizing its potential toxicity.

The determination of the pharmacokinetic parameters of a medication such as the volume of distribution, absorption rate constant, elimination rate constant, half-life, and others is generally a very technical aspect of theoretical pharmacokinetics, which uses sophisticated mathematics or computer programs. Pharmacokinetics can also be applied on a more basic, practical level and actually used in the care of patients. As applied, or clinical, pharmacokinetics, these concepts may be used by pharmacists or physicians to develop or adjust the drug therapy regimens of patients in a number of ways, including the following:

- estimation of an initial, or loading, dose of a drug that will result in a therapeutic concentration of drug in the patient's bloodstream
- estimation of the routine daily maintenance dose of a medication that will achieve continued therapeutic concentrations in the patient's bloodstream
- prediction of the concentration of a drug in the patient's bloodstream based on the amount of medication that has already been received
- identification of patients who may be considered to be at a high risk of having either toxic drug concentrations in the blood or subtherapeutic concentrations

Obviously, in the scope of this book a detailed treatise on the theory and application of pharmacokinetics is inappropriate; however, a basic knowledge of the existence of pharmacokinetics and its major applications in the elderly is necessary in order to better understand that requirements for medication dosage may change as a person ages.

PHARMACOKINETIC CHANGES THAT OCCUR WITH AGE

The discussion of pharmacokinetics in the elderly is pertinent when it examines the various age-related changes in physiology that occur and which therefore affect the pharmacokinetic properties of a medication in the elderly patient. These physiological and pharmacokinetic alterations will frequently influence the dosage requirement and the effect of medications in the elderly patient.

Actually very little is known about the pharmacokinetics of medications in the elderly, although it is possible to speculate on changes that might occur based on a knowledge of the physiological changes of the normal aging process.

Before the significance of the application of clinical pharmacokinetics was understood, medications were frequently administered to patients in "usual doses," making it commonplace for most patients to receive identical or similar medication doses regardless of important variables such as size, age, and kidney function.

Although "usual, or average, doses" are still frequently used today, without considering the effect of these and other patient-related variables it is possible to individualize drug therapy so that doses of certain medications can be tailored to meet the therapeutic needs of the individual patient while significantly reducing the possibility of toxicity. This application has been found to be particularly beneficial in the elderly.

Although there have been major accomplishments in the field of clinical pharmacokinetics and drug dosage adjustment, it is still a new science about which a great deal more needs to be learned before it can be applied to all medications in all patients. A discussion of this subject as it relates to the elderly patient will help the reader acquire the important understanding that many of the age-related changes in drug effect and toxicity are due to identifiable and understandable processes.

Various physiological changes that are associated with the aging process may affect the pharmacokinetic parameters of a medication, resulting in changes in its absorption, distribution, metabolism, or excretion (Greenblatt, Divoll, Abernathy, & Shader, 1982; Greenblatt, Sellers, & Shader, 1982; Lamy, 1982; Ouslander, 1981; Vestal, 1982). Some of these changes are well documented, while some are merely speculative. Some are of a major clinical significance, while some are purely academic. In order to understand these changes, and how they may affect the therapeutic or toxic response to drug therapy in the elderly, the following discussion will review them in relation to the common age-related changes in physiology that may occur.

Changes in Drug Absorption

In order for medications to exert their pharmacological activity they must first be absorbed into the bloodstream. Since most medications are taken by mouth in either a solid dosage form such as tablets and capsules or liquids such as syrups and elixirs, drug absorption usually refers to that which takes place in the stomach or intestine following the medication's administration.

Although most medications that are available in orally administered dosage forms are absorbed quite well, a number of aspects of the function and activity of the gastrointestinal system undergo significant age-related changes. Since drug absorption may be dependent on some of these properties, it is logical to assume that they may potentially affect the absorption of certain medications in the elderly.

The following age-related changes in gastrointestinal function have been documented; however, the effect of these changes on the absorption of medications in the elderly is still largely speculative and may in fact be of little clinical significance.

Increase in Gastric Emptying Time

With age there is a decrease in the activity and motility of the stomach, thus increasing the gastric emptying time, which is the time required for the stomach to empty its contents. This alteration could potentially influence the amount of drug absorbed and the time required before the drug is able to exert its therapeutic effect. Since most medications are absorbed through the stomach to a minor degree, if at all, it is unlikely that decreased gastric motility will result in a significant increase in the absorption of drug through the lining of the stomach, although such an effect is theoretically possible if a drug that has the potential of being absorbed through the stomach remains in contact with that tissue for a prolonged period of time.

The decrease in gastric motility may possibly result in a decrease in drug absorption because some medications, such as penicillin G (Pentids®), are quite sensitive to degradation by the acid present in the stomach. If acid-sensitive drugs are required to remain in an acidic environment for a prolonged period of time, degradation may occur to a greater extent, thus decreasing the amount of drug remaining for absorption. Also, it is possible that this decrease in gastric motility may result in a slower and more prolonged absorption if a drug that is normally absorbed through the intestine is held in the stomach for longer than usual.

Decrease in Intestinal Motility

As is the case with the stomach, the motility of the intestinal tract also decreases with age, resulting in a slower passage of digesting nutrients and unabsorbed medications through the intestines. Since most medications are absorbed primarily in the intestines, it is postulated that the increased transit time through the intestine may alter medication absorption in two very different ways. First, absorption may decrease as the result of the greater amount of time during which the unabsorbed medication remains in contact with the intestinal contents, thus increasing the likelihood that the drug will be bound to some of the components in the digesting food and therefore not completely absorbed or that the drug will be chemically altered so that it is rendered inactive or nonabsorbable.

The other postulated effect of this alteration is the possibility that drug absorption may actually increase, especially in the case of medications that are known to be slowly or poorly absorbed to begin with. The reason for this postulated increase in absorption could simply be that the increased time of passage through the intestine allows the drug to remain in contact with the lining of the intestine for a longer period than usual, thus increasing the possibility that its absorption will be increased.

Decrease in Gastric Acid Production

A well-documented change in the gastrointestinal system of the elderly is a decreased production of stomach acid, resulting in an increase in gastric pH, indicating a less acid environment. This change in the level of acidity might possibly be significant enough to affect the solubility and ionization of certain medications, resulting in either increased or decreased drug absorption in the elderly.

One documented example of this type of effect is seen with orally administered iron preparations such as ferrous sulfate (Feosol®). The absorption of iron salts decreases as the acidity decreases, owing to a change in the ionization of the drug. Therefore, when less acid is present, the absorption of iron decreases.

Decrease in Intestinal Blood Flow

Blood flow to the intestine decreases by as much as 40 to 50 percent with age (Lamy, 1982). It is postulated that as this gradual decrease occurs, drug absorption through the lining of the intestine is delayed or reduced.

Decrease in Capacity to Absorb

A decrease in the number of cells capable of absorbing drugs into the bloodstream may also occur, which could result in a corresponding decrease in drug absorption.

Clinical Significance of Changes in Drug Absorption

In spite of the many age-related changes in the gastrointestinal system that are known, there are very little data available to suggest that significant alterations in the rate and extent of drug absorption actually do occur.

It may be that the numerous physiological changes that occur in the gastrointestinal system of the elderly simply counteract each other, resulting in few clinically significant alterations in drug absorption. Perhaps it is true that most medications are so well absorbed that their absorption is unaffected by the gradual physiological changes that occur with aging. However, problems with drug absorption have been identified in the elderly with medications, such as the cardiac medication digoxin (Lanoxin®), that are not well absorbed, indicating that the issue is not a moot one and that problems resulting in serious clinical implications can arise.

Changes in the Distribution of Drugs in the Body

Following absorption, a medication is then distributed within the body to various tissues and organs, and ultimately to the drug's specific site of activity. Both the rate and the extent of this distribution depend on a number of factors, including the physical and chemical properties of the drug and the physiology of the individual taking the drug. The specific properties of the medication can be considered to be constant; however, as a person ages a number of significant physiological changes do occur, both in body size and composition. These changes may have a significant effect on the distribution of medication within the body.

Changes in Body Size

In general, elderly individuals are of smaller physical stature than younger, healthy individuals. This may be due to both an age-related decrease in the size and height of the individual, resulting from a softening and compression of the spinal column and a loss of muscle tissue, and to the fact that there is a trend for succeeding generations to be larger than those that preceded them.

These changes must be taken into account, and the use of "standard" or "usual" doses that are appropriate for younger and larger individuals is often inappropriate in elderly patients. If these excessive doses are used, the drug may achieve a higher concentration in the patient's body or blood because the same amount of drug is being distributed to a smaller volume of tissue than when it is administered to larger individuals. The higher concentrations achieved could then possibly result in increased drug effect or toxicity.

Changes in Body Composition

With aging, significant, but gradual changes occur in body composition, with an increase in the percentage of fat and a corresponding decrease in the percentage of the body consisting of water (Tables 6-1 and 6-2). These alterations may have a considerable influence on the pharmacokinetics of certain medications within the body because most medications are distributed preferentially to either body fat or body water; hence, the age-related changes in these physiological "compartments" may result in significant alterations in the distribution of medications throughout the body.

Drugs that are distributed in body water may achieve higher concentrations in the bloodstream, resulting from the fact that they are more concentrated in the "smaller" body water compartment of the elderly patient. If an increase in concentration does occur, it could result in increased drug effect or toxicity.

Medications that are fat soluble may actually be more widely distributed in an elderly individual, possibly resulting in a drug effect that is less intense, owing to a

Table 6-1 Approximate Mean Percentage of Total Body Weight
Composed of Fat in Males and Females of Various Ages

	Age	Percent Fat
Male	18–25	18
	25–35	22
	35–45	23
	45–55	27
	55–65	30
	65–85	36
Female	18–25	33
	25–35	32
	35–45	36
	45–55	43
	55–65	44
	65–85	45

Source: Reprinted by permission of the *Journal of Gerontology,* Vol. 27, No. 4., pp. 438–443, October 1972.

Table 6-2 Mean Percentage of Total Body Weight Composed of Water
in Males and Females of Various Ages

	Age	Percent Water
Males	17–34	61
	35–52	55
	57–86	54
Females	20–31	51
	36–54	48
	60–82	46

Source: Adapted from "Further Observations on Total Body Water I. Normal Values Throughout the Life Span," by I.S. Edelman, H.B. Haley, and P.R. Schloerb with permission of *Surgery, Gynecology & Obstetrics,* © 1952.

lower blood concentration, but more prolonged as a result of the gradual release of the drug from the fatty tissue in which it is stored.

The clinical implications of these alterations in body size and composition are not entirely clear, however, loading doses of the water-soluble antibiotic gentamicin, for example, must be administered according to body size, indicating a decreased dosage in smaller elderly patients. Since most sleep-inducing medications such as pentobarbital (Nembutal®) are fat soluble, it is possible that the residual drowsiness that commonly occurs the morning following an evening dose of the drug may be due, at least in part, to the slow release of the drug from the fatty tissue stores, although a decrease in the metabolism of these drugs may also account for their increased effect.

Protein Binding

One factor affecting the distribution of medications within the body and their pharmacological activity is the degree to which they bind in the bloodstream to the protein albumin. Most medications bind to this protein to some extent, and some drugs such as phenylbutazone (Butazolidin®) and warfarin (Coumadin®) are as much as 97 to 98 percent protein bound (American Hospital Formulary Service, 1982).

Protein binding is a reversible phenomenon that reflects an equilibrium between bound and unbound drug in the blood, with drug molecules constantly becoming bound to albumin, or unbound. An important aspect of this phenomenon is that when drug molecules are bound to albumin they are unable to exert any pharmacological activity; thus it is the unbound or "free" drug that is the active form of the drug.

Consequently, the pharmacological activity and toxicity of most drugs may be affected by any factors that are capable of altering the degree to which they are protein bound.

It has been found that elderly persons have a decreased amount of albumin in their bloodstream, most probably resulting from the decreased production of albumin by the liver that results from either the liver's decreased ability to synthesize this protein or perhaps as a secondary effect of the dietary changes in the elderly, characterized by a decreased protein intake from which albumin is synthesized.

It is postulated that the decreased concentration of albumin in the bloodstream of the elderly may result in a decreased percentage of drug that is protein bound, and therefore inactive, and a corresponding increase in the amount of "free" or active drug. Although the relationship between the degree of protein binding of a drug and its therapeutic or toxic effect is rather complex, there is evidence that this relationship will affect the interpretation of the significance of plasma drug concentrations in the elderly patient (Greenblatt, Divoll, Abernathy, & Shader, 1982). This altered pattern may then result in an increase in drug activity, toxicity, or both.

Evidence exists indicating that these alterations in the protein binding of medications may have clinically significant implications.

The fraction of unbound (pharmacologically active) meperidine (Demerol®) in the plasma has been shown to increase with age. This increase may help to explain why elderly patients may demonstrate an increased sensitivity to this drug, resulting in respiratory depression and occasionally an idiosyncratic reaction characterized by stimulation and confusion.

The decreased protein binding of drugs in the elderly may also contribute to the increased incidence of warfarin (Coumadin®) toxicity found in the elderly by resulting in an increase of warfarin that is not bound to protein causing bleeding of the gums, bleeding into the urine, or internal bleeding.

Clinical Significance of Changes in Drug Distribution

Although theories and potential mechanisms explaining the age-related alterations in the distribution of medications within the body have been identified, it is still not possible to identify prospectively all patients in whom this problem may be significant enough to require alterations in their drug therapy.

With a general awareness of these potential problems, extra caution can be exercised in patients who might have an increased likelihood of experiencing significant alterations of drug distribution, such as those patients with small physical stature, those with significantly decreased albumin levels, and those taking medications that are known to be highly protein bound.

Changes in Drug Metabolism

Before they can be eliminated from the body, many medications must first be metabolized by the liver to active or inactive water-soluble metabolites that can then be further metabolized, excreted through the bile, or excreted by the kidneys. Thus, the decrease in liver function that may occur during the aging process may influence the rate at which a medication is eliminated from the body.

Three separate mechanisms have been proposed as potential causes for this change, including a decrease in hepatic (liver) blood flow, a decrease in hepatic mass, and a reduction of hepatic enzyme activity.

The change that is thought to have the most significant impact on hepatic metabolism in the elderly is the decrease in hepatic blood flow, which is the amount of blood pumped through the liver. This decrease is a direct result of the gradual change in cardiac output, which is the amount of blood pumped by the heart in a given period of time. Cardiac output decreases at an annual rate of approximately one percent starting at approximately age 20, when a person reaches physical maturity. As a result of this gradual decrease, cardiac output decreases approximately 40 percent between the third and seventh decades of life (Goldman, 1979). Since it is the blood that normally carries the drug to the liver for it to be metabolized, less blood, and therefore less drug, passes through the liver as cardiac output decreases. This decrease in hepatic blood flow can be further compromised in the presence of disease states that further decrease cardiac output, such as congestive heart failure or myocardial infarction (heart attack).

Another postulated reason for the decreased hepatic metabolism of medications in the elderly is the fact that the mass of the liver decreases with age, which may decrease its ability to metabolize drugs.

Also, a decrease in the amount of certain hepatic enzymes responsible for drug biotransformation may result in a decreased rate of clearance from the body and prolonged biological half-life of some medications. Studies indicate that the liver's ability to metabolize certain drugs does decrease with age; however, this depends largely on the chemical pathways that are involved in the drug's metabolism. It has been found that some of these pathways are significantly altered in the elderly while others are not affected as much (Greenblatt, Divoll, Abernathy, & Shader, 1982).

Clinical Significance of Changes in Drug Metabolism

It is thought that this decrease in hepatic function does in fact result in some clinically significant alterations of drug metabolism in the elderly. For example, the cardiac medication propranolol (Inderal®) and the bronchodilator theophylline (Elixophyllin®) have been found to achieve higher blood levels in the elderly as a result of decreased metabolism by the liver.

Numerous laboratory tests can be used to assess liver damage, and to a certain extent liver function; however, at present it is not possible to predict accurately the degree that drug metabolism will be decreased in a particular individual owing to large intrapatient variability in liver function. These changes can be estimated, however, in the case of certain medications for which a consistent relationship between the pharmacokinetics of the drug and the patient's hepatic function have been determined.

Figure 6-2 is a nomogram that was developed for the bronchodilator drug theophylline, which is eliminated from the body entirely by hepatic metabolism. This nomogram depicts a method in which both a loading and a maintenance dose of theophylline can be determined by using the patient's age and weight. The method provides the prescriber with a suitable theophylline dosage regimen by making the assumption that an age-related decrease in hepatic function occurs that is sufficiently significant by age 50 to necessitate a decrease in the maintenance dose of theophylline that the patient is to receive. Admittedly this method does not provide a dosage adjustment that is precisely tailored to the age-related decrease in liver function of each patient individually; however, it does take these changes into account on a more general basis. This method and others like it have been demonstrated to be effective in reducing the incidence of toxicity resulting from excessive doses of theophylline and other drugs that are metabolized by the liver.

Changes in Drug Excretion

Significant decreases in kidney function also occur as a person ages. This decrease may result from changes in kidney structure; however, it is primarily the

Figure 6-2 Theophylline Dosing Nomogram

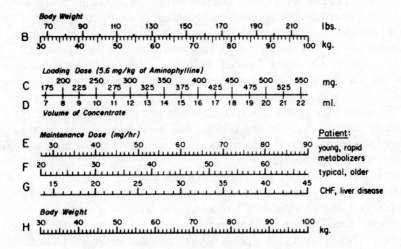

Source: Reprinted from "System for Clinical Monitoring of Theophylline Therapy," by J.R. Koup, J.J. Schentag, and J.W. Vance with permission of the American Society of Hospital Pharmacists, © 1976.

consequence of a decrease in blood flow to the kidneys. As with hepatic blood flow, renal (kidney) blood flow is significantly reduced as a result of the age-related decrease in cardiac output. This decrease is approximately 1 percent per year after the patient reaches maturity. The patient's creatinine clearance, which is an indication of the amount of blood that passes through the kidney, decreases by 35 to 50 percent between the ages of 20 and 90.

Even with this reduced function, the kidneys generally retain the ability to eliminate excess body fluids and wastes; however, the ability to eliminate certain medications may be decreased by a factor of 50 percent or more.

Excretion by the kidney is a major route of elimination for many medications because most drugs that are not normally metabolized by the liver are excreted by the kidneys in the unchanged form. The kidneys are also responsible for excreting some of the pharmacologically active and inactive metabolites of drugs that have been metabolized by the liver.

This age-related decrease in the excretion of medications by the kidneys can be quite significant because unless medication dosage is decreased, the concentration of a drug in the bloodstream will tend to increase as kidney function decreases. With these increased concentrations, an increase in drug effect and toxicity becomes more likely.

Clinical Significance of Changes in Drug Excretion

Age-related decreases in kidney function are probably the single most important reason for altered drug effect in the elderly. Many clinically significant problems have been identified; for example, the cardiac medication digoxin (Lanoxin®) is excreted more slowly in the elderly owing primarily to the age-related decline in renal function (Simonson & Stennett, 1978; Stults, 1982). This decreased excretion is associated with an increased concentration of digoxin in the bloodstream and an increase in adverse effects.

The antibiotics gentamicin (Garamycin®) and tobramycin (Nebcin®) are excreted almost entirely by the kidneys, and it has been determined that age-related alterations in renal function necessitate a significant change in the dosing of these and other medications.

Of all the physiological changes capable of altering the pharmacokinetics of a medication, the age-related decrease in kidney function can be assessed most accurately. Laboratory studies of certain elements in the blood or urine can be used to estimate renal function and the changes that occur with aging. In recent years, a number of highly successful pharmacokinetic methods have been developed that allow the clinician to estimate the patient's renal function. With the use of this information, along with the patient's age, sex, and weight, a specific medication dosage regimen can then be developed.

As an example of one commonly used method is the following formula developed by Cockroft and Gault (1976) that is used to estimate a patient's creatinine clearance, which is a measure of renal function.

$$\frac{(140 - age) \times \text{body weight (kg)}}{72 \times \text{serum creatinine (mg\%)}}$$

(As written, the formula is appropriate for a male; multiply by .85 for a female.)

When the patient's creatinine clearance is determined, this information can then be applied to the dosing method shown in Figure 6-3 developed by Sarubbi and Hull (1978) for the aminoglycoside class of antibiotics.

Pharmacokinetic methods for medications that are eliminated by the kidney are especially valuable because they can be used to take into account both the normal age-related decrease in renal function and also that which results from disease processes such as diabetes, heart failure, and others.

CONCLUSION

The physiological changes affecting the pharmacokinetics of a medication occur gradually, over a period of many years, as a normal part of the aging process. They do not occur at the same rate or to the same degree in all patients,

Figure 6-3 Dosing Chart for Aminoglycoside Antibiotics

1. Select Loading Dose in mg/kg [IDEAL WEIGHT] to provide peak serum levels in range listed below for desired aminoglycoside.

AMINOGLYCOSIDE	USUAL LOADING DOSES	EXPECTED PEAK SERUM LEVELS
Tobramycin Gentamicin	1.5 to 2.0 mg/kg	4 to 10 μg/ml
Amikacin Kanamycin	5.0 to 7.5 mg/kg	15 to 30 μg/ml

2. Select Maintenance Dose (as percentage of chosen loading dose) to continue peak serum levels indicated above according to desired dosing interval and the patient's corrected creatinine clearance.*

PERCENTAGE OF LOADING DOSE REQUIRED FOR DOSAGE INTERVAL SELECTED

C(c)cr (ml/min)	half life† (hrs)	8 hrs	12 hrs	24 hrs
90	3.1	84%	-	-
80	3.4	80	91%	-
70	3.9	76	88	-
60	4.5	71	84	-
50	5.3	65	79	-
40	6.5	57	72	92%
30	8.4	48	63	86
25	9.9	43	57	81
20	11.9	37	50	75
17	13.6	33	46	70
15	15.1	31	42	67
12	17.9	27	37	61
10‡	20.4	24	34	56
7	25.9	19	28	47
5	31.5	16	23	41
2	46.8	11	16	30
0	69.3	8	11	21

*Calculate corrected Creatinine Clearance C(c) cr as:

C(c) cr male = 140-age/serum creatinine
C(c) cr female = 0.85 x C(c) cr male

†Alternatively, one half of the chosen loading dose may be given at an interval approximately equal to the estimated half life.

‡Dosing for patients with C(c) cr≤10 ml/min should be assisted by measured serum levels.

Source: Reprinted from "Amikacin Serum Concentration: Prediction of Levels and Dosage Guidelines," by F.A. Sarubbi and H.H. Hull with permission of the American College of Physicians, © 1978. Originally published in *Annals of Internal Medicine*, Vol. 89 No. 5, pp. 612–618, November 1978.

making it impossible to say that they become significant once a person reaches a certain age, such as age 65. Actually, many of these changes begin to occur during the early 20s, although they obviously become more pronounced and clinically significant in the later years.

Not too much is understood about these changes and much of the existing knowledge is based largely on supposition and speculation. A relative paucity of information is currently available, although as the significance of these changes becomes more widely recognized, methods attempting to individualize drug therapy to meet the needs of each particular patient are becoming increasingly more common. The need to individualize drug therapy is obvious because just as different people require different sizes of clothing, they also require different doses of medication.

In defense of the accomplishments to date it is important to keep in mind the fact that the entire science of pharmacokinetics and dosage individualization is new, and, while the development of these principles and the accumulation of this information is frustratingly slow, it is a tremendous improvement over what was available only a few years ago.

I feel that an increased emphasis on geriatric research is needed so that more of this information can be determined. It is interesting that although many research studies initially investigate the effects of new drugs in healthy young volunteers, those same drugs will probably be used frequently in sick, elderly patients. For this reason it is not at all surprising that the effects of medication in the elderly are sometimes difficult to predict.

In addressing the informational needs concerning the dosage of medications in the elderly it is obvious that more elderly individuals must be included in formal clinical research studies. The concept of drug research may be offensive to some persons working with the elderly, resulting from their unfounded concerns that drug research is coercive and abusive by nature. I believe well-designed, well-controlled, and well-supervised studies can gather valuable information while at the same time provide proper safeguards that respect and guarantee the health, safety, and privacy of the subjects involved. Through geriatric drug research much that we do not know now can be learned while at the same time avoiding any undue risk to individuals.

It is also important that persons working with the elderly report their observations concerning drug toxicity and effect to their colleagues through forums such as society meetings or professional publications so that this body of knowledge will continue to grow.

REFERENCES

American Hospital Formulary Service. Bethesda, Md.: American Society of Hospital Pharmacists, 1982.

Cockroft, D.W., & Gault, M.H. Prediction of creatinine clearance from serum creatinine. *Nephron,* 1976, *16,* 31-41.

Edelman, I.S., Haley, H.B., & Schloerb, P.R. Further observations on total body water: I. Normal values throughout the life span. *Surgery, Gynecology & Obstetrics,* 1952, *95,* 1-12.

Greenblatt, D.J., Divoll, M., Abernathy, D.R., & Shader, R.I. Physiologic changes in old age: Relation to altered drug disposition. *Journal of the American Geriatrics Society,* 1982, *30*(11), S6-S10.

Greenblatt, D.J., Sellers, E.M., & Shader, R.I. Drug disposition in old age. *New England Journal of Medicine,* 1982, *306,* 1081-1088.

Goldman, R. Decline in organ function with aging. In I. Rossman (Ed.), *Clinical Geriatrics* (2nd ed.). Philadelphia: J.B. Lippincott, 1979.

Koup, J.R., Schentag, J.J., & Vance, J.W. System for clinical monitoring of theophylline therapy. *American Journal of Hospital Pharmacy,* 1976, *33,* 949-956.

Lamy, P.P. Comparative pharmacokinetic changes and drug therapy in an older population. *Journal of the American Geriatrics Society,* 1982, *30*(11), S11-S19.

Novak, L.P. Aging, total body potassium, fat-free mass, and cell mass in males and females between ages 18 and 85 years. *Journal of Gerontology,* 1972, *27,* 438-443.

Ouslander, J.G. Drug therapy in the elderly. *Annals of Internal Medicine,* 1981, *95,* 711-722.

Sarubbi, F.A., & Hull, H.H. Amikacin serum concentration: Prediction of levels and dosage guidelines. *Annals of Internal Medicine,* 1978, *89,* 612-618.

Simonson, W., & Stennett, D. Estimation of serum digoxin levels in geriatric patients. *American Journal of Hospital Pharmacy,* 1978, *35,* 943-947.

Stults, B.M. Digoxin use in the elderly. *Journal of the American Geriatrics Society,* 1982, *30,* 158-164.

Vestal, R.F. Pharmacology and aging. *Journal of the American Geriatrics Society,* 1982, *30,* 191-200.

Chapter 7

Adverse Effects of Medications

Modern medicines are now capable of curing many diseases that were major killers just a few years ago. They can alleviate uncomfortable and annoying disease-related symptoms and can control many chronic diseases, such as high blood pressure, diabetes, and arthritis, and drastically extend the life expectancy that would often be cut short by these conditions and others. Unfortunately, in an ironic trade-off, these same medications can create their own symptoms, the consequences of drug-induced disease, and they can even kill.

Robert Butler, M.D., former director of the National Institute on Aging, has estimated that perhaps 30,000 people die each year as the result of adverse drug reactions at a cost of 2 billion dollars in drug-related treatment (U.S. Government Printing Office, 1981), with incalculable human costs; yet it is likely that many of these deaths are contributed to by the weakened condition of the seriously ill patient and are the result of therapy with effective yet toxic medication that frequently represents the patient's only hope for surviving an otherwise fatal illness. Although the adverse effects of medication may have a fatal outcome, they usually do not; but rather they most frequently result in relatively minor symptoms or inconveniences.

Because of a number of factors, which will be discussed in this chapter, the occurrence of adverse reactions to medications can be a significant problem in the elderly patient, occurring more frequently in this age-group than in younger patients. These adverse reactions may at times be well known to health professionals, and therefore easily identifiable, or they may be more subtle, presenting as stereotypical signs of old age. Signs such as confusion, depression, weakness, loss of appetite, constipation, tremor, and others may be mistakenly attributed to a deterioration in the patient's condition as the result of old age, when all of these problems and many more may simply be adverse manifestations of drug effect.

Since most elderly individuals take at least one prescription medication, it is imperative for persons who work with the elderly to be aware of the fact that

125

medications may help the elderly as well as hurt them. However, with the proper patient management these adverse effects can be minimized and drug therapy can be made as safe as possible for the elderly consumer of medications.

DEFINITIONS

In order to better comprehend the types of adverse reactions to medications that can occur, familiarity with the terminology of the subject is necessary.

adverse drug reaction—an unintended, untoward, harmful or noxious response to a drug occurring at dosage levels used in humans for disease prevention, diagnosis, or therapy. Generally this term is used collectively to describe any type of adverse reaction; however, as seen with some of the following definitions, there are a number of specific types of adverse drug reactions.

side effect—an unwanted, predictable pharmacological action unrelated to the therapeutic effect of a drug and not due to overdosage. Many medications may have two or three unique pharmacological actions, although when used in a patient for a specific purpose usually only one of its activities is considered desirable, with the other pharmacological effects considered to be side effects. For example, the drug diphenhydramine (Benadryl®) is an antihistamine that is frequently used to decrease an individual's allergic response and associated symptoms, such as running nose and puffy, irritated eyes. Antihistamines also tend to cause considerable drowsiness in some patients, although this response is highly variable. When drowsiness occurs in a patient for whom diphenhydramine is being used to suppress their allergic response, the drowsiness would be considered to be a side effect because it is an unwanted, yet predictable effect related to the known activity of the drug, which occurs at normal dosages of the drug.

hypersensitivity or allergic response—a reaction, not explained by the pharmacological effects of the drug, caused by altered reactivity of the patient and generally considered to be an allergic manifestation. This type of response is usually not related to the dose of the medication and may occur at doses that are considered to be normal or even subtherapeutic. A hypersensitivity reaction can present as a simple rash or as a severe life-threatening involvement of the skin, pulmonary (lungs) system, and cardiovascular system.

overdose—a characteristic but excessive pharmacological effect of a drug caused by administration of a dose that is larger than the usual therapeutic dose *for the patient's size and age*. An example of this type of response would be residual morning drowsiness resulting from the inappropriately high dosage of sleeping medication administered the preceding evening. It is important to point out that the administration of the "usual dose" of a medication to an elderly person may still be inappropriately large *for that individual* based on the age-related dosage adjustments discussed in Chapter 6.

idiosyncrasy—an uncharacteristic response of a patient to a drug that frequently occurs following administration of the drug at doses that are considered to be appropriate for that patient. Idiosyncratic responses may be directly opposite to the expected activity of the medication. For example, a patient given the narcotic analgesic meperidine (Demerol®) may become agitated and excited rather than experience the analgesia, sedation, and drowsiness that would be expected following the administration of this medication, or a patient given the sleep-inducing medication flurazepam (Dalmane®) may experience agitation rather than drowsiness. An understanding of idiosyncratic reactions is especially important in the elderly because this type of adverse reaction to medications occurs more frequently in this age-group, as well as in the pediatric population.

intolerance—a characteristic pharmacological effect of a drug produced by an unusually small dose, so that a dose considered to be within the normal therapeutic range for a particular patient will tend to induce massive overreaction. An example of this type of reaction can be seen when a patient is extremely sensitive to a diuretic, when a dose normally considered to be therapeutic would elicit a response in urine output much greater than was to be expected. This excessive fluid loss could consequently result in dehydration in the elderly patient.

These definitions have been presented to provide the reader with a basic familiarity with some of the more common nomenclature used in the discussion of adverse drug reactions. Although the definitions cited could be contested by some, I believe that they adequately describe the major types of adverse drug reactions that are most pertinent to the following discussion.

Actually the semantics involved can be quite confusing. For example, a "side effect" is definitely an adverse drug reaction, but an adverse drug reaction is not necessarily a side effect!

Further complicating the issue is the interchangeability of some of these terms. As previously mentioned, drowsiness resulting from the administration of diphenhydramine (Benadryl®) is a side effect when the drug is being used to treat an allergy. However, diphenhydramine may also be used to induce sleep, especially in the elderly. In that case the primary pharmacological activity of the drug is to induce drowsiness, with the accompanying ability to dry nasal secretions, perhaps resulting in a dry nose or mouth becoming a side effect!

INCIDENCE OF ADVERSE DRUG REACTIONS

It is difficult to determine precisely the incidence of adverse drug reactions in the elderly population because their occurrence varies, depending on a number of factors such as type and amount of medication taken, the patient's health status, and whether the individual is institutionalized. In addition, adverse reactions may frequently go undetected and therefore unreported in the elderly population, with symptoms or changes in behavior being attributed to disease states or senility rather than to the adverse effect of medications.

Although this uncertainty exists, few will argue that the greatest incidence of adverse drug reactions is among the institutionalized elderly population, in particular those elderly patients who have been admitted into short-stay hospitals for treatment of acute health problems such as a broken hip or a heart attack or of recurrence of a chronic problem such as arthritis or diabetes.

It is generally more likely that patients in the hospital environment will be taking greater amounts of medications than those who are either in nursing homes or who are not living in institutional settings. It is also more likely that the medications that are taken by the hospitalized patient tend to possess a greater potency, such as intravenously administered antibiotics, potent cardiac drugs given to control the rhythm of the heart, and powerful injectable drugs to regulate the patient's cardiac output and blood pressure.

The health status of the patient cannot be understated as an extremely important factor that influences the occurrence of adverse drug reactions in hospitalized patients.

The illnesses that have resulted in the patient's admission to the hospital, such as a recent heart attack or severe pneumonia, may compromise the physiological response of a patient to various environmental factors, including drug therapy, and therefore patients suffering from these diseases and others will be much more prone to experiencing an adverse reaction to a medication.

Some of the most comprehensive data available indicates that approximately four percent of hospital admissions are either caused or significantly influenced by adverse drug reactions (Miller, 1973); however, this figure may be somewhat higher in the elderly population. Results of a study of almost 2,000 admissions to geriatric medicine departments in the United Kingdom concluded that an adverse drug reaction contributed to 12.9 percent of these admissions (Williamson & Chopin, 1980).

Hospital-based studies indicate that the incidence of adverse drug reactions within the hospital also increase with age. In a study of 1,160 hospitalized patients given medication, the rate of adverse reaction in those under 60 years of age was 6.3 percent while 15.4 percent of those 60 years and older experienced adverse drug reactions (Hurwitz, 1969).

Data gathered through the comprehensive *Boston Collaborative Drug Surveillance Program* are shown in Table 7-1, which also reveals an age-related increase in the incidence of adverse drug reactions in hospitalized patients ranging from 19.4 percent in the 16- to 25-year-old group to a high of 32.8 percent in those aged 66 to 75. It is important to point out, however, that 50 percent of these adverse reactions were considered to be minor and only 10.5 percent were determined to be of major significance (Miller, 1973).

Similar findings were revealed by an often-cited 1966 study of 714 hospitalized patients in which 9.9 percent of those patients between the ages of 21 and 30 experienced adverse drug reactions compared with 24.0 percent of those 81 years of age or older (Seidl, Thornton, Smith, & Cluff, 1966). These two studies also determined that adverse drug reactions occur more commonly in females than in males.

A great deal of uncertainty exists concerning the incidence of adverse drug reactions in the noninstitutionalized elderly. Undoubtedly the incidence is lower in this group because three of the major factors that are responsible for the relatively high incidence of adverse drug reactions in the hospitalized elderly do not apply to the same extent to patients living at home. Namely, noninstitutionalized patients are generally in better health than those who are hospitalized. On the average they take fewer medications, and the medications that they do use are generally less toxic than those used in hospitals, although many of the medications that are used in the home certainly possess considerable toxicity and should always be used cautiously.

Table 7-1 Age and Sex Distribution of Hospitalized Patients with an Adverse Drug Reaction

Category	Percent of patients with adverse reactions among all patients in category
Age 16–25	19.4
26–35	21.9
36–45	25.4
46–55	27.1
56–65	31.8
66–75	32.8
76–85	30.4
86+	29.8
Sex Male	25.4
Female	28.1
Total population	28.1

Source: Adapted from "Drug Surveillance Utilizing Epidemiologic Methods: A Report from the Boston Collaborative Drug Surveillance Program," by Russell R. Miller, *American Journal of Hospital Pharmacy,* Vol. 30, No. 7, pp. 584–592, July 1973, with permission of the American Society of Hospital Pharmacists.

A thorough review of adverse drug reaction studies points out the difficulty in assessing the real magnitude of adverse drug reactions in the elderly because of the fact that many of the previously performed studies have either significant methodological weaknesses or are prone to misinterpretation (Klein, German, & Levine, 1981). This review further points out that data on adverse drug reactions gathered from hospitalized patients cannot easily be applied to studies of ambulatory individuals, although both casual conversation and interviews by health professionals with elderly individuals living in their homes or apartments reveal that adverse drug reactions do occur frequently enough to be considered a significant problem in the elderly.

IDENTIFYING THE PATIENT AT RISK

In reviewing the various aspects of the aging process that can influence the occurrence of adverse reactions to medication among elderly patients, a few simple criteria can be developed to help health care providers in identifying patients who may be at greater risk of experiencing adverse drug reactions (Exhibit 7-1) (Simonson & Pratt, 1981). By using these simple criteria when taking medical or drug histories, dispensing medications, or monitoring a patient's drug therapy, health professionals involved in geriatric patient care can pinpoint incompatible drug therapy regimens and prevent or manage adverse drug reactions or interactions quickly and appropriately. The following points constitute criteria that can help to identify a patient who is at high risk of experiencing an adverse response to medications.

Exhibit 7-1 Factors Associated with an Increased Incidence of Adverse Reactions to Medication

- Patient is 75 years of age or older.
- Patient is of extremely small physical stature.
- Patient is receiving an excessive number of medications.
- Patient has developed new symptoms or changes in overall condition after modification of drug therapy regimen.
- Patient has developed kidney dysfunction.
- Patient is taking high risk medication.

Source: Reprinted from *Assessing Geriatric Patients and Their Drug Therapy Regimens* by William Simonson and Clara Pratt with permission of the Joint Commission on Accreditation of Hospitals, © 1981.

Is the Patient Older Than 75 Years of Age?

Although age by itself is probably not a risk factor for the occurrence of adverse drug reactions, numerous physiological and pharmacokinetic alterations generally have an increasingly greater effect on the drug therapy regimen of older patients, placing the "old old" (i.e., persons older than 75) at an even greater risk than the "young old" (i.e., persons between 65 and 74). In addition, older persons take more medications than the young, thus increasing their chances of experiencing an adverse reaction. Furthermore, persons over age 75 are more likely to have suffered sensory and social losses, such as relocation and widowhood. Economic losses also are more common in the "old old." These sensory, social, and economic factors may have a direct effect on an elderly person's ability to comply with medication regimens, thus increasing the possibility of adverse response.

Is the Patient of Extremely Small Physical Stature?

Many elderly individuals are of small physical stature compared with the young, a phenomenon that is partially due to age-related changes in body structure and musculature and partially because successive generations are increasing in average height. To be effective and nontoxic, a specific dose of medication may have to be adjusted to a patient's physical stature. An elderly person weighing 85 pounds, for example, will usually require a smaller dose of medication than a 210-pound individual.

Is the Patient Taking Several Medications?

As the number of medications taken by an individual increases, the associated risks of adverse drug reactions, drug interactions, and improper compliance to drug therapy also increase. Since consumption of both prescription and non-prescription medications increases with aging (see Chapter 2), so does the chance of experiencing an adverse drug reaction.

Has the Patient Developed Any New Symptoms?

Recent changes in an individual's drug therapy may result in adverse drug reactions that cause new symptoms or significant changes in a person's condition, such as confusion or depression. These changes or new symptoms should not be dismissed simply as characteristics of aging or as the result of age-related changes in physical condition. Rather, assessment of the patient may identify drug therapy as the source of these new symptoms. Failure to recognize such drug-induced conditions may result in inappropriate treatment, including the addition of even more unnecessary medications.

Has the Patient Experienced Kidney Dysfunction?

In addition to the gradual age-related decline of kidney function that occurs in all people, elderly persons may experience acute or chronic conditions that result in a further decline in kidney function. A geriatric patient who suffers from diabetes, for example, may experience long-term vascular changes that affect kidney function. Kidney function is an important consideration in drug therapy, because many drugs are eliminated from the body through the kidneys. If a patient with poor kidney function is given a drug dose that is inappropriately high, toxicity may occur.

Is the Patient Taking High-Risk Medications?

Certain medications taken more frequently by elderly patients are known to be associated with a relatively high degree of toxicity. Warfarin (Coumadin®), for example, which is frequently prescribed to manage certain disorders of blood clotting in elderly patients, is associated with potentially severe bleeding problems. Digoxin (Lanoxin®) is associated with a relatively high incidence of loss of appetite, confusion, depression, and potentially lethal disturbances of the rhythm of the heart. Combinations of several different medications also may precipitate high levels of toxicity in elderly individuals.

PRESCRIPTION MEDICATIONS COMMONLY CAUSING ADVERSE DRUG REACTIONS IN THE ELDERLY

As mentioned previously, certain medications that are commonly used by the elderly are responsible for a relatively large percentage of the adverse drug reactions that occur in this segment of the population (Table 7-2). The following discussion briefly reviews some of these drugs and the particular adverse effect(s) that may result from the use of these drugs in the elderly. This is not meant to be a thorough review of all the drugs that frequently cause adverse effects in the elderly, nor is it meant to review every adverse effect of each drug mentioned, but rather it is meant to provide the reader with a general understanding of the common adverse effects that occur in this group and how these effects may present themselves in the elderly (Abel, 1981; Crooks & Stevenson, 1979; Conrad & Bressler, 1982; Petersen, Whittington, & Payne, 1979 ; Practical Guide to Geriatric Medication, 1980).

Table 7-2 Significant Adverse Reactions to Medications in Elderly Patients

Type of drug	Generic name	Brand name example	Adverse effect(s)
Prescription drugs			
Cardiac	Digoxin	Lanoxin®	Loss of appetite, vision disturbances, depression, confusion, breast enlargement in males, abnormal heart rhythm
	Propranolol	Inderal®	Slow pulse, low blood pressure, complicates diabetic monitoring
Diuretic	Hydrochlorothiazide Chlorothiazide Furosemide	HydroDIURIL® Diuril® Lasix®	Potassium loss, dehydration, low blood pressure, diabetes, gout
	Spironolactone	Aldactone®	Excess potassium levels, breast enlargement in males
Antihypertensive	Methyldopa	Aldomet®	Drowsiness
	Reserpine	Serpasil®	Depression, sedation, gastrointestinal distress, abnormal heart rhythm
Antiarthritic	Phenylbutazone	Butazolidin®	Gastrointestinal irritation, fluid retention, serious blood disorders
	Indomethacin	Indocin®	Headache, gastrointestinal irritation, dizziness, mental confusion, ringing in ears
Anticoagulant	Warfarin	Coumadin®	Bleeding problems
Corticosteroids	Prednisone	Deltasone®	Fluid retention, diabetes, decreased immunity, ulcers, softening of bones, glaucoma, cataracts, confusion, psychosis
Bronchodilator	Theophylline	Elixophyllin ®	Nausea, seizures, abnormal heart rhythm
Gastrointestinal	Cimetidine	Tagamet®	Confusion, disorientation
	Atropine	Donnatal®*	Dry mouth, blurred vision, constipation, urinary retention, confusion, psychosis
Narcotic Analgesic	Codeine	Empirin® with Codeine* Tylenol® with Codeine*	Constipation, sedation
Sedative-Hypnotic	Pentobarbital	Nembutal®	Confusion, residual drowsiness, agitation, psychosis
	Flurazepam	Dalmane®	Drowsiness, confusion, unsteady walking
Antianxiety	Diazepam	Valium®	Drowsiness, sedation, confusion, dizziness

Table 7-2 continued

Type of drug	Generic name	Brand name example	Adverse effect(s)
Prescription drugs			
Antidepressant	Amitriptyline	Elavil®	Dry mouth, confusion, low blood pressure, constipation, increased pulse, heart rhythm disorders, glaucoma
Antipsychotic	Chlorpromazine	Thorazine®	Sedation, low blood pressure, dry mouth, blurred vision, constipation, urinary retention, extrapyramidal effects, including: restlessness, exaggerated facial movements, and symptoms of Parkinson's disease
	Haloperidol	Haldol®	Less toxicity than chlorpromazine but increased extrapyramidal effects
Nonprescription medication			
Analgesic	Aspirin	Bayer Aspirin®	Nausea, gastrointestinal irritation, ulcers, confusion, drowsiness, metabolic disturbances
Antacids	Magnesium hydroxide		Diarrhea
	Aluminum hydroxide		Constipation
	Calcium carbonate		
	Sodium bicarbonate		Can worsen high blood pressure, congestive heart failure, kidney disease
Laxatives			Dehydration, electrolyte loss

*contains more than one active ingredient

Note: This table does not include all important adverse drug effects that occur in the elderly nor does it list all drugs capable of causing adverse effects.

Cardiac Drugs (Heart Medications)

Digoxin (Lanoxin®)

Digoxin is one of the most commonly prescribed medications taken by the elderly. It is one member of a family of drugs called digitalis glycosides, which are extracted from the digitalis or foxglove plant. Similar medications include digitoxin (Crystodigin®) and digitalis leaf.

Digoxin may be used in the management of atrial fibrillation, a disorder in heart rhythm, although it is most commonly used in elderly patients to manage congestive heart failure, because it is capable of increasing the strength of contractions of the heart.

In addition to being commonly used it is also one of the most frequent causes of adverse drug reactions in the elderly, partially because of its frequency of use and partially due to its inherent toxicity. One of the major causes of digoxin toxicity is the fact that elderly patients are frequently given doses that are inappropriately high. The dangers of this practice are compounded by the fact that digoxin and all of the digitalis glycosides have a low therapeutic index, meaning that the dose that will result in toxicity is only slightly greater than the therapeutic dose.

The half-life of digoxin in a normal healthy adult is approximately 36 hours; however, in a sick elderly patient the half-life of digoxin may be twice that or longer, largely because the body's ability to excrete digoxin decreases in proportion to the decrease in kidney function that occurs with aging.

Traditionally, toxicity to digoxin and the other digitalis glycosides has been commonly described as nausea, vomiting, and diarrhea; however, digoxin toxicity in the elderly more commonly presents as more subtle symptoms, such as anorexia (loss of appetite), vision disturbances, fatigue, bad dreams, confusion, and depression. The patient may also experience different types of potentially fatal disorders in heart rhythm as a result of digoxin toxicity. Use of this drug may also cause gynecomastia (breast enlargement) in elderly men (see Chapter 9 for a more detailed discussion of this problem).

Even though digoxin may commonly cause toxicity it may be used safely if proper geriatric principles are followed when the dosage is being determined and the drug is being administered.

Propranolol (Inderal®)

Propranolol is a commonly used member of the family of drugs called beta-receptor blockers. This name is derived from the fact that these drugs act by blocking the beta receptors in the heart, which usually results in a decrease in heart rate and cardiac output; therefore, these drugs are used to treat angina, high blood pressure, and numerous other cardiac and noncardiac diseases.

Studies have demonstrated that the metabolism of propranolol in the elderly is decreased, resulting in higher blood concentrations of this drug.

Owing partially to existing cardiovascular disease, elderly patients are predisposed to certain toxicities of propranolol, such as hypotension (low blood pressure) and bradycardia (slow pulse), both of which could cause weakness, dizziness, and fainting. Propranolol may also mask the signs and symptoms of hypoglycemia (low blood sugar) in diabetic patients who are using either insulin or oral hypoglycemic (antidiabetic) drugs.

Diuretics

Diuretics are used to eliminate excess fluids from the body in many elderly individuals with congestive heart failure, cirrhosis of the liver, and various other conditions that result in accumulation of fluid (edema). Diuretics are also used to treat high blood pressure. Two basic types of diuretics are most commonly used: the potassium-wasting diuretics and the potassium-sparing variety, both of which may cause a variety of adverse reactions (Smith & Steele, 1983).

Potassium-Wasting Diuretics

Potassium-wasting diuretics include hydrochlorothiazide (HydroDIURIL®, Esidrix®), chlorothiazide (Diuril®), and furosemide (Lasix®). This class is so named because the action of these drugs on the kidney causes the body to lose (waste) an important electrolyte, potassium. They are potent diuretics to which the elderly may experience many possible adverse reactions, including hypokalemia (loss of potassium); hypovolemia (excessive loss of fluid); impaired glucose tolerance, which can sometimes precipitate or worsen adult-onset diabetes; and hyperuricemia, which is an increased level of uric acid in the patient's bloodstream that may result in gout.

Hypovolemia can be an especially significant problem in the elderly because the reduced amount of fluid available for circulation may cause postural hypotension, a condition in which an individual's blood pressure drops significantly when rising from a sitting or lying position, causing dizziness or fainting and possible severe injury resulting from a subsequent fall. Severe hypovolemia, or dehydration, may also occur, especially in the elderly who already have decreased amounts of water in their bodies and who may be likely to stop or reduce food and fluid intake when they are ill.

Hypokalemia, symptoms of which include lethargy, irritability, numbness, and muscle weakness, may be a significant problem in some patients who take potassium-wasting diuretics, necessitating the ingestion of potassium-rich foods such as citrus fruits and juices or the use of potassium supplementation by prescription. Although the problem of hypokalemia is variable and not all persons will require additional potassium, the problem does appear to be greater in elderly women than in elderly men (Clark, Wheatley, Rawlings, & Vestal, 1982).

Hypokalemia can also be a major problem when it occurs in patients who are taking some form of digitalis because it markedly increases that individual's chance of experiencing digitalis toxicity. This common and potentially lethal drug interaction is discussed more fully in Chapter 8.

Potassium-Sparing Diuretics

Potassium-sparing diuretics, one of which is spironolactone (Aldactone®), generally have few adverse effects, but one major problem associated with their use in the elderly is hyperkalemia, or too much potassium in the system. This is most likely to occur due to the age-related decrease in kidney function that decreases the kidneys' ability to eliminate potassium from the body. Hyper-kalemia, if serious, can lead to cardiac arrest. It is almost never necessary to administer potassium supplementation to patients taking spironolactone or other potassium-sparing diuretics and, in fact, their concurrent use may be extremely detrimental to the patient. Spironolactone may also cause gynecomastia (breast enlargement) in elderly males (see Chapter 9).

Antihypertensives

High blood pressure is relatively common in the elderly, and although it usually is present without the patient experiencing any symptoms, it is a serious problem because it increases the risk of various cardiovascular diseases, such as angina pectoris (chest pain) and myocardial infarction (heart attack); it also increases the incidence of stroke.

As a result of the decrease in sensitivity of physiological regulatory systems in elderly persons, it becomes difficult to treat high blood pressure with drugs without a considerable risk of toxicity.

In the elderly there frequently also exists a decreased flow of blood to the brain as the result of hardening of the arteries, which further complicates the treatment of high blood pressure.

When antihypertensive drugs are used to decrease blood pressure there is a corresponding decrease in blood flow to the brain as systemic blood pressure falls. The decreased capacity of elderly individuals to compensate for this decrease in blood pressure increases their likelihood of experiencing mild symptoms such as dizziness or lightheadedness or more severe problems such as orthostatic or postural hypotension, which is a significant fall in blood pressure when rising from a lying or sitting position, possibly resulting in fainting and a subsequent dangerous fall. Because of these problems it is important that blood pressure in the elderly not be treated too aggressively. The therapeutic goals for antihypertensive therapy in the elderly must often be significantly more conservative than if the patient were younger, making it necessary to settle for a somewhat higher blood pressure in order to avoid the potentially significant adverse reactions associated with this therapy.

Methyldopa (Aldomet®)

The antihypertensive agent methyldopa may cause drowsiness and sedation in elderly patients, although this problem may resolve somewhat after several weeks of therapy. In rare instances methyldopa may cause hemolytic anemia, a destruction of red blood cells within the body.

Reserpine (Serpasil®)

Reserpine should be used with great care in the elderly because of the large number of adverse effects that it may cause, including sedation, decreased libido, gastric distress and ulceration, nasal congestion, and disorders of heart rhythm. Perhaps the most serious complication of reserpine is its ability to cause depression in the elderly. This depression may be severe enough to require hospitalization and is especially dangerous because it may occur insidiously, with its cause remaining unrecognized. Depression induced by reserpine may also persist for several weeks following the discontinuation of the drug.

Antiarthritics

Phenylbutazone (Butazolidin®)

Phenylbutazone may result in severe toxicity in the elderly. It is quite irritating to the gastrointestinal tract and may cause significant ulceration. In addition, elderly persons who take phenylbutazone for prolonged periods of time have an increased risk of developing aplastic anemia, a critical deficiency of blood cells.

Indomethacin (Indocin®)

Although indomethacin is not uncommonly used in the elderly, it is capable of causing significant adverse reactions in the elderly. Headache is not uncommon, and gastrointestinal ulceration can occur. A wide variety of additional effects can also be seen, including dizziness, mental confusion, and ringing or buzzing in the ears.

Anticoagulants

Warfarin (Coumadin®)

Warfarin is an anticoagulant that decreases the synthesis of clotting factors produced by the liver in order to prevent the occurrence of thrombosis (clotting inside the body). It is not used by a large percentage of the elderly population; however, its potency and the fact that it is more likely to cause toxicity, primarily in the form of bleeding problems, warrant a discussion of its potential toxicity in the elderly.

Warfarin may possess greater toxicity in the elderly for a number of reasons, including the fact that it is less bound to protein in the bloodstream in the elderly and thus may exhibit increased activity and toxicity (see Chapter 6 for a more detailed discussion). Its toxicity may also be related to age-related alterations of the blood clotting mechanism in the presence of degenerative vascular disease.

Improper nutrition or alteration in nutritional patterns may also affect the activity and toxicity of warfarin, both of which are related to the intake of vitamin

K. An increase of dietary vitamin K, from leafy green vegetables or other sources can actually counteract the effectiveness of warfarin, whereas a decrease in vitamin K intake may result in an increased bleeding tendency.

Warfarin toxicity may also be increased by certain health conditions, such as recent eye surgery or other types of surgery, or other diseases, such as liver disease or gastric irritation or ulceration, which would predispose the patient to experience a bleeding episode.

Additionally, other medications commonly taken by the elderly, such as various sleeping medications, aspirin, and certain antibiotics, may interact with warfarin, resulting in toxicity.

Elderly patients may require reduced doses of warfarin and should be closely monitored for possible toxicity caused by inappropriately high dosage, drug interactions, or as the result of concurrent disease states.

Corticosteroids

Prednisone (Deltasone®)

Prednisone and numerous related corticosteroids may be used for a wide variety of conditions from arthritis to cancer but should be used judiciously in the elderly, owing to the wide variety of serious adverse reactions that may occur.

These adverse reactions can be divided into two general classes: (1) those that occur following short-term administration of these drugs for a period of several days or weeks and (2) those that generally result from administration over a prolonged period of time, ranging from several weeks to years.

Short-term problems include the following:

- *fluid retention*. This results from corticosteroid-induced retention of sodium in the body. This accumulation of fluids can be quite extreme and may be especially detrimental in patients with congestive heart failure, angina, or other types of heart disease. Fluid retention may also raise blood pressure significantly, making it a problem in persons with high blood pressure.
- *psychological problems*. Corticosteroids are capable of causing a wide variety of behavioral or psychological effects, ranging from an increased sense of well-being, or euphoria, to agitation and even extreme psychotic behavior.
- *diabetes*. Corticosteroids also tend to decrease the control of blood sugar in diabetic patients and may precipitate diabetes in patients who are predisposed to diabetes, especially obese elderly individuals.
- *decreased immune response*. These drugs have the capacity of decreasing an individual's immune response, thus making them more susceptible to infection. They may also reactivate tuberculosis in patients who have previously been infected with this disease.

- *ulceration*. Corticosteroids may also cause gastrointestinal irritation and even ulceration.

Long-term problems include two major adverse effects: osteoporosis and ocular changes. Osteoporosis is the softening of a person's bones, making them weak and more likely to fracture. Long-term corticosteroid use is capable of causing significant osteoporosis, especially in elderly individuals, resulting in fractured vertebrae of the spine, a broken hip, or other fractures. The ocular effects of corticosteroids that may result from long-term administration include the development of glaucoma and the formation of cataracts.

Many of the adverse effects of corticosteroids may occur in younger persons as well as the elderly, however, the types of effects that occur, and their relationship to preexisting problems, gives them special significance in the elderly patient.

Bronchodilators

Theophylline (Elixophyllin®)

It is questionable whether an inherent sensitivity to theophylline and similar drugs exists in elderly patients, although patients with heart disease, which of course includes many elderly individuals, may be more likely to experience theophylline-induced disturbances in heart rhythm. It has been determined, however, that the elimination, or clearance, of theophylline from the body decreases with age, resulting in increased blood levels in the elderly if doses are not decreased accordingly. If blood levels increase into the toxic range, various adverse effects can occur, including nausea, seizures, and disturbances of the heart rhythm.

Gastrointestinal Drugs

Cimetidine (Tagamet®)

Cimetidine effectively reduces gastric acid secretion and for that reason is used in a variety of gastrointestinal disorders.

It has been determined that the clearance of cimetidine from the body is decreased in the elderly, resulting in higher blood levels that are related to an increase in the incidence of adverse drug reactions.

Elderly individuals, especially those with impaired kidney function or associated severe medical illness are more prone to the drug's complications, which include alterations in the patient's mental status. Delirium, confusion, disorientation, agitation, and other problems can occur. These adverse effects tend to become evident within 48 hours of the start of the drug's administration. Patients with other types of mental impairment, such as Alzheimer's disease, may be particularly prone to these adverse effects of cimetidine (Jenike, 1982).

Atropine

Atropine (found in Donnatal®) is one of the members of the class of drugs called anticholinergic agents. This name is derived from the pharmacological activity that these drugs possess. They are used for a variety of purposes, including dilation of the pupil. They are also used to decrease spasms in the stomach and intestines and prior to surgery to prevent excessive salivation and secretions in the lungs.

The adverse effects of drugs with anticholinergic properties can be severe in the elderly and include dry mouth; blurred vision; constipation, possibly leading to fecal impaction in the intestine; and urinary hesitancy or urinary retention, especially in elderly males with an enlarged prostate gland. These drugs can also cause confusion, disorientation, and psychosis.

It is important to be aware of the adverse effects that are associated with the anticholinergic properties of a medication because many medications that are commonly taken by the elderly, including antipsychotic drugs, antidepressants, and drugs used to treat Parkinson's disease, possess strong anticholinergic properties and consequently may frequently cause these types of adverse reactions.

Narcotic Analgesics

Codeine

Potent narcotics such as codeine (in Empirin No. 3® and Tylenol No. 3®) and others may cause mental confusion in the elderly and may worsen any preexisting mental impairment. The use of narcotics, especially their excessive use, can also cause significant depression of the central nervous system and may depress respiration. They can immobilize the patient as a result of oversedation, resulting in dehydration and leading to pressure sores. Narcotics, especially codeine and oxycodone (found in Percodan®), may also be quite constipating.

Lower narcotic doses in the elderly provide good pain relief with less depression of the central nervous system and respiratory system.

Sedative-Hypnotics (Sleep Inducers)

Pentobarbital (Nembutal®)

Pentobarbital is a member of the class of drugs known as the barbiturates. The use of pentobarbital and other barbiturates for inducing sleep in the elderly is generally to be avoided because of the significant adverse reactions that may occur. The metabolism of the barbiturates is decreased in the elderly, and it has been found that elderly persons have an increased sensitivity to the effect of these drugs. Their use may cause confusion, possibly resulting in a fall, and the patient may experience significant residual drowsiness the morning following their use to induce sleep. The elderly may also experience a paradoxical response, and instead of sleeping may develop symptoms ranging from mild restlessness to a major psychotic episode.

Persons using pentobarbital or any barbiturate should not drink alcohol, because a serious and often fatal drug interaction may occur.

Flurazepam (Dalmane®)

Flurazepam is used frequently to induce sleep in the elderly; however, it does have adverse effects. It can cause a number of effects, especially drowsiness, confusion, ataxia (inability to walk steadily), and sluggishness. These effects may be observed the morning after the use of this drug.

Most of these adverse effects, however, are dose related and can be decreased or avoided by using the recommended geriatric dose of 15 mg, rather than the standard adult dose of 30 mg.

As with other sedative drugs, patients taking flurazepam should avoid drinking alcohol.

Antianxiety Drugs

Diazepam (Valium®)

Diazepam is a popular representative of the class of drugs known as the benzodiazapines, which are frequently used in the elderly to treat anxiety.

It has been found that the elimination of diazepam is decreased in the elderly; therefore, increased sensitivity to the adverse effects of this drug results.

Elderly patients commonly experience drowsiness and sedation from diazepam, especially resulting from the use of inappropriately high doses of the drug. Other similar problems that may occur are confusion, dizziness, and fatigue.

Although they may seem minor to some, these adverse effects can have a profound effect on the life of elderly patients and their ability to care for themselves and function independently. It is recommended that doses of diazepam and other benzodiazepine drugs be reduced in the elderly.

Antidepressants

Amitriptyline (Elavil®)

Amitriptyline belongs to a family of drugs called the tricyclic antidepressants. These drugs can be quite effective in treating depression, which is not uncommon in the elderly individual.

The elimination of amitriptyline and other tricyclic antidepressants from the body has been found to be decreased in the elderly population, resulting in drug concentrations in the bloodstream that are higher in the elderly than they are in younger persons following comparable doses.

Unfortunately, amitriptyline and the other tricyclics are capable of causing a wide variety of adverse drug reactions that are both annoying and serious. Most of these adverse reactions that are problems in the elderly are related to the anticholinergic properties of this family of drugs and include dry mouth, confusion, postural hypotension (significant lowering of blood pressure on standing, which may cause lightheadedness or fainting, resulting in a fall), and constipation with possible paralytic ileus (paralysis of a portion of the intestine resulting in severe constipation and fecal impaction). Adverse reactions may also involve the heart, causing tachycardia (increased pulse rate), congestive heart failure, and disturbances of the heart's rhythm. In addition, amitriptyline may cause sedation; may increase pressure within the eye, thus aggravating glaucoma; and may also cause confusion or behavioral problems, including psychosis.

Antipsychotic Drugs (Psychiatric Drugs)

Antipsychotic agents are commonly used in the elderly to treat major mental disorders such as psychosis, major personality disorders, severe agitation, delusions, and hallucinations.

Many different antipsychotic drugs are available; however, their therapeutic effects and pharmacologic activities are similar, with the major differences between the different agents being the adverse effects that they may cause.

Because antipsychotic drugs are capable of causing large numbers of serious adverse reactions in the elderly, some clinicians recommend that elderly individuals should receive doses that are one third to one half those administered to younger patients. A detailed discussion of the adverse reactions to this class of drugs is beyond the scope of this book; however, the reader is referred to one of the *1983 U.S.P. Dispensing Information* reference books (see Appendix 5-1 for ordering information) for excellent summaries of the adverse effects that are caused by these drugs and many others.

For the purposes of this chapter the major toxicities of two well-known antipsychotic drugs will be briefly discussed.

Chlorpromazine (Thorazine®)

One of the significant adverse reactions to chlorpromazine is sedation, which can have great significance in the elderly, who, when sedated, are at risk of experiencing a fall. The drug also has a propensity to cause hypotension (low blood pressure), which may be more likely to occur when a patient stands quickly, resulting in lightheadedness, dizziness, and possibly an injurious fall.

Chlorpromazine may also cause annoying and sometimes serious anti-cholinergic (atropinelike) side effects, such as dry mouth, blurred vision, constipation, and urinary retention. The use of chlorpromazine may also result in a significant incidence of adverse effects known as extrapyramidal effects. Extrapyramidal effects are numerous, and those that are most severe in the elderly can be divided into three major categories as follows:

1. *parkinsonian effect*. Antipsychotic drugs can cause a series of symptoms that are identical to Parkinson's disease, with the patient exhibiting decreased motion, a lack of facial expression, a shuffling gait, a "pill rolling" hand movement, and tremor and muscle rigidity. These effects are considered to be related to the dose of the drug and are usually reversible following discontinuation of the drug; however, they may continue for a long period of time following discontinuation of the drug (Murdoch & Williamson, 1982).
2. *akathesia*. This problem is characterized by the patient's subjective desire to be moving constantly and may result in restlessness or other types of continuous motion.
3. *tardive dyskinesia*. This is characterized by exaggerated movements of the tongue, mouth, jaw, or face. It may be seen as a chewing, lip smacking, or tongue rolling motion and can be quite debilitating to the patient from a social standpoint. Tardive dyskinesia is a serious problem that is most likely to occur in elderly females, although it may occur in males and in patients under 60 years of age. The syndrome often occurs in patients who have been taking antipsychotic drugs for prolonged periods of time such as three to six months or longer; however, it may occur soon after a patient starts taking the drug. Unfortunately this problem may be irreversible and may persist, even following discontinuation of the drug. There is no effective treatment for tardive dyskinesia aside from the discontinuation of the offending agent (Portnoi & Johnson, 1982). Attempts have been made to treat tardive dyskinesia with various compounds, most notably lecithin (Crismon, 1982; Jenike, 1983).

Haloperidol (Haldol®)

Haloperidol is as effective as the other antipsychotic drugs but possesses a significantly different spectrum of adverse reactions than does chlorpromazine. This drug has the advantage of being one of the least sedating antipsychotic agents, while also resulting in less hypotension and fewer anticholinergic effects. Haloperidol does, however, induce more adverse extrapyramidal effects than do most of the other antipsychotic drugs.

NONPRESCRIPTION MEDICATIONS COMMONLY CAUSING ADVERSE DRUG REACTIONS IN THE ELDERLY

Nonprescription medication is frequently used by the elderly to treat various complaints such as minor pain, upset stomach, or constipation, and while most nonprescription medications can be used safely it must be realized that they may have adverse effects just as prescription drugs do (see Table 7-2).

Aspirin

Aspirin is frequently used by elderly individuals for minor pain, either as aspirin tablets or in combination ingredient products, which the individual may or may not know contain aspirin. It may also be used in large doses ranging from ten to sixteen 325-mg tablets daily for the treatment of rheumatoid arthritis.

Aspirin is quite irritating to the stomach and frequently causes symptoms of gastrointestinal distress such as nausea, vomiting, and abdominal pain. Its use may cause the individual's stool to become black and sticky, indicating severe blood loss from the stomach or upper intestine. In fact, most elderly individuals who habitually take aspirin do experience blood loss, which, if allowed to continue, may be significant enough to cause severe anemia, requiring hospitalization and blood transfusions. This gastrointestinal irritation is increased if the patient ingests alcohol.

Other manifestations of aspirin toxicity in the elderly result from relatively moderate doses and may occur insidiously, causing confusion, drowsiness, dizziness, temporary deafness, ringing in the ears, hallucinations, and severe metabolic disturbances (Vivian & Goldberg, 1982).

Antacids

Antacids usually consist of one or more of the following chemicals: aluminum hydroxide, magnesium hydroxide, or calcium carbonate. The adverse effects that antacids have depend on which of these particular ingredients are in the product that is being used.

Antacids that contain primarily aluminum hydroxide tend to be constipating, as do those with calcium carbonate as their chief ingredient. Magnesium hydroxide on the other hand causes diarrhea to such an extent that it is not used by itself as an antacid but rather used, as milk of magnesia, to treat constipation. Many antacids contain a mixture of two or more of these chemicals in an effort to balance their constipating and diarrhea-inducing properties.

Sodium bicarbonate is used by some elderly individuals as an antacid, but this practice is not wise and its use for this purpose should be discouraged. The large amount of sodium in this product can have a detrimental effect in elderly individuals with a number of health conditions, including high blood pressure, congestive heart failure, kidney disease, and other conditions.

Laxatives

Laxatives are used frequently by the elderly, but they should be used in moderation because excessive or routine use can result in dehydration and loss of important electrolytes such as sodium or potassium.

THE CONSEQUENCES OF ADVERSE REACTIONS TO MEDICATIONS

Adverse reactions to medications may impact on the patient in many ways. The following points briefly outline some of the major detrimental effects of such adverse reactions.

Morbidity

The most obvious negative aspect of adverse drug reactions is the actual physical manifestation of the reaction. The effect may be physically harmful to the patient, such as when an individual experiences gastrointestinal irritation and blood loss resulting from the administration of the antiinflammatory medication indomethacin (Indocin®), and may even lead to further and more serious problems, such as iron deficiency anemia resulting from the occurrence of such blood loss over a prolonged period of time.

Adverse effects of medications may also be harmful to the patient in a more personal way, by creating relatively minor, but annoying problems such as blurred vision or dry mouth resulting from the atropinelike effect of medications, including certain antidepressants, or in a social way, such as when a liquid antacid preparation causes diarrhea and a sense of urgency, perhaps even resulting in fecal incontinence.

Mortality

The patient may actually experience an adverse drug reaction and die, although this is rare. An individual's death may also be an indirect result of an adverse reaction to a medication, such as described in the following scenario: An elderly woman, who is experiencing residual morning drowsiness resulting from the administration of an excessive dose of a sleeping medication the previous night, experiences a fall in her bathroom as a result of this drowsiness. From the fall the patient sustains a broken hip, for which she is admitted to a nursing home for recuperation. While in the nursing home, and as a result of her injury, the patient is largely confined to her bed, where she develops a blood clot in her leg, which travels to her lungs, causing a fatal pulmonary embolism.

I believe that situations similar to this fictional scenario occur on a relatively frequent basis. I have seen many elderly patients who have died with multiple problems with their medications, and while their deaths are not usually thought to be specifically the result of the adverse effects of their medications, I am sure that they are often contributing factors.

Polypharmacy

Adverse reactions to medications may result in the addition of more medications to the patient's drug therapy regimen, especially if the initial adverse effect experienced by the patient is not identified as the cause of the signs or symptoms being experienced by the patient (see Chapter 2 for a detailed discussion of polypharmacy).

Financial Expense

If patients experience an adverse drug reaction as an outpatient, it may be necessary for them to return to their physician for assessment, perhaps even requiring additional prescription or nonprescription medication or other types of therapy to treat the adverse reaction. In extreme cases the adverse reaction may contribute to or directly result in admission to a hospital or nursing home.

If patients who are already in an institution such as a hospital or a nursing home experience an adverse reaction, they, too, may require additional therapeutic measures, including the use of additional medications to treat the adverse drug effect or additional laboratory tests. In addition, the duration of the patient's stay in the facility may be prolonged.

All of these consequences and interventions mentioned above have the potential of adding a significant financial burden to the patient, who in the case of the elderly may be on a limited fixed income, or to the third-party payer who is responsible for the patient's expenses.

Clinical Manifestations

The clinical manifestations of adverse reactions to medications range from mild to fatal and depend on many factors, including the medication causing the adverse response, the dose of the medication that is being administered, and, of course, the patient's clinical status.

The overwhelming majority of adverse reactions to medications are mild and are usually self-limiting and of little consequence. Examples of this type of adverse reaction include the mild diarrhea caused by some antibiotics such as ampicillin (Polycillin®). Adverse reactions may also be quite serious, and if not managed and reversed, they may sometimes become life threatening.

In their most severe form, adverse reactions to medications may result in fatality, although it has been estimated that such fatal episodes occur in only three-tenths percent of hospitalized patients (Miller, 1973), with the frequency most likely being significantly less than that in noninstitutionalized patients. Most fatal adverse reactions are caused by a relatively small number of medications that have a known risk of toxicity. In some cases, such as with certain anticancer medications that have a very great potential for toxicity, the risk of the patient experiencing a severe or even fatal adverse reaction could be considered justifiable, considering the lifesaving potential of the medication.

COMMON MANIFESTATIONS OF ADVERSE REACTIONS TO MEDICATIONS

Adverse drug reactions may present in the elderly as a wide variety of signs and symptoms, ranging from a very subtle presentation such as a mild residual drowsiness in the morning to an acute episode of urinary retention.

Although I would not say that most medications are highly toxic, it is true that almost any prescription and nonprescription medication is capable of causing some types of adverse effect, depending on the basic pharmacology of the drug and the health status of the patient. The occurrence of an adverse reaction also relates strongly to how that particular individual responds to the medication that he or she is taking, since that response may vary significantly between patients, resulting in a situation in which a specific medication might be very beneficial in one individual while at the same time being highly toxic in another.

Since a large number of medications may cause similar adverse effects in the elderly, I believe that it is important to review these basic types of adverse reactions and how they may present in the elderly.

Along with each symptom, I have listed and briefly described one or more medications that may cause the problem mentioned, although it must be emphasized that neither the list of adverse drug reactions nor the list of offending medications is complete (Table 7-3).

Confusion

Many different medications may result in a confusional state in the elderly patient. One example is the medication atropine, which can cause a variety of adverse symptoms involving the patient's mental state, ranging from mild confusion to major psychoses with severe agitation. The use of atropine per se is now

Table 7-3 Examples of Adverse Effects of Medications That Commonly Occur in the Elderly with Selected Medications That May Cause These Problems

Adverse effect	Drug name	
	Generic name	*Brand name*
Confusion	Atropine	Atropisol®
	Amitriptyline	Elavil®
	Chlorpromazine	Thorazine®
	Propantheline	Pro-Banthine®
	Cimetidine	Tagamet®
Depression	Reserpine	Serpasil®
Anorexia	Digoxin	Lanoxin®
Weakness	Furosemide	Lasix®
	Hydrochlorothiazide	HydroDIURIL®
Lethargy	Flurazepam	Dalmane®
Ataxia	Flurazepam	Dalmane®
	Diazepam	Valium®
	Phenytoin	Dilantin®
Forgetfulness	Pentobarbital	Nembutal®
	Secobarbital	Seconal®
Tremor	Haloperidol	Haldol®
Constipation	Codeine	Tylenol #3®*
	Oxycodone	Percodan®*
Diarrhea	Magnesium hydroxide	Maalox®*
Urinary retention	Amitriptyline	Elavil®
	Chlorpromazine	Thorazine®
	Propantheline	Pro-Banthine®

*contains more than one active ingredient

largely limited for use in surgery, when it prevents excessive salivation and secretions in the respiratory tract, thus reducing the chance that the patient will accidentally aspirate any of those secretions into the lungs, which could cause pneumonia. Atropine is also used to treat various disorders of the eye when it is necessary to dilate the pupil. However, many medications that are commonly used by the elderly possess strong atropinelike (anticholinergic) activity. These medications include antidepressants such as amitriptyline (Elavil®); antipsychotics, such as chlorpromazine (Thorazine®); and medications used to reduce gastric activity and acid production such as propantheline (Pro-Banthine®). Another medication that has been found to cause a significant amount of confusion and delirium in the elderly is cimetidine (Tagamet®), which is used to inhibit the production of gastric acid in patients with ulcers.

Depression

One of the medications that is capable of causing depression in an elderly individual is reserpine (Serpasil®), which has been used primarily to treat high blood pressure. The depression that is caused by reserpine can be quite severe, even to the point at which the patient may become suicidal. Depression does not develop in all patients who take reserpine, and it may be possible to detect the onset of depression by observing the patient for sleep disturbances, physical weakness, or a decreased ability to concentrate (Holloway, 1974). Reserpine-induced depression can be a serious problem in the elderly; however, the knowledge of its potential occurrence is fairly widespread, and that, combined with the availability of a large assortment of newer, less toxic and possibly more effective antihypertensive medications, has reduced the use of this drug in the elderly. A number of other medications, including propranolol (Inderal®) and digoxin (Lanoxin®), may cause depression in the elderly.

Anorexia

Anorexia (loss of appetite) can occur as a result of toxicity from the digitalis glycosides, such as digoxin (Lanoxin®). Anorexia can be a difficult symptom to detect because its onset can be very subtle, and it may at first present simply as a patient's disinterest in food. It may also be more pronounced and may have a significant effect on the patient's state of nutrition, especially if allowed to continue for a prolonged period. Health professionals frequently look for nausea, vomiting, diarrhea, and bradycardia (slow pulse) as signs of digitalis toxicity but not for anorexia, even though it may be of as great or greater significance to the patient than the other more well-recognized symptoms.

Weakness

Weakness in the elderly can be the result of the depressive effect of certain medications on the central nervous system, or it may result from other mechanisms, such as a drug-induced disturbance of serum electrolytes in the body, most notably potassium.

Certain diuretics such as furosemide (Lasix®) or hydrochlorothiazide (Hydro-DIURIL®) that are commonly taken by the elderly to control high blood pressure or to eliminate excess body water in congestive heart failure and other conditions result in the loss of potassium from the body. Although the individual response to these drugs is highly variable, some elderly patients may be quite sensitive to both their diuretic and potassium-depleting effect, resulting in dehydration and hypokalemia (potassium deficiency). One of the more prominent signs of hypokalemia is weakness, which may occur if the hypokalemia is not corrected. Potassium levels in the body can be easily replenished with the oral administration of potassium chloride; however, the dosage form of potassium chloride that is most commonly given to the patient is a liquid, the taste of which most will agree is quite unpalatable, thus contributing to poor compliance, the continuation of the low potassium levels, and therefore a continued weakness.

Lethargy

Lethargy, or drowsiness, can be caused by many different medications that have a depressant effect on the central nervous system. This includes the sleep-inducing medications that may be used in the elderly, such as flurazepam (Dalmane®) and others. For example, in one major study (Greenblatt, Allen, & Shader, 1977) it was determined that 39 percent of the elderly patients who had taken flurazepam in doses of 30 mg or more per day experienced residual drowsiness on arousal the next morning, although it was also found that low doses of the drug, that is, less than 15 mg per day, were well tolerated without excessive drowsiness.

Although drowsiness is generally considered to be a side effect of little consequence, it may have significant implications in the elderly individual if it interferes with self-care. For example, the effect of drowsiness could be tragic if it results in a fall and perhaps a broken hip.

Ataxia

Ataxia is a rather unsteady pattern of walking in which an individual may have a wide and irregular gait. It may look somewhat like the person is intoxicated. Ataxia may be caused by medications that can cause lethargy and drowsiness including sleeping medications such as excessive doses of flurazepam (Dalmane®) and other similar medications such as diazepam (Valium®), which can depress the central nervous system. Phenytoin (Dilantin®) may also cause ataxia, which may be quite dangerous to the patient because it may cause the patient to fall.

Forgetfulness

Barbiturates such as secobarbital (Seconal®) and pentobarbital (Nembutal®) may cause forgetfulness. This annoying problem could have a significant impact on many of the patient's daily activities, including the patient's ability to comply properly with prescribed drug therapy.

Tremor

Various neurological conditions such as Parkinson's disease or a condition known as senile tremor occur with increased frequency in the elderly; however, some medications may also result in significant tremor in some patients. For example, the use of certain antipsychotic medications, such as haloperidol (Haldol®), may result in a drug-induced Parkinson's disease that is thought to be biochemically related to Parkinson's disease, manifesting itself with symptoms, including tremor, that are strikingly similar to the actual disease. This drug-induced Parkinson's disease can usually be corrected with a reduction of drug dosage or the addition of a medication to treat the Parkinsonian symptoms.

Constipation

Some medications that are used by the elderly may cause constipation due both to the effect of the medication and to the fact that age-related alterations in the gastrointestinal tract may predispose the elderly individual to constipation. For example, certain narcotic analgesics such as codeine (an ingredient in Tylenol #3®) and oxycodone (an ingredient in Percodan®) may cause severe constipation and even fecal impaction in the elderly bedridden patient.

Diarrhea

Another gastrointestinal complaint that can result from medications is diarrhea. Although various oral antacid preparations containing magnesium hydroxide and aluminum hydroxide (Maalox®) are taken by persons of all ages, some of these products may cause diarrhea as a result of their magnesium hydroxide content.

Urinary Retention

Medications with atropinelike (anticholinergic) properties may cause or worsen the retention of urine in the bladder, making it difficult for the patient to void completely. Medications possessing this property act by inhibiting the neural impulse to the bladder sphincter muscle, subsequently inhibiting urine flow from the bladder. Drug-induced urinary retention may be especially annoying or even dangerous to an elderly male who is experiencing some urinary problems due to the enlargement of his prostate gland, resulting in a partial restriction of urine outflow. The ability of the elderly male to urinate may be decreased by medications possessing anticholinergic properties, such as antidepressants like amitriptyline (Elavil®); antipsychotics, such as chlorpromazine (Thorazine®); and gastrointestinal antispasmodics, such as propantheline (Pro-Banthine®).

THE ELDERLY STEREOTYPE

The adverse drug reactions just described are certainly not the only ones that can occur in the elderly, nor are these medications the only ones that can be the cause of these problems; yet as identified they represent what I have observed to be a fair representation of those adverse effects that may occur more commonly in the elderly.

In a review of Table 7-3 it can be noted that while these signs and symptoms are identified as examples of adverse effects of medications, they also comprise what could be considered as the "stereotypical signs of aging," or more appropriately, "the unfair stereotype of old age."

Because of the similarity between the signs and symptoms of adverse medication reactions and those making up the unfair stereotype of old age, it is of paramount importance for those persons who work with the elderly to have a thorough understanding of the aging process so that they may better differentiate between those changes in behavior and health status that are caused by medications and those that are, in fact, truly associated with the aging process.

It is frequently impossible to make this distinction without some difficulty because one patient may simultaneously experience some problems that are drug related and some that are age related. This awareness must be based on the understanding that an elderly individual may, for example, be confused and constipated but does not *have to be* confused and constipated simply because they are old. Yet at the same time we must realize that some of the changes that could be attributed to the aging process may in fact be aggravated by or entirely caused by the patient's medications.

For example, a particular elderly male patient may be experiencing a slight degree of confusion, due to his organic brain syndrome; yet the confusion could be made worse by the addition of an atropinelike drug. In an instance such as this, it is very important to the patient's well-being that the additive adverse effects of the drug-induced confusion be differentiated from the preexisting organically based confusion. Admittedly this may be a difficult task, requiring the input and expertise of the entire health care team.

THE DANGER OF NOT RECOGNIZING AN ADVERSE DRUG REACTION

In spite of the fact that the majority of adverse drug reactions do not represent an immediate or even a major threat to the patient's emotional or physical well-being, it must be remembered that these adverse reactions may have serious and even life-threatening consequences in some patients. However, what I believe to be the most dangerous potential outcome of adverse reactions to medications in the elderly is the distinct possibility that they may occur and inadvertently be allowed to continue without being properly recognized as a potentially reversible drug effect.

If the sometimes difficult distinction between age-related and disease-related signs and symptoms and those due to the adverse effect of medications is not properly made, a strong likelihood exists that the problem might be treated with one or more additional medications, each having its own potential for inducing additional adverse effects, which may also go unrecognized, perhaps resulting in the use of even more medication.

An example of a hypothetical scenario that could occur, and probably has, is that of an elderly male nursing home patient who experienced a mild recurrence of his longstanding peptic ulcer disease. Consequently the physician ordered the antiulcer medication cimetidine (Tagamet®) to treat the flareup. Shortly after the cimetidine was begun, the patient became quite agitated and confused. The physician then ordered chlorpromazine (Thorazine®) for what was thought to be psychosis, and the patient quieted down considerably. A few days after the chlorpromazine was ordered, the patient complained of experiencing difficulty urinating. He was examined and was found to have a distended bladder, so a urinary catheter was then inserted to drain his bladder. Four days after the insertion of the catheter the patient developed shaking and chills, his temperature rose to 105°F, and he was found to be in shock with a massive infection, most likely resulting from the spread of a urinary tract infection caused by the presence of the urinary catheter. The patient was subsequently sent by ambulance to the local hospital for appropriate intravenous antibiotic therapy.

In reviewing this fictional case, we can see that the problem that initiated this patient's course of events was the recurrence of his peptic ulcer disease. The physician chose to treat the patient with cimetidine (Tagamet®), which has been shown to be very effective in decreasing acid production by the stomach. Within a few days the patient developed signs of cerebral dysfunction. At that point a thorough effort should have been made to determine the cause of this new development; however, apparently this was not done, and the patient was treated symptomatically and his agitation and confusion, which were most likely the result of an adverse drug reaction, were overlooked. Subsequently the patient's therapy became more complex, his condition worsened, and even more medications were used. Had the appropriate intervention taken place when the patient first developed the agitation and confusion the treatment with cimetidine would have been implicated as a probable, or at least potential, cause of this condition, and steps could have been taken to manage the toxicity through measures such as decreasing the cimetidine dose, or perhaps even discontinuing the medication and placing the patient on antacid therapy, which can also be quite effective in the management of peptic ulcer disease.

I have seen versions of this scenario occur at numerous different occasions in elderly patients. Although the occurrence of adverse drug reactions may result in a great deal of discomfort and harm to the patient, I must emphasize my belief that the overlooking of drug-related problems does not represent an active, purposeful neglect of the elderly patient by the health professional but rather an error of omission resulting from both the very real difficulty of determining whether a symptom, complaint, or change in condition is in fact related to the patient's medication. It also results from the existing shortcomings of the process of drug regimen review.

Persons who are not familiar with the common alterations associated with the aging process will obviously have considerable difficulty in detecting drug-related problems. However, this lack of recognition may also be a problem with health professionals who are quite familiar with these alterations. One component of this problem stems from the fact that it is very easy to lose sight of the possibility that changes in the condition of the patient may be secondary to medications when numerous other factors that may be more obvious, such as familial, social, financial, or physical problems, could be the source of these changes. Additionally, a great deal of expertise and understanding of the manifestations of adverse medication reactions in the elderly is required to identify problems that may be very subtle or of gradual onset or that may present in an apparently unlikely fashion. After all, as in the previous case study, would it be normal for someone who did not have an understanding of adverse drug reactions in the elderly to expect agitation and confusion to be caused by a medication that is used to treat an intestinal ulcer?

I believe that a necessary component of drug therapy review in the elderly should include either a designated member of the health care team or a step in the review process that routinely raises the question, ''Is this change in the patient's condition related to the individual's medications?''

For example, as a pharmacist, a significant component of my activities in the drug therapy review of elderly patients centers around my efforts to attribute recent or longstanding changes in the patient's physical or mental status to their drug therapy. To properly execute this function I must continuously remind myself to play the role of ''devil's advocate.'' Sometimes my attempts to indict a drug as the cause of a patient's complaints necessitate my taking a position that is counter to the opinions of the nurses, physicians, and other members of the health care team with whom I work; however, I fully realize the value of this process, as do the other health professionals. Although I will sometimes devote a significant amount of energy attempting to relate a new symptom to a medication while everyone else thinks that the symptom in question is a clear-cut manifestation of the patient's disease, I feel that the effort is valuable and rewarding. If this effort is applied routinely to all patients, the likelihood of a drug-related problem being overlooked will be greatly diminished.

ROLE OF HEALTH PROFESSIONALS

As I have already mentioned, the team approach to patient care can be an effective way to prevent the occurrence of adverse reactions to medications, although this approach may be more of a concept than a standardized approach and may vary considerably in format, depending on the patient care environment (e.g., acute care hospital, nursing home, outpatient care) and the willingness of the members of the team to participate.

I have experienced the team concept as applied in major medical centers where more than a dozen different health professionals, including attending and resident physicians, clinical pharmacists, psychologists, staff nurses and nurse practitioners, occupational therapists, nutritionists, social workers, and medical, pharmacy, and nursing students met together to combine their individual areas of expertise in the evaluation of a patient's total therapy. I have also worked with effective teams that rarely actually sat down together but nonetheless were able to share their combined expertise for the benefit of the patient. This type of team could consist simply of a nurse and a pharmacist in a nursing home, who, after communicating with nurses' aides, physical therapists, or others, could contact the physician to share their findings and develop a plan for the care of the patient.

An effective team can accomplish a great deal toward promoting the rational use of medications and preventing or managing the adverse medication reactions that do occur. However, owing to the uniqueness of some of the functions of the various team members working toward that effort, each member may have a different role or responsibility. The following is a brief review of the different types of activities that team members might participate in as a part of their efforts to prevent, detect, and manage adverse reactions to medications in the elderly.

Physicians

Use Appropriate Geriatric Doses

The physician should be aware of those medications for which a geriatric dosage recommendation exists. In some cases the manufacturer explicitly provides such recommendations, as is the case with the hypnotic (sleep-inducing medication) flurazepam (Dalmane®), for which the manufacturer recommends an initial dose of 30 mg for normal healthy adults and an initial dose of 15 mg for elderly individuals. In most instances the manufacturer does not provide such information, as demonstrated by the fact that only 17 percent of the 200 most commonly prescribed medications in the United States have a specific recommendation for a geriatric dose. Therefore, resources such as professional journals, geriatric textbooks, or pharmacists may have to be used to obtain this information.

Avoid Excessive Prescribing

The excessive use of unnecessary medication is sometimes referred to as polypharmacy. This practice is unwise and dangerous in any patient but especially in the elderly, in whom it will inevitably result in an increased incidence of drug-related problems, such as drug interactions, an unnecessary financial burden, and an increased incidence of adverse reactions to medications. In some instances these problems contribute directly to the patient's admission to a hospital or nursing home and may even result in a significant deterioration of the individual's health status.

Obtain Accurate Patient Histories

Many patients, including the elderly, are poor historians when asked about their past medical history and are especially inept when asked to identify their history of medication use, including the names and dosages of medications that they have taken, the condition(s) for which they were being used, and any adverse reactions or medication allergies that have occurred.

This last item is especially important in determining which medications should be avoided in a particular patient. It is important for the physician to realize that since many individuals are such poor historians, the histories that they do provide should not be accepted as totally accurate based solely on the information that is volunteered by the patient. Proper interviewing techniques, such as not "leading" the patient to provide an answer that the interviewer expects and the use of questions that are repeated in a somewhat different fashion, can help the interviewer to assess the validity of the information that the patient is providing. In evaluating information about a patient's history of allergies to medications it is important that not only the offending agent be properly identified but also a description of the allergic manifestation be provided, in order to determine whether a true allergy actually did occur. For example, I have heard many patients say that they are "allergic" to penicillin, only to find that they had experienced a minor adverse reaction such as a slight upset stomach when they were taking penicillin a number of years ago. It is important to differentiate between true allergies and other adverse drug reactions because just as it is important to avoid rechallenging patients with a medication that they are truly allergic to, it is also important not to eliminate the possibility of using a potentially lifesaving medication, such as penicillin, because of a supposed allergy that, in fact, does not exist.

Observe the Patient for Adverse Drug Reactions

The patient should be observed for any signs or symptoms that might be the result of an adverse drug reaction. As mentioned previously the prescriber must develop an awareness of the common clinical manifestations of adverse medication reactions as they appear in the elderly. It is also extremely important not to misinterpret an adverse drug reaction as a ''sign of aging.'' In addition, when any significant or potentially life-threatening changes in the patient's condition are noted, the possibility of these changes being related to the patient's medication therapy should be ruled out before the diagnosis is established. It must be remembered that, in addition to causing minor or annoying side effects, medications may cause serious problems in the elderly, including congestive heart failure, kidney failure, shock, and other major disorders.

Listen to Patients' Complaints

Patients should be encouraged to inform the prescriber or others if they develop any new signs that may possibly indicate the occurrence of an adverse medication reaction. It is also important that the prescriber take the time to listen to these complaints and not simply dismiss them as the insignificant and nonspecific complaints of a senior citizen whom it is believed has nothing better to do but complain.

When the prescriber has determined that a patient's complaint or symptom may be the result of his or her drug therapy, efforts should be made to reduce or eliminate the problem.

First, the medication that is responsible for the problem should be discontinued. I have frequently observed that, in many instances, medications that are causing side effects in an elderly patient can be permanently discontinued and the patient suffers no apparent ill effect resulting from a lack of the medication, with the added advantage of the resolution of the adverse effect.

If a patient is on a number of medications that may be causing the adverse response it may be necessary to discontinue more than one of them, subsequently restarting them one at a time and observing the patient closely for the recurrence of an adverse drug effect. I have even seen cases in which a patient's problems were considered to be related to medications and as many as six or eight or even more medications were abruptly discontinued. Following this action an impressive improvement in the patient's condition may occur even to the point that only a minimal number of medications have to be reordered, leading to the obvious conclusion that, in addition to creating unnecessary toxicity, the majority of some patients' medications are apparently unnecessary.

Adverse reactions to medications may also be reduced in severity or eliminated by changing the dosage of the offending agent (usually by decreasing it) to one that is more appropriate for the particular patient experiencing the adverse effect. This is generally not an effective step in the management of adverse reactions that are idiosyncratic or those that are caused by a hypersensitivity or allergic response to a drug, because these types of adverse drug reactions generally occur independently of the dose of the drug administered. Some types of adverse reactions to medications are, however, related to the dosage of drug administered, and these will frequently respond to a reduction in drug dosage to one that is more appropriate for that patient. Examples of adverse drug reactions that may be reduced or eliminated by a decrease in drug dosage include the anorexia (loss of appetite) and confusion that can result from administration of digoxin (Lanoxin®) and the oversedation and drowsiness that may occur after the administration of inappropriately high doses of medication used to induce sleep.

Still another intervention that can be used to reduce or eliminate an adverse medication effect is simply to change the patient's medication from the agent that is causing the problem to an entirely different drug. This practice is frequently successful in the case of antipsychotic drugs. Since there are a large number of different antipsychotic medications that may be effective, the use of different agents can be tried until one is found that is both effective and nontoxic.

Nurses

Be Familiar with the Patient's Diagnosis

In understanding the diagnosis of the patient the nurse will usually be in the position to know whether a patient's complaint is to be expected with the particular disease state that has been diagnosed or if it is rarely associated with that condition, and therefore more likely to be the result of some other factor, such as the adverse effect of a medication.

The nurse should also be familiar with the most common manifestations of adverse medication reactions in the elderly in order to be better able to differentiate between the patient's disease condition(s) and the possibility that the patient is experiencing an adverse reaction to one or more medications.

Be Familiar with Appropriate Doses

Since nurses are usually the health professionals who are most likely to have responsibilities for the administration of medications to the patient, they should be familiar with both the standard and the geriatric dosages of all medications administered.

This is especially true for medications that are known to cause frequent or severe adverse effects in the elderly patient and also those medications for which specific geriatric dosage recommendations exist. With this knowledge nurses will be able to identify medication dosages that may be inappropriate for a particular patient, thus alerting the pharmacist or the prescriber to this potential problem.

Report and Document Adverse Drug Reactions

Should an adverse medication reaction occur, it is important that it be documented, along with its sequelae, so that the chance of inadvertent rechallenge with that medication will be reduced. Such documentation can be included in the nurses' notes on charts of patients who are hospitalized or who are residing in nursing homes. Documentation could also be included in physicians' office records of outpatients, in the nurses' records used for home health care patients, and in other similar formats.

Use P.R.N. (As Needed) Medications Properly

When a patient in an inpatient setting such as a hospital or nursing home has an existing p.r.n. (as needed) order for any medication, a great deal of responsibility lies with the nurse who must determine whether the particular medication that has been ordered is truly "needed."

The nurse must be familiar with the patient's condition and must also understand how the medication is to be used in the management of that condition. For example, in a patient who is experiencing pain, the nurse should be familiar with the source of that pain and how aggressively it should be treated. It is the nurse's responsibility to determine at what level the patient's pain should be considered unacceptable and therefore when the patient should be medicated for that pain.

Nurses must be careful to be as objective as possible in regard to the administration of p.r.n. medications and should prevent their own biases, such as their fear of pain or their stoicism and high tolerance for pain, from having too great an influence on the medications that they administer to the patient, because the overuse or unnecessary use of medications may result in adverse reactions.

Nurses should also make an effort to administer p.r.n. medications only when they are truly needed, to avoid exposing the patient to any unnecessary risks of experiencing drug side effects. For example, if a patient has a standing p.r.n. order for a sleeping medication it should not be given routinely but rather should be given only when the patient cannot sleep without it; yet I have seen instances in which entire groups of patients were given their p.r.n. sleep medication before they were even given a chance to sleep without them.

The Nurse As a Prescriber

The nurse's role discussed here represents those functions that are more traditional and are not entirely representative of the practice functions of nurse clinicians or nurse practitioners. Since the newer nursing roles include a greater responsibility to the patient, perhaps even the privilege to prescribe medications (Baker, 1981), the nurse's role in the detection, prevention, or management of adverse drug reactions may be much more involved and may include many of the responsibilities that are listed previously as those of physicians.

Pharmacists

Since the primary responsibilities of pharmacists relate to drug therapy, their involvement in the efforts to detect, manage, and prevent adverse medication reactions in the elderly will, by definition, be extensive. Some of these responsibilities may occasionally appear to duplicate those of physicians and nurses; depending on various situations or practice environments, these responsibilities may actually be interchangeable between various health professionals. Some of these functions, such as observing the patient for the occurrence of adverse reactions to medications, may very well be the simultaneous responsibility of all of the team members.

The professional role of pharmacists has changed significantly within the past decade from one that is primarily product oriented to one that possesses a strong patient orientation. This approach, often termed *clinical pharmacy*, more fully uses the knowledge of the pharmacist concerning medications and drug therapy for the patient's benefit.

One important aspect of the professional role of pharmacists is their drug therapy monitoring function. The responsibilities within this function will vary somewhat depending on factors such as the training of the pharmacist performing the monitoring and the location of the practice environment (i.e., is the pharmacist practicing in a large nursing home and participating in a formalized drug therapy review process, or is the pharmacist working in a small community pharmacy where the drug therapy review would then take place whenever a patient visits to purchase a new prescription or refill an existing prescription?)

Although the scope of this review will vary, it usually includes some of the following responsibilities that are designed, in part, to identify, reduce, or eliminate the occurrence of adverse reactions to medications.

Review Medication Histories

Pharmacists are especially well suited for the performance of patient medication histories because of their familiarity with both the generic and the trade names of prescription and nonprescription products. They are also quite familiar with the appearance of most medications, and this knowledge is especially helpful when patients are trying to describe the white "heart pill" or the green "nerve pill" that they have been taking.

Monitor Patient Medication Profile

In many inpatient and outpatient pharmacy practice environments a written profile of the medications taken by each patient is kept by the pharmacist. When a new medication or a change in the dose of an existing medication is ordered, the pharmacist records this information on the medication profile in order to have available the most correct information regarding the patient's medication therapy. With this information the pharmacist is then able to evaluate the patient's drug therapy for problems that could possibly result in adverse reactions. Some of the more common problems of this nature include the following:

- *Drug-drug interactions*. Two or more medications may interact in the patient resulting in an adverse response.
- *Drug allergy*. The profile lists the specific allergies to medications that have occurred in a patient. With this information the pharmacist can alert the prescriber when a medication that may cause an allergic response is ordered.
- *Inappropriate medication doses*. With the use of medication dosage recommendations provided by the manufacturer, or doses calculated by the pharmacist, inappropriate (usually too large) doses of medication can be identified and altered to prevent the adverse effects that may result from excessive doses. A patient medication profile can be used to determine whether a prescribed medication is being consumed at a rate greater than that intended by the prescriber. For example, a patient may have an order for three acetaminophen with codeine (Tylenol® with Codeine) tablets a day for pain but may actually be taking twice that many, placing the patient at a greater risk of experiencing toxicity from that medication. In addition, pharmacists can quickly scan a patient medication profile to determine the total number of medications, both prescription and nonprescription, that a patient may be taking. Those patients identified as taking a large number of medications can then be studied more closely, since their high rate of consumption would indicate an increased likelihood that they would experience an adverse reaction to one or more of their medications.

Observe for Adverse Reactions

The pharmacist may also observe the patient for adverse medication effects. In an institutional setting the pharmacist may choose to visit patients with another health professional to observe those individuals who may be suspected of experiencing adverse reactions to their medications, or the pharmacist may choose to make solo visits to individual patients while observing them for obvious signs of toxicity, such as tremor, confusion, or drowsiness. The pharmacist may also question the patients directly to see if they might be experiencing constipation, diarrhea, or other adverse physical manifestations of drug therapy.

In this process the pharmacist must be careful not to overlook signs of medication toxicity by attributing these signs to signs of aging, rather than adverse reactions to medication. The pharmacist should also be constantly on the lookout for major changes in the patient's condition, such as kidney or heart failure that could also be a very serious and life-threatening complication of drug therapy.

I also believe that the pharmacist is the most likely member of the health care team to play the previously mentioned role of ''devil's advocate'' in an attempt to attribute new signs or symptoms to drug therapy.

If one individual, such as the pharmacist, continuously tries to attribute these changes to patient behavior to adverse medication effect, there is little chance that such adverse reaction will often go unnoticed.

Provide Drug Information

Especially on the outpatient basis, pharmacists should be willing to provide the patient with information regarding the proper use of both prescription and non-prescription medications in order to reduce the possibility that the improper use of the medications by the patient will result in adverse effects.

Dietitians

Dietitians, or nutritionists, should have an awareness of some of the more significant adverse drug-nutrient interactions that a patient may experience. Even though their formal training does not usually include the study of pharmacology or adverse drug reactions, they should be able to perform a basic evaluation for this type of problem in patients receiving special diets. For example, if a diabetic patient is receiving a diet that is low in sugar, the dietitian would be able to determine whether any of the patient's medications were being administered in a dosage form that contained a great deal of sugar, such as is the case with many syrup forms of medications.

Physical and Occupational Therapists and Activity Directors

Since the nature of the work of physical and occupational therapists and activity directors includes observing the patient at work or at play, they would be able to identify patients who are experiencing alterations in activity or mobility that may be a result of adverse reactions to medications, alerting the physician or pharmacist to these problems (Simonson, 1978).

ROLE OF FAMILY MEMBERS

In addition to the efforts of health professionals, the patient's family members, friends, and social contacts have a responsibility to ensure that the patient is not under any undue risk of experiencing adverse medication reactions. This can be accomplished by four simple steps:

1. *Assure proper compliance.* They should encourage the patient to take medications as prescribed, providing supervision or assistance if necessary.

2. *Understand adverse drug reactions.* Family members should become acquainted with the common and the serious adverse medication reactions that might be expected from the medication(s) that the patient is taking, so that they will not go unnoticed if they occur.
3. *Observe for adverse reactions.* The patient should be observed for any changes in activity, behavior, or mental or physical functions that could possibly be attributed to the adverse effects of medications.
4. *Report suspected adverse reactions.* If any suspicion exists that the patient is experiencing an adverse reaction to one or more of their medications, the family member or person supervising the patient should promptly contact the patient's pharmacist, nurse, or physician. In some cases an adverse reaction may not exist, but in some the patient's medication therapy may have to be altered.

REFERENCES

Abel, S.R. Drug-induced potentiation of glaucoma, *U.S. Pharmacist,* 1981, 6(11), 37-44.

Baker, N. Prescriptive authority for nurse practitioners. *Geriatric Nursing,* 1981, 2, 420-421.

Clark, B.G., Wheatley, R., Rawlings, J.L., & Vestal, R.E. Female preponderance in diuretic-associated hypokalemia. *Journal of the American Geriatrics Society,* 1982, 30, 316-321.

Conrad, K.A., & Bressler, R. *Drug therapy for the elderly.* St. Louis: C.V. Mosby, 1982.

Crismon, M.L. Drug-induced extrapyramidal syndromes. *U.S. Pharmacist,* 1982, 7(1), 33, 34, 36-42.

Crooks, J., & Stevenson, I.H. *Drugs and the elderly: Perspectives in geriatric clinical pharmacology.* Baltimore: University Park Press, 1979.

Greenblatt, D.J., Allen, M.D., & Shader, R.I. Toxicity of high dose flurazepam in the elderly. *Clinical Pharmacology and Therapeutics,* 1977, 21, 355-361.

Holloway, D.A. Drug problems in the geriatric patient. *Drug Intelligence and Clinical Pharmacy,* 1974, 8, 632-642.

Hurwitz, N. Predisposing factors in adverse reactions to drugs. *British Medical Journal,* 1969, 9, 536-539.

Jenike, M.A. Cimetidine in elderly patients: Review of uses and risks. *Journal of the American Geriatrics Society,* 1982, 30, 170-173.

Jenike, M.A. Tardive dyskinesia: Special risk in the elderly. *Journal of the American Geriatrics Society,* 1983, 31, 71-73.

Klein, L.E., German, P.S., & Levine, D.M. Adverse drug reactions among the elderly: A reassessment. *Journal of the American Geriatrics Society,* 1981, 29, 525-530.

Miller, R.R. Drug surveillance utilizing epidemiologic methods: A report from the Boston Collaborative Drug Surveillance Program. *American Journal of Hospital Pharmacy,* 1973, 30, 584-592.

Murdoch, P.S., & Williamson, J. A danger in making the diagnosis of Parkinson's Disease. *Lancet,* 1982, 1, 1212-1213.

Petersen, D.M., Whittington, F.J., & Payne, B.P. *Drugs and the elderly: Social and pharmacological issues.* Springfield, Ill.: Charles C Thomas, 1979.

Portnoi, V.A., & Johnson, J.E. Tardive dyskinesia. *Geriatric Nursing,* 1982, 3, 39-40.

Practical Guide to Geriatric Medication. Oradell, N.J.: Medical Economics, 1980.

Seidl, L.G., Thornton, G.F., Smith, J.W., & Cluff, L.E. Studies on the epidemiology of adverse drug reactions III. Reactions in patients on a general medical service. *Bulletin of the Johns Hopkins Hospital,* 1966, *119,* 299-315.

Simonson, W. Medication of the elderly: Effect of response to physical therapy. *Physical Therapy,* 1978, *58,* 179-180.

Simonson, W., & Pratt, C.C. Assessing geriatric patients and their drug therapy regimens: Evaluation using high-risk criteria. *Quality Review Bulletin,* 1981, *7*(9), 19-24.

Smith, W.E., & Steele, T.H. Avoiding diuretic-related complications in older patients. *Geriatrics,* 1983, *38,* 117-119, 124.

U.S. Government Printing Office. Federal health programs. In *Developments in aging: A report of the Special Committee on Aging, United States Senate* (Vol. 1). Washington, D.C.: Author, 1981.

Vivian, A.S., & Goldberg, I.B. Recognizing chronic salicylate intoxication in the elderly. *Geriatrics,* 1982, *37*(11), 91-97.

Williamson, J., & Chopin, J.M. Adverse reactions to prescribed drugs in the elderly: A multicentre investigation. *Age and Aging,* 1980, *9,* 73-80.

Chapter 8

Drug Interactions

Drug interactions may occur in persons of any age; however, for a number of reasons that will be discussed in this chapter, their occurrence is especially significant in the elderly population. Anyone working with the elderly should have a basic understanding of what drug interactions are, why they occur, and what their significance is in the elderly patient.

Three basic types of drug interactions exist: (1) drug-drug interactions, (2) drug-nutrient interactions, and (3) drug-laboratory test interactions.

A *drug-drug interaction* could be defined as the modification of the therapeutic or toxic effect of one drug by the prior or concurrent administration of another drug. A simpler, yet still accurate definition is "the modification of the effect of one drug by another drug" (May, Stewart, & Cluff, 1977, p. 322).

A *drug-nutrient interaction* can be defined as "the situation in which a food or nutrient alters an individual's response to a drug or in which a drug interferes with an individual's nutrition" (Hartshorn, 1977, p. 1).

Drug-laboratory test interactions occur when a medication has an effect on a patient's laboratory test, such as a urinalysis or a blood chemistry profile. Although extremely interesting and important, drug-laboratory test interactions require a detailed knowledge of pharmacology and biochemistry and are therefore beyond the scope of this text and will not be discussed further. The reader is referred to *Drug Interactions* by Philip Hansten (1979) for more information on this subject.

What makes this aspect of drug therapy so complex is that there are thousands of different prescription and nonprescription medications available in the United States that can be taken in millions of different combinations.

Another confusing factor is that the occurrence of a drug interaction is not absolute, that is, the same combination of medications that may result in a life-threatening drug interaction in one individual may have little or no clinical effect in a different person.

167

THE DISCOVERY OF DRUG INTERACTIONS

Prior to final approval for human use, the U.S. Food and Drug Administration requires extensive testing of medications, including laboratory testing and clinical trials in both animals and humans. This research is designed to determine the drugs' safety and efficacy; however, it does not necessarily serve to detect possible drug interactions. Although it would be desirable that potential interactions could be detected before a drug reaches the market, the task is simply too overwhelming to be feasible at present. Consequently, significant drug interactions are usually detected after a medication has been used in humans long enough to gain sufficient clinical experience regarding the medications or nutrients with which it may interact. When a new drug reaches the market and is prescribed for use in humans, health professionals such as physicians, pharmacists, and nurses should be alert to the possibility of the occurrence of a drug interaction. When a significant interaction is suspected, often a letter describing the possible drug interaction will be sent by the health professional who noticed the interaction to a scientific journal for the purpose of alerting other health professionals to this potential problem. If others happen to observe the same problem, they may follow up with additional letters, perhaps containing more detailed information about the interaction. Frequently then, a review of the reports of the interaction or perhaps even an organized human study will be performed and published to inform health professionals about the interaction, why it occurs, and, more importantly, how it can be prevented. Then the documented interaction can be included into drug interaction textbooks and other resources so that its occurrence will become "common knowledge."

Unfortunately the process of "spreading the word" about a drug interaction may be painfully slow. Perhaps one of the best examples of the inefficiency of this method is the now well-documented interaction between the two cardiac medications digoxin (Lanoxin®) and quinidine (Quinora®). In the late 1970s, numerous letters to the editors of various medical and pharmacy journals alerted health professionals to the fact that quinidine will sometimes cause a significant elevation of the concentration of digoxin in the bloodstream, possibly resulting in a serious episode of digoxin toxicity. Once people were alerted to this possibility, many more instances of this interaction were quickly reported and review articles appeared in the literature (Leahey, Reiffel, Giardina, & Bigger, 1980) fully describing the interaction and how to adjust the dosage of the drugs involved to allow their concurrent administration while at the same time preventing the serious consequences of this interaction. Once alerted, the word spread quickly; however, it must be noted that the concurrent use of digoxin and quinidine for the treatment of certain rhythm disturbances of the heart has been in common practice for over three decades, during which most of that time the interaction was essentially unrecognized! Obviously the interaction did not just start happening within the past five years, but rather it has been occurring unrecognized for years.

This makes me wonder about two things. First, how many individuals suffered toxicity, and possibly even death, resulting from this interaction that was unknown to themselves, the health profession, and their families? Second, how many significant drug interactions are occurring now, but simply have yet to be recognized as such?

While this is certainly of great concern, I do not want to give the impression that nothing can be done to predict whether a drug may be capable of causing interactions. Indeed, as we understand the mechanisms of drug interactions more fully, it is possible to identify in advance certain general types of drug interactions involving particular classes of drugs that may potentially occur, so that these interactions can be anticipated, observed, and detected as soon as they occur.

THE INCIDENCE OF DRUG INTERACTIONS

The realization that thousands of potentially significant drug interactions exist is a frightening thought, so it is important to place the incidence of occurrence of significant drug interactions in its proper perspective.

Clinically significant drug interactions certainly may occur, but they usually do not. It is important to realize that most drug interactions are only *potentially significant* interactions that do not in fact result in an observable effect; yet each potential interaction must be treated as if it could be significant, as is certainly the case. When drug interactions do occur, their clinical significance may range from a minor effect, such as a dry mouth, to a major life-threatening problem, such as a fatal bleeding episode. It is comforting to realize that the overwhelming majority of drug interactions that do occur are of minor clinical significance and that it is possible for an individual to take four or five or even more medications without experiencing the adverse effects of a drug interaction.

DRUG INTERACTIONS IN THE ELDERLY

Drug interactions may occur in any population, but they are probably more likely to occur in the elderly for a number of reasons.

Incidence

The actual incidence of drug interactions in the elderly is difficult to assess because the studies that have attempted to determine this have used different methodologies and different definitions of significant versus potential interaction; however, some understanding of the extent of the problem does exist.

Based on the studies that have been performed, it appears that potentially significant drug interactions may occur in 10 to 15 percent of the elderly population in nursing homes (Cooper, Wellins, Fish, & Loomis, 1975; Simonson, 1981). The incidence is most likely lower in noninstitutionalized patients because they generally consume less medication than those in institutions.

One study performed in California determined that nursing home patients who received an average of approximately 42 prescriptions per year, including both new and refill prescriptions, had an incidence of potential drug-drug interactions that was more than three and one-half times greater than that of noninstitutionalized patients, who received only 9 prescriptions per year (Laventurier, Talley, Hefner, & Kennard, 1976).

In a nursing home study that I performed with a colleague, we determined that there was one potentially significant drug interaction for every 50 medications that were dispensed. Since most of the patients in this study were taking more than one medication, these same figures also indicated that approximately 17 percent of the patients involved had combinations of medications that could result in potentially significant drug interactions (Simonson & Sturgeon, 1979).

Reasons for Increased Incidence

The reasons that the elderly may experience a greater incidence of potential drug interactions are discussed below (Hussar, 1977; Simonson, 1981).

Increased Medication Consumption

The risk of experiencing a drug interaction increases with the number of medications an individual takes. Since the consumption of both prescription and nonprescription medications increases in the elderly, the chance of experiencing a drug interaction increases accordingly.

Changes in Physiology

Since the changes in physiology that are associated with age may affect the absorption, distribution, metabolism, and excretion of medications, the occurrence of drug interactions may be affected. For example, two different medications that are normally eliminated from the body through the kidneys may be eliminated more slowly in an elderly individual, resulting in increased amounts of both medications in the body, causing a drug interaction.

Types of Medications Consumed

Elderly individuals more commonly consume certain types of medications that are more frequently implicated in drug interactions. For example, warfarin (Coumadin®) known as a ''blood thinner,'' digoxin (Lanoxin®), a cardiac medication, and cimetidine (Tagamet®), an antiulcer medication, are medications that are taken more frequently by the elderly and are capable of causing significant drug interactions.

Visiting More Than One Physician

Elderly patients visit their physicians more frequently than younger patients (Hussar, 1977; U.S. Government Printing Office, 1982) and they may also frequently visit more than one physician; yet each physician may be unaware of the medications prescribed by the others or the fact that the patient is even seeing other physicians, resulting in potentially significant drug interactions.

Noncompliance

Although noncompliance to prescribed drug therapy is a problem that is not unique to the elderly it is a problem that occurs in the elderly that may contribute to the occurrence of drug interactions. For example, individuals who do not properly comply with instructions provided to them regarding their drug therapy may take one of their medications at the wrong time of day, resulting in an interaction with another medication or nutrient that they might be taking.

Presence of Disease States

Certain chronic disease states that are more commonly associated with old age may increase the incidence of drug interactions. For example, an elderly patient with longstanding diabetes may have some degree of kidney damage that is frequently associated with that disease, therefore making the individual more likely to experience drug interactions between medications that are eliminated by the kidneys.

Concurrent Use of Prescription and Nonprescription Medications

Occasionally, elderly individuals will use prescription medications that they have borrowed from friends or relatives without fully realizing that these drugs could interact adversely with their prescribed therapy. This practice is unwise and should be avoided because prescription drug therapy is tailored to meet the needs of the individual patient and is not meant to be shared with another person who may have similar symptoms but a different disease.

Interactions may also result from the concurrent use of nonprescription medications that the patient has decided to use without the prescriber's knowledge. Persons taking prescription medications must realize that the interaction between prescription and nonprescription medications can be significant, and they should adopt the wise practice of consulting their pharmacist prior to using any nonprescription drugs.

THE MECHANISMS OF DRUG INTERACTIONS

Interactions between medications may occur as the result of mechanisms that are quite different from each other. These mechanisms include alterations in the absorption of drugs into the bloodstream, alterations in the distribution of medication within an individual's body, changes in the metabolism or excretion of medications, and alterations in the effect of medications at their site of action within the body (Simonson, 1981).

In order to understand, detect, and ultimately prevent drug interactions, a thorough knowledge of these mechanisms, requiring a strong background in pharmacology, pharmacokinetics, and biochemistry, is needed.

Because of their expertise in these areas and their knowledge of drug products, it is my belief that pharmacists are the key health professionals who should be involved in drug interaction detection and prevention; however, all persons who work with the elderly should be aware of the existence of drug interactions and the problems that they can create. Although professionals such as nursing home administrators, social workers, activity directors, and others will not ordinarily be directly involved in the drug interaction screening process, they should be aware of the fact that these different mechanisms exist to help them understand the complexity of this potentially serious problem.

Drug Absorption

One mechanism of drug-drug interactions is the interference with the absorption of one medication into the patient's bloodstream by another medication. This type of interaction usually occurs when two or more interacting medications are taken at the same time, so that they are in the stomach or small intestine together. One example of this type of interaction, as it may occur in an elderly individual, is the drug-drug interaction between the cardiac medication digoxin and many common nonprescription antacid preparations. The interaction between these compounds decreases the amount of digoxin that is absorbed into the patient's bloodstream, which can then result in a decreased therapeutic effectiveness of digoxin.

Since drug-drug interactions of this type usually only occur when the interacting agents are present in the stomach or small intestine at the same time, it is frequently possible to avoid the problem by alternating the time of administration of the interacting medications. In the case of the digoxin-antacid interaction, the potential interaction could be effectively avoided by having the patient take the digoxin on arising at 7 A.M., and then not taking any antacid until four to six hours later, thus allowing sufficient time for the absorption of digoxin to take place in the stomach and the intestine.

Drug Distribution

After a medication is absorbed into the bloodstream, it then distributes through-out various parts of the body, depending on a number of factors relating to the medication, such as its tendency to bind reversibly to the protein that is found in the bloodstream and the degree to which the drug is fat or water soluble.

Most medications are bound to a certain extent to the protein albumin, which circulates in the bloodstream. The extent of this binding varies from very little to almost 100 percent. This binding is a reversible and dynamic event, with drug molecules continuously binding with albumin molecules and becoming unbound. It is interesting and important to realize that when a drug molecule is bound to an albumin molecule it is not able to exert its pharmacological effect, whereas an unbound molecule is pharmacologically active. Thus the bound molecules are inactive and the unbound or "free" molecules are active, and consequently anything that is capable of altering the ratio of bound to unbound drug can actually alter the effect of that drug.

This is an important consideration in drug interactions because it has been found that one medication may actually compete for these protein binding sites with another medication, resulting in a decrease in the amount of protein binding of one or both of the drugs involved.

One example of this type of interaction occurs when the antiinflammatory agent phenylbutazone (Butazolidin®) is given to a patient who is taking the anti-coagulant warfarin (Coumadin®). Since both of these medications are bound to albumin to a significant extent they compete for the available binding sites, resulting in a displacement of some of the previously bound warfarin. Conse-quently, the increase in the amount of unbound and pharmacologically active warfarin may accentuate its normal effect, which is to decrease the production of certain clotting factors in the blood. The extent of this interaction may be so great that the individual experiencing it may develop a potentially severe bleeding episode.

Another way in which a drug interaction may have an effect on the distribution of a drug within the body is by the alteration of a drug's volume of distribution. The volume of distribution is actually an estimate that is used to tell whether the drug is widely distributed throughout the body, in which case it would usually have a large volume of distribution, or whether it is distributed instead to only select body tissues, which would generally be indicated by a small volume of distribution. Volume of distribution is discussed in greater detail in Chapter 6.

This type of interaction can be exemplified by the interaction that occurs between the two cardiac medications digoxin (Lanoxin®) and quinidine (Quin-ora®). When quinidine is given to an individual who is already taking digoxin, the concentration of digoxin in the person's blood may more than double (Doering, 1979), thus seriously increasing the risk of digoxin toxicity, which could include effects such as nausea, vomiting, confusion, or depression and may even cause lethal abnormalities in the individual's heart rhythm.

Drug Metabolism

Many medications are broken down, or metabolized, in the body in order that they may be inactivated and eliminated from the body. This metabolism usually takes place in the liver but may also occur in other parts of the body. Occasionally the rate or extent of the metabolism of one medication may be altered significantly by another medication.

A good example of this type of drug interaction would be that between ethyl alcohol (ethanol) and disulfiram (Antabuse®). When taken concurrently, disulfiram inhibits the metabolism of ethanol, causing an accumulation of acetaldehyde, one of the breakdown products of ethanol metabolism.

Since the presence of acetaldehyde in the blood is part of the reason why people experience hangovers after drinking too much alcohol, the elevated acetaldehyde levels resulting from the interaction between alcohol and disulfiram will have the same effect, causing extremely unpleasant symptoms such as nausea, vomiting, sweating, flushing, throbbing headache, and others, which may last for several hours or longer. This interaction is particularly interesting because the potential for this interaction is precisely why disulfiram is given to alcoholics. The hope is that as long as the individual takes the disulfiram, he or she will abstain from drinking alcohol to avoid the extremely unpleasant effects of this interaction.

Drug Excretion

Most of the medications that are not metabolized are eliminated by excretion through the kidneys. Alteration of this pathway of elimination may also be a mechanism of drug-drug interaction. The interaction between the antigout medication probenecid (Benemid®) and the antibiotic ampicillin (Polycillin®) occurs through this mechanism, because probenecid interferes with ampicillin's elimination through the kidneys, resulting in higher and more prolonged ampicillin concentrations in the blood. This interaction is a good example of how drug interactions may be used therapeutically to benefit a patient because a combination ingredient product named Polycillin-PRB® actually contains 1 gm of probenecid and 3.5 gm of ampicillin in the same bottle. When these powders are reconstituted by the addition of water and taken by an individual, the high ampicillin concentrations in the blood allow for the successful treatment of gonorrhea after a single dose of this product, thus eliminating the need for the administration of repeated doses of the antibiotic over a period of days.

Site of Drug Action

A patient may ingest more than one medication with similar therapeutic effects or side effects. For example an individual could be taking chlorpromazine (Thorazine®), a medication used to control agitation or psychotic behavior, and benztropine (Cogentin®), a medication that is used to control some of the adverse effects of chlorpromazine, such as tremor or muscle rigidity. This drug interaction may result in the increase of annoying atropine like (anticholinergic) symptoms that can be caused by the use of either of these medications alone, including dry mouth, blurred vision, or constipation.

Another example of this type of drug interaction that might commonly be noted in the elderly is the additive sedative effects that may be found with concurrent administration of combinations of sedatives, tranquilizers, antihistamines, narcotic analgesics, or alcohol.

DRUG-ALCOHOL INTERACTIONS

Although the interaction between medications and alcohol could be considered to be a drug-drug interaction, the potential serious consequences of this type of interaction deserve special comment.

Alcohol intake and even alcoholism are not uncommon in elderly individuals and the fact that alcohol can be obtained both without a prescription and without the knowledge of the physician increases the possibility of the concurrent administration of alcohol and medications without the knowledge of health professionals.

Alcohol may interact with many medications, both prescription and nonprescription, and these interactions may be of greater significance in the elderly because of both the physiological alterations that occur with aging and the decreased tolerance to alcohol that may occur in the elderly.

The toxic manifestations resulting from these interactions include a wide range of adverse effects, such as irritation and ulceration of the stomach lining, pneumonia resulting from the accidental aspiration of contaminated mucus into the lungs, confusion, excessive sedation, coma, and even death.

Whenever an elderly individual is taking a medication that may interact with alcohol, the possibility of such an interaction must be kept in mind (Seixas, 1979).

CONSEQUENCES OF DRUG-DRUG INTERACTIONS

Significant drug-drug interactions may have consequences that result in a detrimental effect on the patient's health status.

Interference with Therapeutic Effect of Drug

Some drug-drug interactions result in the reduction of the therapeutic effect of one or more of the medications involved. This lack of or decrease in effect, although not toxic to the patient per se, may deprive the patient of the therapeutic effect that was desired when the medication was ordered.

Increased Financial Burden

If an interaction does in fact negate or reduce the effect of a medication, resulting in inadequate response to that therapy, patients may incur additional expense when they find it necessary to return to the physician for continuing therapy of the original, unresolved complaints, in addition to having spent money on ineffective medications. It is also possible that individuals may have to be admitted to an inpatient care facility owing to the continuing effects of their health condition that were unsuccessfully treated.

Toxicity

Another possible consequence of drug-drug interactions is a range of toxic effects that may present as nothing more serious than a minor upset stomach or rarely, in extreme cases, as life-threatening problems such as severe hemorrhage. The toxic effects of drug interactions may also mimic the unfair "elderly stereotype," with signs such as confusion, drowsiness, or weakness, thus making their identification more difficult.

DRUG-NUTRIENT INTERACTIONS

One aspect of the study of drug interactions that is receiving a considerable amount of attention, yet is still poorly understood, is that of interactions between drugs and nutrients. Because of the increased frequency of nutritional deficiencies in the elderly it is more likely that they would experience the effect of interactions between medications and their nutritional status than would younger, healthier persons with proper nutrition (Lamy, 1980).

Examples of Drug-Nutrient Interactions

It has been found that some medications and nutrients may interact causing various effects (Table 8-1).

Table 8-1 Major Types of Drug-Nutrient Interactions Including Examples of Selected Interactions and Their Consequences

| Interacting agents | | Mechanism of interaction | Consequence |
Drug	Nutrient		
Most antibiotics	Food	Decreased absorption of medication	There are decreased levels of antibiotic in the bloodstream.
Mineral oil	Oil-soluble vitamins	Decreased absorption of nutrient	Deficiency in vitamins A, D, E, and K may result after prolonged use of mineral oil.
Tetracycline	Iron, calcium, magnesium	Decreased absorption of medication and nutrient	There is a decreased amount of drug and nutrient in the body. Interaction may result in decreased tetracycline levels. Decreased nutrient levels are unlikely to be significant with short-term drug administration.
Griseofulvin (Fulvicin®)	Fatty food	Increased absorption of medication	Levels of griseofulvin in the body increase with concurrent administration of fatty food.
Warfarin (Coumadin®)	Foods containing vitamin K	Decreased effect of medication	Increased intake of vitamin K containing food in patients taking warfarin may decrease effect of the drug.
Monoamine oxidase (MAO) inhibitors (Eutonyl®, Eutron®, Nardil®, and Parnate®)	Foods containing tyramine	Increased toxicity of medication	Concurrent intake of MAO inhibitors and tyramine-containing foods may cause hypertensive crisis.
Nitrofurantoin (Furadantin®)	Milk	Decreased toxicity of medication	Concurrent intake of milk may decrease the gastrointestinal irritation frequently caused by nitrofurantoin.

Decreased Absorption of Medication

Some nutrients may decrease the absorption of certain medications. This is true with most antibiotics when they are taken with food. The presence of food in the stomach tends to decrease both the rate of antibiotic absorption into the bloodstream and the amount of antibiotic absorbed. To ensure maximal absorption, most antibiotics should be taken on an empty stomach, either one hour before or two hours after meals.

Decreased Absorption of Nutrient

Some medications may decrease the absorption of certain nutrients. This is true with mineral oil, a nonprescription medication that acts as a laxative by lubricating intestinal contents so that they may pass through the bowel more easily. After mineral oil is taken by mouth, it mixes with digesting food that may be present in the stomach or intestine. Since vitamins A, D, E, and K are fat soluble they may then be extracted from the digesting food by dissolving in the mineral oil, thus passing through the intestine without being absorbed. This decrease in vitamin absorption is of little concern with the occasional use of mineral oil or products that contain mineral oil; however, a significant decrease in the absorption of these vitamins could result when mineral oil is used on a regular basis over an extended period of time.

Decreased Absorption of Both Drug and Nutrient

Occasionally, drug-nutrient interactions may result in a decrease in absorption into the bloodstream of both the drug and the nutrient. The antibiotic tetracycline readily combines with certain ions, including iron, calcium, and magnesium, to form an insoluble complex that is not absorbed. Thus, if an individual takes tetracycline with meals, there will be suboptimal absorption of both the medication and the nutrients to which it may bind, although it is unlikely that significant nutritional deficiencies could result from this interaction. Administration of tetracycline on an empty stomach, one hour before meals or two hours following a meal, will prevent this problem; however, tetracycline may cause symptoms of gastrointestinal irritation, such as cramps or a burning sensation in the stomach when it is taken on an empty stomach. It is advisable that tetracycline should therefore be taken with a full glass of water to reduce the possibility of such irritation. It is important that tetracycline not be taken with milk, or other dairy products, because of their high calcium content and tetracycline's previously discussed ability to form an insoluble complex with calcium and other elements found in food.

Increased Absorption of Medication

Instead of decreasing medication absorption, the absorption of certain medications may actually be increased by the presence of certain nutrients. One good example is that of the antifungal medication griseofulvin (Fulvicin®), whose absorption may be significantly enhanced by the concurrent intake of foods that are rich in fat.

Decreased Effect of Medication

Drug-nutrient interactions may also result in a decrease in the effect of the medication involved in the interaction. If the therapeutic effect of the medication is important for the patient, this interaction could have serious consequences. For example, warfarin (Coumadin®) is an orally administered anticoagulant that is used to reduce the risk of certain internal blood clotting disorders that may result in stroke, pulmonary embolism, or other major problems. The activity of warfarin in the bloodstream is indicated by a laboratory test called the prothrombin time, which is performed on a blood sample. The results of this test indicate if the patient's warfarin dosage is sufficient for an appropriate therapeutic response or is within the toxic range. Since the activity of warfarin is partially dependent on the presence or absence of vitamin K, there is a chance that the amount of this vitamin that is included in the patient's diet could possibly have a significant effect on the activity or toxicity of this medication. Because of this relationship, the effectiveness of warfarin may be decreased if a patient consumes an excessive amount of food with a high vitamin K content, such as liver or leafy green vegetables, or even after tube feedings that have a high vitamin K content. As mentioned, this interaction could be significant because it may lead to the recurrence of the clotting problems that were the original reason why the warfarin was being given. Of course this interaction may also cause an increase in the toxicity of warfarin if a patient who was stabilized on an effective dose of this drug suddenly reduces his or her ingestion of foods containing vitamin K.

Increased Toxicity of Medication

As already mentioned, drug-nutrient interactions may result in the increased toxicity of a medication. One of the most serious drug-nutrient interactions known involves the class of prescription antihypertensive medications (used to lower blood pressure) called monoamine oxidase (MAO) inhibitors, which include Eutonyl®, Eutron®, Nardil®, and Parnate®.

When a patient is taking one of these potent medications it is important that they avoid the intake of foods that contain the compound tyramine, owing to the possibility of a significant increase in blood pressure, which may even reach crisis levels. Foods that contain tyramine include cheese, raisins, yogurt, bananas, avocados, soy sauce, and beers and wines, especially hearty red wines such as chianti.

Decreased Toxicity of Medication

Drug-nutrient interactions may also decrease the toxicity of a medication and may in fact be desired for that reason. A simple example of this type of interaction would be the recommendation that a person drink a full glass of milk or eat some food when taking a dose of the urinary tract antiinfective nitrofurantoin (Furadantin®). In this case the milk or food serves the purpose of reducing the degree of gastrointestinal irritation that is commonly associated with this medication.

MANAGEMENT OF DRUG INTERACTIONS BY HEALTH PROFESSIONALS

Certainly some drug interactions remain undiscovered for a long period of time, such as the recently discovered interaction between digoxin and quinidine. However, there is adequate documentation of many drug interactions, with many reference books, pamphlets, and scientific articles listing and describing thousands of known interactions. Since so many drug interactions have been identified, they should also therefore be preventable, either by avoiding certain combinations of medications or by "managing" the potential interaction so that it does not occur, remembering that most interactions are not "absolute" but rather involve combinations of medications that can be used concurrently when consideration is given to factors such as proper dosage, time of administration, condition of the patient, and other factors.

The two health professionals with the greatest potential impact on the prevention and management of drug interactions are the physician and the pharmacist, although their effectiveness in this task can be augmented greatly by nursing personnel and others and is severely hampered without the cooperation of the patient.

Physicians

It is the physician's responsibility to understand a medication fully before it is prescribed. Certainly one of the important aspects for a physician to understand about a medication is the medications or nutrients with which it may potentially interact. When new medications are added to a patient's preexisting drug therapy regimen the physician should be especially concerned about the possibility of the new medication interacting with the medications that the patient is already taking.

Because the patient may be taking medications that were ordered by another prescriber, the patient should be asked about any medications that are being taken either routinely or occasionally, before additional medication is prescribed. This list of medications should also include nonprescription medications, some of which are capable of causing interactions with severe effects.

The physician should also consider the patient's personal and family history. Persons with a documented history of experiencing a particular drug interaction should be carefully evaluated before the use of the same combination is considered again. Additionally, the physician should be more cautious of drug interaction if the patient has a family history of diabetes or other diseases that occur more frequently in offspring, which might possibly place the patient at a greater risk of experiencing a drug interaction.

Once the patient begins taking medications the physician should keep in mind the possibility of the occurrence of a drug interaction and monitor the patient for this possibility with the understanding that drug interactions may present in a variety of ways, including an unusual response to a medication, the lack of response, or a toxic effect.

The physician should also warn the patient of the possibility that the prescribed medication may interact with other prescription medications, nonprescription medications, alcohol, and nutrients.

If a patient is identified as having experienced a drug interaction, the physician may be able to manage the interaction so that it would not be a problem to the patient. These efforts could include the alteration of the dose or dosage schedule of one or more of the interacting medications, modification of the patient's nutrient intake, or perhaps even the discontinuation of one of the interacting agents, prescribing instead an effective noninteracting, alternate medication.

Pharmacists

Since pharmacists have a comprehensive education in the pharmacological, chemical, and pharmacokinetic aspects of medications, they can be of obvious assistance in the detection and prevention of drug interactions. Through the use of an up-to-date patient medication profile, which is a record of all the medications that a patient is receiving, pharmacists can compare new orders for prescription and nonprescription medications with the medications that the patient may already be taking (Cadwallader, 1979; O'Hara, 1976). A distinct advantage of a patient medication profile is the fact that all of the prescription medication obtained at that pharmacy, regardless of the physician who ordered the medication, will be listed to provide the pharmacist with the opportunity to evaluate thoroughly the patient's entire drug therapy for the possibility of interactions. A routine review of this medication profile will allow the pharmacist to assess a patient's drug therapy each time a new medication or refill is received or a nonprescription medication is purchased.

Since individuals frequently rely on the pharmacist to recommend the use of specific nonprescription medications, this opportunity can be used by the pharmacist as a chance to discuss with the patient their other drug therapy, in an effort to detect potential drug interactions. Pharmacists can caution patients about potential drug interactions involving prescription medications or nonprescription medications. They can also educate the patient about drug interactions involving alcohol and nutrients.

When a patient experiences a drug interaction, the pharmacist may be able to assess whether it is a minor problem, requiring no medical intervention, or whether the patient should contact the physician for further management of this drug interaction.

When a patient presents to a pharmacist a new prescription that has the potential to interact with existing medications the pharmacist may be able to manage this interaction successfully by recommending that the patient take the medication at a particular time of day that will prevent the interaction from occurring.

The pharmacist may be able to manage interactions involving nonprescription medications either by recommending an alteration of dosage schedule or by suggesting the substitution of an alternative nonprescription product that would be appropriate for the patient's medical complaints, yet would not be involved in a drug interaction.

Nurses

Nursing personnel may also be able to assist in the detection of drug interactions in a number of different ways. In the more traditional nursing roles, nurses can assist in the identification of potentially harmful combinations of medications that their patients are taking by being aware of the medications that they are taking and notifying a patient's physician for appropriate action if a potential interaction exists. Nurses should also be observant of their patients' responses to medications in order to detect atypical responses to combinations of medications that may in fact indicate a drug interaction.

As new practice roles in nursing evolve, the nurse practitioner or nurse clinician will most likely have a greater individual responsibility to patients and to their drug therapy. These new roles may allow for the prescribing of medications by the nurse (Baker, 1981), in which case their responsibilities for the detection, prevention, and management of drug interactions would more closely parallel those mentioned earlier for physicians.

Nutritionists or Dietitians

Nutritionists or dietitians can also become involved in the detection or prevention of drug-nutrient interactions by familiarizing themselves with the more common and more serious interactions of this type that may occur. Thus, if patients are taking particular medications that are known to interact with nutritional status, or if the patient's nutritional intake is likely to interfere with a particular drug therapy, the pharmacist or prescriber may be notified so that the proper intervention can be taken.

Other Professionals

Other persons who work with the elderly, such as physical therapists or social workers should be alert to the fact that an alteration in the patient's behavior or an apparent deterioration in the individual's condition may be the result of a drug interaction, especially in patients who are taking a large number of different medications. If such a problem is suspected, they should notify the patient's pharmacist or physician for further evaluation.

REFERENCES

Baker, N. Prescriptive authority for nurse practitioners. *Geriatic Nursing,* 1981, *2,* 420-421.

Cadwallader, D.E. Drug interactions in the elderly. In D.M. Peterson, F.J. Whittington, & B.P. Payne (Eds.), *Drugs and the elderly.* Springfield, Ill.: Charles C Thomas, 1979.

Cooper, J.W., Wellins, I., Fish, K.H., Jr., & Loomis, M.E. Frequency of potential drug-drug interactions. *Journal of the American Pharmaceutical Association,* 1975, NS *15*(1), 24-31.

Doering, W. Quinidine-digoxin interaction: Pharmacokinetics, underlying mechanism and clinical implications. *New England Journal of Medicine,* 1979, *301,* 400-404.

Hansten, P.D. *Drug interactions* (4th ed.). Philadelphia: Lea & Febiger, 1979.

Hartshorn, E.A. Food and drug interactions. *Guidelines to Professional Pharmacy,* 1977, *4*(3), 1, 4.

Hussar, D.A. Optimizing drug therapy—the patient's need to know. *American Journal of Pharmacy,* 1977, *149*(3), 65-77.

Lamy, P.P. Drug interactions and the elderly—a new perspective. *Drug Intelligence and Clinical Pharmacy,* 1980, *14,* 513-515.

Laventurier, M.F., Talley, R.B., Hefner, D.L., & Kennard, L.H. Drug utilization and potential drug-drug interactions. *Journal of the American Pharmaceutical Association,* 1976, NS *16*(2), 77-81.

Leahey, E.B., Reiffel, J.A., Giardina, E.V., & Bigger, T. The effect of quinidine and other oral antiarrhythmic drugs on serum digoxin. *Annals of Internal Medicine,* 1980, *92,* 605-608.

May, F.E., Stewart, R.B., Cluff, L.E. Drug interactions and multiple drug administration. *Clinical Pharmacology and Therapeutics,* 1977, *22,* 322-328.

O'Hara, G.L. Patient medication profile monitoring. *Journal of the American Pharmaceutical Association,* 1976, NS *16*(5), 48-49, 70.

Seixas, F.A. Drug/alcohol interactions: Avert potential dangers. *Geriatrics,* 1979, *34*(10), 89-102.

Simonson, W. Geriatric considerations for drug interactions. *Pharmacy Times,* 1981, *47*(12), 60-66.

Simonson, W., & Sturgeon, C.K. The evaluation of a pharmacy based drug interaction detection system in a long term care facility. *American Health Care Association Journal,* 1979, *5*(5), 6-12.

U.S. Government Printing Office. Part IV Health. In *Developments in Aging:* A report of the special Committee on Aging, United States Senate (Vol. 1). Washington, D.C.: Author, 1982.

Chapter 9

Sexual Implications of Drug Therapy in the Elderly

Certain medications are known to have major detrimental effects on the psychological and physiological aspects of an individual's sexuality, affecting both their attitudes and perceptions of their own sexuality and their ability to engage successfully in sexual activity, making coitus difficult or impossible. Although these negative effects may occur in persons of all ages, society seems to assign a greater importance of these effects in individuals of the age at which procreation is likely or sexual activity is assumed to be a "normal" activity.

Since procreation is not usually a significant consideration in the elderly, unless the woman is considerably younger than the man, the major remaining consideration in the elderly population is that of the effect of medications on the individual's sexuality, including the psychological and physiological aspects, and the individual's willingness or desire to participate in sexual activity.

My observations have led me to conclude that although medications may have an impact on sexual function in persons of any age, health professionals generally consider this to be a greater problem in younger patients. For example, I once saw a 19-year-old man who was given the diagnosis of malignant hypertension. This condition, in which the term *malignant* means "severe" rather than its usual meaning of "cancerous," is a life-threatening acute rise in blood pressure that can result in severe kidney damage, stroke, and death within a period of months if it is not brought under control.

The patient was placed on medications to bring the condition under control by reducing his high blood pressure; however, soon after starting the therapy, the patient noticed that he was no longer able to achieve an erection, and, consequently, the patient's compliance to his drug therapy diminished considerably. Because of both the potential consequences of this disease and the patient's drug-induced sexual impotence, a great deal of attention was devoted to this case to design a drug therapy regimen that would control the patient's blood pressure without inhibiting his ability to perform sexually. Fortunately, it was found that the patient's high blood pressure was caused by a kidney-related disorder that was surgically correctable.

Even though the situations are not totally analogous, I find it interesting that elderly patients may often be placed on antihypertensive drugs, antidepressants, or antipsychotic medications, all of which may result in sexual impotence, without any attention being given to the possibility that this inhibitory effect on sexual performance may be unacceptable to the patient. Perhaps in the case of elderly patients it is often assumed that their drug-induced sexual impotence will not be noticed!

Although the major focus of this chapter concerns the effect that medications may have on an individual's sexuality, the more general issue of sexuality and the sexual aspects of aging must first be addressed to lend the proper perspective to the subject.

In other words, if sexuality is not important to the elderly individual, then the effects that medications may have on that sexuality would be strictly academic. However, through my observations, I am convinced that sexuality is important in persons of all ages and that while it may receive a different emphasis in the elderly, it is important just the same.

I have found that many of the health professionals with whom I have worked are sensitive to both this issue and to the needs of the elderly individual in general; however, I have also seen instances in which the sexuality of the elderly person has been misunderstood.

For example, I had the opportunity to see a 74-year-old man who developed suicidal depression after his wife left him. He and his wife had been sexually active until shortly before their separation and he had not had any apparent problem with his sexual performance. After the patient was placed on therapy with antidepressant drugs he was unable to achieve an erection. At the patient's request, diagnostic studies were performed to determine whether this inability to function was a complication of his drug therapy or whether it was a neurological problem, in which case consideration could have been given to the implantation of a penile prosthesis.

I found it interesting that most staff members who worked with this patient did not voice any disagreement with these efforts to assist this man; yet one nurse indicated that the procedure was a waste of time and money and that there was no need to take such drastic measures for something so ''unimportant'' to this patient. In my perspective, this nurse's assessment of the situation was a value judgment based not on what was important to the patient but rather what was important, or perhaps what was considered to be proper, by her, perhaps based on her own morals or experience with sexuality.

I have received interesting reactions from students who have enrolled in my university courses in which this aspect of aging has been discussed. These reactions have ranged from positive, stating that this is an important aspect of a person's life, to negative, with comments indicating that it is too personal or too unimportant a subject to be discussed in class.

With this discussion I am not advocating sexual activity for the elderly, nor am I advocating promiscuity, but rather am simply pointing out that it is important for persons who are presently working with the elderly, or who are planning such a career, to realize that a person's sexuality may continue to be an important aspect of life even in the later years and that this sexuality may be significantly influenced by medications.

In many ways, societal, professional, and familial attitudes toward sexual activity and aging are generally negative and based on inaccurate information and suppositions concerning sexual potency and activity. Such misinformation includes the belief by some that with age comes an inevitable cessation of sexual activities. This is untrue. Certainly changes in one's sexuality and sexual behavior and physiology do occur; however, while these changes do have an effect on sexual activity, they do not have to be the cause of its elimination.

PATTERNS OF SEXUAL ACTIVITY IN THE ELDERLY

Major studies of sexual activity and aging indicate that approximately one half of individuals over age 65 engage in coitus regularly (Pearlman, 1972; Pfeiffer, 1974).

Pfeiffer (1978) has also determined that 70 percent of 68-year-old men and 25 percent of 78-year-old men are sexually active, although the best predictors of sexual activity for older men are lifelong patterns of sexual behavior and current health status. Therefore, men who have been sexually active in their younger years tend to continue to be active as they age if failing health does not prevent it (Masters & Johnson, 1966; Pfeiffer & Davis, 1972).

Similar patterns of continued sexual activity exist for older women, although because of their husband's failing health or death, older women are more likely than older men to report a decline in sexual activity earlier in life. Women tend to marry older men, and men generally die at a younger age than women, leaving the older widowed woman without a sex partner for a number of years. This trend is further affected by the low ratio of elderly men to elderly women and the fact that elderly men also tend to marry women younger than themselves, making it even less likely that the elderly woman will remarry or find a suitable partner.

Sexual expressiveness may also be affected by the institutional environment that some elderly individuals may live in (Miller, 1978; Wasow & Loeb, 1978). These environments generally have high female-to-male ratios, and they usually lack the privacy that most would find necessary for sexual encounters. In addition, individuals living in an institutional environment may perceive themselves as being unattractive as a result of their health status. Furthermore, institutional policies or the responses of staff members may prohibit or limit the opportunity for individuals to express themselves sexually.

I have observed this last factor to be a significant one that tends to vary considerably between facilities and staff members. Some facilities, for example, allow for the husband and wife to share the same room and to have privacy when requested, while some do not adopt such a policy. Some staff members may make an effort to respect the privacy of consenting adults, while some may intervene to prevent such sexual encounters.

SEXUAL RESPONSE IN THE AGING MALE

Age-related changes in sexual physiology and responsiveness do occur; however, as with other physiological changes these changes reflect tremendous individual differences and occur very gradually (Kart, Metress, & Metress, 1978; Weg, 1978):

- *decreased testosterone formation.* A gradual decline in production of the male hormone, testosterone, by the testes occurs, beginning at about age 50. This decrease results in lowered rates of spermatogenesis, the formation of sperm.
- *alterations of the prostate gland.* With age, the prostate gland, which is among other things responsible for the secretion of seminal fluid, enlarges, but its force of contraction weakens, resulting in a decreased force of ejaculation and a reduction in the volume of seminal fluid produced.
- *changes in erection.* Older men are generally not able to achieve an erection as quickly as younger men, but they are able to maintain their erection longer than younger men. An additional change in erection includes an increase in the refractory period, which is the time period following ejaculation that is necessary before another erection can be achieved.
- *changes in orgasm.* With age there is generally a decreased sensation of ejaculatory inevitability, a reduced capacity and urgency for orgasm with intercourse, and a decreased length of orgasmic period when it occurs.

In spite of these normal, age related changes, a functional sexual capacity continues in most healthy older males.

SEXUAL RESPONSE IN THE AGING FEMALE

Age-related changes in sexual physiology that occur in the woman are significant and begin in the late 30s with the onset of the climacteric. This period extends approximately 20 years and occurs as a result of a gradually diminishing production of estrogen and progesterone, which ultimately results in the following features (Masters & Johnson, 1966; Rossman, 1978; Weg, 1978):

- *menopause*—the cessation of menses (menopause) and the associated loss of fertility
- *decreased elasticity of skin*—a decrease in the elasticity of all skin in general, and a decrease in the amount of subcutaneous fatty tissue in the genitalia
- *changes in uterus and vagina*—a gradual atrophy of the uterus and vagina, which is often accompanied by atrophy of the urethra and bladder
- *decreased vaginal lubrication*—a decrease in the number and activity of the Bartholin glands, which lubricate the vagina
- *other physical changes*—a wide variety of signs, symptoms, and complaints including hot flashes, sweating, an increase in blood pressure, anxiety, depression, and insomnia.

The decreased hormonal levels do not affect the capacity for the woman to experience an orgasm, or multiple orgasms, however a greater time for stimulation to arousal and orgasm may be required. Additionally, coitus may become painful as a result of decreased vaginal lubrication.

DISEASE CONDITIONS INTERFERING WITH SEXUALITY

Numerous diseases and physical conditions that are associated with the aging process or that occur more commonly in old age may affect sexual performance in the elderly (Renshaw, 1981) through a number of different reasons such as fear of further physical injury, pain, or discomfort; fear of sexual failure; concern that the sexual activity will cause further physical problems; and the belief by one or both sexual partners that sexual contact is not possible.

To familiarize the reader with some of the more common problems of this type I will briefly discuss a few particular disease states and how they may impact on sexual performance. Subsequently, I will discuss some of the interventions that may be used to compensate for the condition's negative effect on sexuality. This discussion is pertinent to the issue of medication effect because drug therapy may be involved in two unique ways. First, drugs used to control or manage the condition may by themselves have a negative impact on sexuality and, second, alterations in existing drug therapy may reverse some of the negative sexual implications of the disease state.

Diabetes Mellitus

One of the major long-term complications of diabetes is neuropathy, which is a condition in which damage to nerve pathways occurs. Diabetic neuropathy usually involves peripheral nerves, such as those in the hands and feet; however, it may involve any portion of the nervous system, resulting in a wide range of manifestations, including decreases in the sense of touch and muscle weakness. It may also cause a decrease in sexual function. In the male, diabetic neuropathy may cause sexual impotence and may also cause retrograde ejaculation, a condition in which the man's semen is ejaculated into the bladder rather than externally through the penis. The man may also experience reduced sexual responsiveness resulting from the increased fatigue that may accompany diabetes. In spite of these inhibitory effects on sexual performance, libido, or sexual desire, persists.

Diabetes may also have an effect on the woman's sexual response as a result of neuropathy and fatigue, and a decrease in vaginal lubrication may also occur, although some evidence exists indicating that diabetes does not cause significant sexual dysfunction in the female (Ellenberg, 1980).

Although the ability of diabetes to produce sexual impotence has been reported frequently in the scientific literature, some questions exist concerning the extent of that impotence and its inevitability.

One medical textbook reports that approximately 25 percent of young male diabetics and 50 percent of male diabetics in their 40s develop sexual impotence as a consequence of diabetic nerve damage (Thorn, 1977), although their interest in sex generally persists. A more recent study, however, has shown that the impotence of 2 to 7 years' duration that was supposedly due to diabetes in patients who had been taking insulin for 15 to 17 years was reversible within two to seven weeks (Renshaw, 1978a)! This finding indicates that there is most likely a strong psychological component to the impotence that occurs in diabetic males, although decreases in nerve conduction velocity in diabetic patients have been documented and may be at least partially reversible with proper therapy (Judzewitsch, Jaspan, Polonsky, Weinberg et al., 1983).

It may also be possible to reverse some cases of the sexual impotence that occur with diabetes by maintaining good control of the patient's blood sugar, although if any improvement does occur it may take weeks or months to become evident.

Another intervention that is possible in the diabetic male is the implantation of a penile prosthesis, which is discussed in more detail later in this chapter.

In the diabetic female experiencing discomfort due to insufficient vaginal lubrication, a lubricant such as Lubafax® or KY Jelly® may be used.

Cardiac Disease

Patients with cardiac disease, such as angina, or those who are recovering from a myocardial infarction (heart attack), may have significant problems with sexual activity, not as much from a decrease in their physical ability to perform sexually but rather resulting from their fears of the risk associated with sexual activity. For example, a male or female patient who has experienced a myocardial infarction may have serious doubts about the resumption of normal sexual activity or whether he or she can ever have sex again. This hesitancy may be related to the fear of failure or the possibility of overexertion and experiencing angina or causing further cardiac damage or even dying during the sexual act.

Most cardiac patients, including those who have suffered from myocardial infarctions, are able to resume normal sexual activity. Patient education is crucial so that they may be made aware of the fact that their renewed activity will not be harmful and may even be beneficial by decreasing anxiety and reducing the conflict that may exist between the patients and their partners.

The patient should be made aware of the fact that normal sexual activity is roughly equivalent to climbing two flights of stairs, and if they are able to accomplish that task without major discomfort, then sexual activity will most likely not be too strenuous.

Patients with angina may also engage in sexual activity without endangering their health or cardiac function, although they should not do so while experiencing an anginal attack. Appropriate therapy with the antianginal drug nitroglycerin (Nitrostat®) or other similar product is likely to control and prevent their cardiac pain. Patients may even decide to take an extra dose of nitroglycerin before engaging in sex. The drug is quite safe, with headache being one of the major signs of excessive dosage, and the administration of this additional dose, although perhaps not absolutely necessary from the standpoint of the patient's cardiac disease, may instill enough confidence in the patient to reduce or eliminate any anxiety before sexual activity.

Patients with angina may also use a medication from a class of drugs called beta blockers (e.g., propranolol [Inderal®]), although this class of drugs has been associated with loss of libido or difficulty in achieving erection. They may also use a class of medications known as calcium channel blockers, which include nifedipine (Procardia®), verapamil (Isoptin®), and diltiazem (Cardizem®). One potential advantage of these medications over the beta blockers is that the calcium channel blockers are said to have a low incidence of sexual inhibitory effects.

Other medications, including antihypertensive agents, diuretics, antiar-rhythmics, and digitalis preparations, that may be used in the therapy of various heart conditions may also have negative effects on sexual function, as shown in Table 9-1. This consideration makes it important that those who work with the elderly realize that one cause of sexual problems in cardiac patients may in fact be their medications.

Arthritis

The two major forms of arthritis, rheumatoid arthritis and osteoarthritis, may result in a considerable degree of pain and discomfort, creating a significant disincentive for sexual activity.

Table 9-1 Medications That May Induce Sexual Dysfunction

Drug class with selected examples	Decrease or loss of libido	Erectile problems	Ejaculation difficulty	Gynecomastia	Decreased vaginal lubrication
Antihypertensives					
Methyldopa (Aldomet®)	+	+	+	+	
Propranolol (Inderal®)	+	+			
Nadolol (Corgard®)	+	+			
Reserpine (Serpasil®)	+	+	+	+	
Clonidine (Catapres®)		+	+		
Hydralazine (Apresoline®)		+			
Diuretics					
Spironolactone (Aldactone®)	+	+		+	+
Chlorthalidone (Hygroton®)	+	+			+
Thiazide Diuretics (HydroDIURIL®)	+	+			+
Antihistamines					
Diphenhydramine (Benadryl®)	+	+			+
Chlorpheniramine (Chlor-Trimeton®)	+	+			+
Antidepressants					
Amitriptyline (Elavil®)	+	+	+	+	
Imipramine (Tofranil®)	+	+	+	+	
Doxepin (Sinequan®)	+	+	+		
Psychiatric					
Chlorpromazine (Thorazine®)	+	+	+		
Haloperidol (Haldol®)		+	+	+	
Thioridazine (Mellaril®)	+	+	+		
Narcotics (for pain)	+	+			

Table 9-1 continued

Drug class with selected examples	Decrease or loss of libido	Erectile problems	Ejaculation difficulty	Gynecomastia	Decreased vaginal lubrication
Anticholinergic (Atropinelike drugs including Donnatal® and others)	+	+			+
Antiparkinson					
Benztropine (Cogentin®)	+	+			+
Trihexphenidyl (Artane®)	+	+			+
Antiulcer					
Cimetidine (Tagamet®)	+	+		+	
Cardiac					
Digoxin (Lanoxin®)		+		+	
Disopyramide (Norpace®)		+			

Note: This table identifies only a small portion of the drugs that possess the potential of causing sexual dysfunction. Not all persons taking these drugs will experience the problems identified.

Source: Adapted from "Drug Induced Sexual Dysfunction," by Sylvia A. Aldridge, *Clinical Pharmacy*, Vol. 1, No. 2, pp. 141-147, 1982, with permission of the American Society of Hospital Pharmacists; "Drug Related Sexual Dysfunction," by J.W. O'Connor and J.M. Scavone, *The Apothecary*, Vol. 94, No. 1, pp. 20-30, 1982, with permission of Health Care Marketing Services; "Sexual Effects of Cardiovascular Drugs," by Chris Papadopoulos, *Archives of Internal Medicine*, Vol. 140, No. 10, pp. 1341-1345, 1980. Copyright © 1980, American Medical Association.

It may be possible to circumvent some of this pain and discomfort if the couple follows the following recommendations (Renshaw, 1981):

- make love when rested in the morning after a warm bath, perhaps taken together
- take needed analgesics (pain medication) 30 minutes before sex
- try alternative comfortable positions within the limits of mobility

Arthritis sufferers should be careful to comply with their drug therapy in an effort to avoid as much pain and discomfort as possible. It is important to remember that the analgesics used may have an impact on sexual performance; for example, narcotic analgesics may cause decreased libido or sexual impotence while antiinflammatory drugs (e.g., sulindac [Clinoril®]) would be less likely to do so.

Alcoholism

Alcoholism is certainly not unique to the elderly, however, it may occur late in life as a result of the fear of aging, of personal losses of companions and physical prowess, or of the individual's boredom resulting from retirement and an excess of free time.

Some may think of alcohol as a sexual stimulant, but pharmacologically it is a depressant that can seriously inhibit sexual response. It may also cause nerve damage that can result in a decrease of sexual functioning. The reason why some people seem to experience an increased libido or interest in sex as a result of alcohol ingestion is because alcohol first depresses the "higher" functions of the brain, which include the social inhibitions that individuals might have that normally inhibit them from engaging in sexual activity; therefore, it has been said that alcohol increases the desire for sexual contact but decreases the ability to perform.

Severe alcoholism can cause liver damage, which may have many detrimental biochemical effects, including a decrease in the liver's ability to metabolize estrogen. Although estrogen is known as a female hormone, it is also produced in the male and normally metabolized in the liver so the male does not develop feminine characteristics. If the metabolism is significantly decreased by liver damage or other processes, the effects of estrogen can be seen in males, including breast enlargement, shrinking of the testicles, and a generalized loss of body hair. Obviously these changes can have a significant physiological and psychological effect on the sexuality of the alcoholic male.

It may be possible to reverse the sexual impotence resulting from alcohol abuse if the alcohol ingestion is discontinued; however, it may take several months, and as many as 50 percent of former alcoholics may not regain their ability to perform sexually (Lemere & Smith, 1973).

Antidepressant medication may help to renew sexual desire if the individual's impotence is related to alcohol-induced depression rather than neurological damage or other toxic effects of the drug (Renshaw, 1981), but it must be remembered that antidepressants may cause impotence in some individuals.

Mental Disorders

Various mental problems that may occur with old age include depression, hallucinations, or psychotic behavior. Each of these disorders may depress or interfere with sexual function, but depression is more likely to cause these problems. Antidepressant drugs may be used effectively for depression, and various tranquilizers or antipsychotic drugs may be helpful with other mental problems; however, many of the medications that are used to treat these disorders have the potential to decrease sexual performance.

Hysterectomy or Mastectomy

A hysterectomy or mastectomy may cause a woman to develop an impaired self-image and feelings of sexlessness. It is possible for women to have breast implants or cosmetic surgery following mastectomy so that they may look and feel more like they did before their surgery.

Prostate Disorders

As a man ages, his prostate gland frequently increases in size, restricting urine flow through the urethra, with a resultant decrease in the ability to form a continuous stream of urine. The prostate may enlarge to the point that surgery is necessary to remove a portion of the enlarged gland.

The most common form of prostatic surgery is the transurethral resection of the prostate, which is known as TURP. The technique involved in this type of surgery involves the insertion of an instrument through the opening of the urethra in the penis. This tubelike instrument is of small enough diameter to fit through the urethra and long enough to reach the area of the prostate, which is just below the urinary bladder. When the instrument is at the level of the prostate, a small knife blade in the instrument is unshielded and a portion of the gland is cut away along with a section of the urethral lining. The urethral lining is then able to grow back again, leaving the prostate gland smaller than before the surgery, so that it no longer interferes with urine flow.

Although prostate surgery may result in sexual impotence, this problem is not common after transurethral resection and is usually psychogenic when it does occur, necessitating understanding and attention from health professionals and the patient's partner. Sexual potency and ability may be more commonly inhibited after more drastic types of prostate surgery.

SEXUAL IMPOTENCE

Sexual impotence can be defined in general terms as "the loss of libido or the inability to achieve or maintain erection and/or the decreased or absent ability to ejaculate."

Masters and Johnson (1966) also define impotence as the inability to achieve or maintain an erection quality sufficient to accomplish successful coitus.

Usually the term *impotence* implies continued difficulty in sexual function, although an individual may experience temporary or periodic impotence as a result of alcohol intoxication, effect of medications, fatigue, acute illness, or lack of sexual desire.

In order to more fully understand the factors that influence impotence in the male it is first necessary to briefly review the nerve pathways responsible for penile erection and ejaculation.

Penile erection is governed by two basic mechanisms, one psychogenic, the other reflexogenic. Psychogenic erection is mediated by nerve impulses descending from the brain that are stimulated by auditory (hearing), visual, olfactory (smell), tactile (touch), and imaginative stimuli. Reflexogenic erections are dependent on a local reflex arc that is stimulated by tactile stimulation of the genital area, such as stroking the penis or bladder fullness.

Ejaculation of semen is controlled by nerve fibers in the lumbar (lower back) segment of the spine, which activate neuronal receptors, inducing contractions of the organs involved in ejaculation, including the seminal vesicles, the vas deferens, and the bulbar muscle (Horowitz & Goble, 1979; Lording, 1978).

Many causes of impotence exist in men of all ages, but even though there is an increased number of reasons in older men it has been estimated that 80 to 90 percent of impotence in older men may result from the fear of sexual failure and from their self-fulfilling expectations of impotence.

A number of disease conditions such as those mentioned earlier can also cause impotence. However, since the psychogenic aspect of impotence is so important, it is frequently difficult to determine whether the problem is caused by the disease process itself or by the patient's reaction to the disease (e.g., depression and feelings of unattractiveness).

Some of these disease states include atherosclerosis (hardening of the arteries), thyroid disease, prostatitis (inflammation of the prostate), neurological disease (multiple sclerosis), and various diseases with associated neuropathies (degeneration of nerves). Serious diseases associated with the failure of major organ systems, such as the heart, liver, lungs, and kidneys, can also cause impotence, although it must be emphasized that while all of the conditions mentioned, and many more that were not mentioned, can be the cause of impotence, their presence does not dictate impotence because some patients may have serious or extensive illness and still have a healthy libido and ability to perform sexually.

The Prosthetic Penis

One important intervention that may be used successfully in males experiencing sexual impotence is the surgical insertion of a penile prosthesis. A prosthesis that is permanently rigid is available; however, the device that seems to be the most effective is a prosthesis that can be inflated or deflated as desired (Scott, Byrd, Karacan, Ollson, Beutler, & Attia, 1979). On inflation, an erection that mimics a natural erection is achieved, although it does not provide the man with the ability either to reach sexual climax or to ejaculate; however, if he could do so before the prosthesis was implanted, he will continue to be able to do so (Renshaw, 1979). Persons who work with the elderly should be aware that such a prosthesis exists, and they may be able to inform a patient or client of the existence of these devices, thus referring them to their urologist for additional information.

Drug-Induced Impotence

Prescription and nonprescription medications may also be the cause of impotence. The mechanism of this impotence varies considerably between medications, depending on their pharmacological activity and toxicity, and may inhibit libido, erection, and ejaculation. As in disease-induced impotence, there is a large variation in response between patients, so that some will experience impotence after using a particular medication and some will not have any such problem from the same medication. Drug-induced impotence is not an absolute occurrence.

Some of the types of medications commonly used by the elderly that may cause impotence are discussed in the following sections.

Antihypertensive Medications

There are many different drugs used to treat high blood pressure, and their mechanisms of action vary tremendously. For example, some act directly on the blood vessels, some affect the heart, and others act on various parts of the nervous system. In spite of this wide range of effects, many of the medications used to treat high blood pressure possess the potential for causing impotence. Some of the antihypertensives that are most likely to cause impotence include guanethidine (Ismelin®), methyldopa (Aldomet®), and clonidine (Catapres®).

Psychiatric Medications

A wide range of drugs are used to treat psychiatric disorders; however, two common groups, the antidepressants and the antipsychotics, are most likely to cause problems with sexual function. Antidepressants that may cause impotence include amitriptyline (Elavil®) and imipramine (Tofranil®). Although these and similar drugs may be the cause of sexual impotence, it is difficult to differentiate between decreased sexual functioning resulting from the drug or that resulting from the patient's depression. Antipsychotic medications, such as thioridazine (Mellaril®), are used to treat agitation, delusions, hallucinations, and other manifestations associated with psychosis. These medications may also cause impotence.

Drugs of Addiction

Alcohol, narcotic analgesics such as morphine, amphetamines (Dexedrine®), barbiturates (Nembutal®), and other drugs with a high abuse potential may cause sexual impotence. Alcohol is probably the single most common cause of drug-induced impotence and is frequently involved in an individual's first episode of impotence, which, if not understood, can result in serious doubts about one's ability to perform and may create fears about the possible permanence of the condition.

Anticholinergic Drugs (Atropinelike Drugs)

Many prescription and nonprescription medications have properties that are similar to those of the drug atropine. These are referred to as anticholinergic properties and may cause a number of symptoms such as dry mouth, blurred vision, and difficulty in urination. Examples of drugs with anticholinergic properties include some that are used to treat Parkinson's disease, such as benztropine (Cogentin®), and some antidepressants, such as amitriptyline (Elavil®). These drugs may also inhibit sexual arousal in both men and women. Both penile erection and vaginal lubrication may be affected by some of these agents, although libido generally remains unaffected (see Table 9-1).

INHIBITION OF SEXUAL RESPONSE IN THE FEMALE

In the body of literature concerning the effect of medications on sexual response it is rare to find even brief mention concerning the manifestation of these effects in the female. This fact is emphasized as a note in a review of the subject of drugs and impaired sexual function by Horowitz and Goble (1979). The authors noted that their original intention was to review drug-induced sexual dysfunction in both men and women; however, they found very little information regarding these effects in men and virtually no information relating to women. Therefore, the title of their excellent article when finished was ''Drugs and Impaired *Male* Sexual Function.''

It appears that most of the studies that have been performed have been with men, as have the case studies that have been reported in the literature. Perhaps this obvious absence of the effect of medications on the sexual performance of women stems from the traditional male-oriented view that the most important requirement for sexual activity is an erect penis, and since the majority of researchers are male, their studies reflect that attitude.

Perhaps it is because the absence of an erection in a male is simply an easier and more qualitative observation to make than it is to observe the degree of vaginal lubrication or sexual excitement in the female.

Another possible reason for the male orientation of the overwhelming majority of this knowledge of the effect of medications on sexual function may simply be that aging or elderly men are more apt to complain openly about noticeable changes in their sexual performance whereas women might be a bit more reticent to discuss this issue, perhaps reflecting the social or sexual mores that were predominant when they were younger.

While it is true that an erect penis is generally recognized as a requirement for traditional sexual activity, this certainly does not mean that the female is not entitled to keep her sexuality or ability to perform sexually at the level that she desires.

Physiologically there are many direct correlations between male and female sexual physiology and response, so it is likely that many of the drug effects that are seen in the male may also have an effect, albeit somewhat different, in the female.

For example, vaginal lubrication in the female is the direct physiological correlation of a penile erection in the male, involving analogous nerve pathways and blood vessels. Therefore it is entirely possible that medications that have an inhibitory effect on the ability of the male to achieve an erection may also decrease the ability of the female to achieve vaginal lubrication. In the small body of literature that does exist on this subject, some information regarding drug effect on vaginal lubrication has been summarized and is presented in Table 9-1, although no concerted attempt has been made to correlate that response in the female with inhibition of erectile response in the male.

Another area that may have implications in both sexes is the following question, If a medication will prevent ejaculation in the male, will it then therefore inhibit or abolish the orgasmic response in the female?

I am unaware of any information in the literature that discusses this comparison, and in fact this and the analogy between vaginal lubrication and penile erection are both still speculative. In the small amount of information that is available concerning drug effect on female sexual response it has been reported that certain central nervous system depressants, such as high doses and chronic abuse of alcohol, barbiturates, sedatives and narcotics, and high blood pressure medications, may depress sexual activity in the female (Aldridge, 1982; Jaffe, 1979; O'Connor & Scavone, 1982; Weg, 1978). Additionally, androgens (male hormones), which may occasionally be used in the female to manage breast cancer and a variety of other conditions, may promote the development of masculine secondary sex characteristics in the woman, such as an increase in body and facial hair, and may also decrease libido.

DRUG-INDUCED GYNECOMASTIA

Gynecomastia can be defined as the excessive size or development of the male breast. It may occur in one or both breasts and is usually painless, although soreness and tenderness may be present. Extreme cases of gynecomastia may actually be associated with the ability of the male breast to produce milk! Since the male breast includes a mammary gland that is analogous to the gland in the female, this is physiologically possible, although this degree of breast development in the male is extremely rare and is usually associated with major endocrine (hormonal) disturbances. Some degree of gynecomastia is quite common and may occur in 30 to 40 percent of the male population although it is usually not associated with any symptoms such as pain or tenderness and frequently goes unnoticed.

The prevalence of gynecomastia appears to increase moderately with advancing age and is more common in men over age 65 because a decrease in testicular function in older men results in a decreased production of the male hormone testosterone (Carlson, 1980). This condition results from an alteration in the balance between the influence of androgens (male hormones) and estrogens (female hormones) and may be caused by a number of disease processes, including hyperthyroidism (hyperactive thyroid gland), liver disease, and various hormonal disturbances.

Perhaps the single most common identifiable cause of gynecomastia is that of the effect of medications, which can be manifested through a variety of mechanisms. Some medications may have an estrogenlike structure, thus stimulating breast development, and others may affect the binding or metabolism of hormones in various ways, resulting in gynecomastia. A partial list of drugs that have been shown to be capable of causing gynecomastia is presented in Table 9-1, although it must be emphasized that gynecomastia will not occur in all patients taking these medications.

Management of Gynecomastia

Gynecomastia may be caused by hormonal disturbances and may indicate serious underlying disease; however, drug-induced gynecomastia is rarely a serious physical threat, although it may have significant psychological and emotional implications, as demonstrated by the following example.

Several weeks after beginning therapy with digoxin (Lanoxin®) for congestive heart failure, a 72-year-old man began refusing to undress in front of his wife and resisted affectionate hugs from her and from his adult children. He would not discuss the reason for this change in his usually affectionate nature. When an appointment for a routine physical checkup came, he said he did not want to go. He stated he did not want to undress in front of a nurse. In conversation with his wife, he finally admitted that his reluctance to be nude or to be hugged stemmed from the enlargement of his breasts. He was confused and embarrassed by ''looking like a woman.'' He did not understand the source of this recent change and feared this process. When finally contacted, the physician explained that breast enlargement is a known side effect of digoxin therapy. The patient then questioned continuing treatment. The physician and family encouraged him to comply with the drug therapy, reassuring him that the physical change in appearance was not noticeable. He continued the treatment reluctantly.

This case demonstrates the impact that gynecomastia can have on an individual, including his physical appearance, self-esteem, and his willingness to continue complying with necessary drug therapy. Imagine how an aging male might react to the development of gynecomastia. He may already be concerned about his changing role in life. After retirement he is no longer the primary provider and may be relegated to a self-perceived ''lesser'' role in his wife's domain, the home. His children are now married and have their own children and their own responsibilities. He has noticed that his musculature is nothing like it used to be, and he may also notice that he has less body hair than when he was younger, causing further doubts about his role as a father, and perhaps even raising questions about his masculinity and virility. Then, in addition to all of these events, he notices that his breasts are developing! This is indeed a situation that requires a great deal of understanding and counseling.

As in the previous example, a man who notices gynecomastia must be counseled. If it is not a serious problem he should be told that it is not noticeable or unattractive, which is usually the case. If it is a significant physical problem, a physician should be consulted to determine whether the condition might be related to a disease process or whether it is drug induced.

If it is drug induced, the patient should be made aware of the situation and the fact that some drugs may cause this problem. If this is unacceptable to the patient, it may be possible for the prescriber to reduce or eliminate the gynecomastia by altering the patient's drug therapy by switching to a different medication or by decreasing the dose of the existing medication. It may also be possible to completely discontinue administration of the offending drug; however, it must be realized that although this will usually result in a resolution of the gynecomastia, it may be at the expense of the therapeutic reason for which the medication was originally prescribed.

This discussion of gynecomastia has been limited to the male for the obvious reason that it is in the male that even a slight degree of breast enlargement will be most easily noticed. Generally, gynecomastia is not considered to be a significant problem in the female; however, it is possible that such a problem could occur in the form of breast tenderness or soreness or breast enlargement (O'Connor & Scavone, 1982). If the problem did occur to an unacceptable degree, the same steps could be taken in the female that were implemented in the male, that is, decrease the dose of the drug, switch to a different drug, or discontinue the therapy entirely.

MEDICATIONS USED FOR THEIR POSITIVE EFFECT ON SEXUALITY

In some instances various medications may be used in elderly individuals in an attempt to provide benefit from the drug's potentially positive effect on sexuality by either reversing some of the age-related changes in sexual physiology or function or by reversing sexual impotence.

Hormonal Replacement

Estrogens (female hormones) may be administered to women who are experiencing menopausal symptoms or to those who are postmenopausal in an effort to arrest the physiological changes that are associated with menopause. Women may take conjugated estrogen tablets (Premarin®) for this purpose, which are often quite effective in reducing the symptoms of menopause, such as hot flashes and sweating. However, the general popularity of the use of estrogens for this purpose has declined significantly in recent years, partially because they have not been as effective as originally hoped and also because of their possible association with an increased risk of uterine cancer.

Topical administration of estrogen in the form of a vaginal cream (Premarin®) can reduce painful intercourse and facilitate lubrication by the direct effect that it exerts on the vaginal tissue. The principle behind this topical application is that the hormone will maintain or restore youthful qualities to vaginal tissue by administering a relatively small estrogen dose locally rather than giving a larger dose systemically. Ideally this will result in positive effects on vaginal tissue while avoiding systemic estrogen effects.

The use of intravaginal estrogen cream is not without hazard, however, as evidenced by the 70-year-old man who developed gynecomastia following his wife's use of the cream two to three times a week as a lubricant before sexual intercourse. Apparently enough of the female hormone was absorbed through his penis to have a systemic effect. As mentioned earlier, lubricants may be helpful, but hormone creams are not meant to be used as lubricants to facilitate sexual intercourse (DiRaimondo, Roach, & Meador, 1980).

Systemic testosterone or testosterone derivatives (male hormones) have been given to men in order to counter some of the effects of aging and to increase sexual responsiveness and ability to perform. Their use is not without problems, however, due to side effects of edema, gynecomastia, liver problems, and an increased risk of prostatic cancer. In addition to being potentially dangerous, this practice is not very rational since the overwhelming majority of men who experience sexual impotence do not have low testosterone levels and are therefore suffering impotence from psychogenic rather than physiological causes.

Testosterone has also been given to women in small doses to increase their libido; however, this practice is quite controversial and may result in masculinizing signs in the woman such as beard growth, lowering of the voice, and enlargement of the clitoris (Renshaw, 1978b).

Aphrodisiacs (Sexual Stimulants)

For as long as recorded history humans have attempted to rely on an assortment of ''love potions,'' ''tonics,'' or other ''remedies'' that would increase sexual interest or response in themselves and their prospective mate. Cantharides (also known as Spanish fly), dried shark fin, powdered rhinocerous horn, and raw oysters have been touted and used as aphrodisiacs. Supposed sexual stimulants such as strychnine, bromocriptine (an ergot derivative), gerovital (see Chapter 10), and vitamin E have also been used.

The most interesting aspect of aphrodisiacs is that while none of them have really been demonstrated to be effective based on their supposed pharmacologic activity, they frequently provide the user with the desired results. When a compound or medicine is found to be an effective sexual stimulant, that effect is most likely due to its ''placebo'' or psychological effect. This is especially true with drugs used to treat impotence, since the problem is frequently psychological in origin.

The strong placebo effect of sexual stimulants, and their popularity, can be demonstrated by an advertisement that appeared in a popular magazine with an offer for some capsules that were supposedly effective sexual stimulants. The advertisement described the capsules as ''placebos'' that would increase sexual drive and performance. Apparently the seller was depending on the likelihood that many of the potential customers did not understand that *placebo* means a drug that has no pharmacologic activity. However, I suspect that in spite of that fact there were many satisfied customers who thought that the capsules would work for them and, consequently, they did work.

In this situation it is academic to refer to a medication as a placebo if it actually works. Perhaps the best assessment of the effectiveness of a ''drug'' or ''supposed drug'' is whether or not it works, rather than whether or not it is supposed to work.

Although the use of aphrodisiacs, ''placebo'' or not, may actually help some persons with their sexual problems, their use is not totally without risk, however, for the following reasons:

- *financial rip-off*. Aphrodisiacs and sex stimulants may cost significantly more than they are worth, although a look at the cost versus benefit is important. If an individual pays ten dollars for sugar pills that are worth only ten cents, they are not getting their money's worth; however, if those same ''sugar pills'' enable that individual to reach his or her goal of renewed sexual activity as a result of the pill's psychological effect, the purchase could be considered to be a bargain.

- *failure to recognize an underlying problem.* An individual, failing to achieve satisfactory response to the product, may accept that failure as a permanent problem of aging and not bother to find the underlying and possibly reversible cause of that problem.
- *toxicity.* Not all aphrodisiacs are harmless placebos. For example, strychnine and cantharides may both cause peripheral nerve damage, which could further aggravate any problem with sexual response.

INTERVENTIONS BY HEALTH PROFESSIONALS

Health professionals and other persons working with the elderly patient will most likely have the opportunity to work with individuals whose sexuality is in some way being influenced by their medications. They may either be experiencing drug-induced impotence or gynecomastia or they may be considering the use of, or may actually be using, prescription medications or nonprescription aphrodisiacs to counter the age-related changes in their sexuality or to stimulate their sexual response.

It is important that this sensitive subject be handled in an understanding way, and in spite of any preconceived notions by the health professional it must be realized that the loss of sexuality may be perceived by the elderly individual as a very significant loss. Care must be taken to understand the changes in sexual physiology and sexual expression that take place with aging, understanding that in spite of those changes sexual expression remains a viable option; however, that expression may be significantly altered by drug therapy.

Health professionals may have many different types of interactions or interventions with the patients whose sexuality is being affected by drug therapy. These interactions will necessarily vary, depending on the professional and personal relationship between the professional and the elderly individual. They will also depend on the responsibilities of the health professional. The following are possibilities:

Avoid Suggesting That Impotence or Gynecomastia Will Occur

When patients are placed on a medication that is new to them, or when the dosage of existing therapy is altered, it is generally unwise to inform them of the possibility that they may experience impotence or gynecomastia, even though it is a known effect of the particular medication(s) in question. If a male is informed that a particular drug is likely to impair his sexual function, that information will probably become a self-fulfilling prophecy. Many individuals will not experience impotence even from medications that are well known to cause that problem, so in this case the patients' right to know about the effects of their drug therapy may be outweighed by their right to be free from unwanted side effects. It is also quite likely that compliance with that drug therapy will decrease if the patient anticipates impotence or gynecomastia.

Observe the Patient for Altered Behavior

Impotence or gynecomastia should be suspected if a patient does not comply well with drug therapy, especially if previously exhibited compliance was good. Other behavioral changes such as the patient's reluctance to be hugged or to undress in front of others could possibly indicate gynecomastia. Additional attention to these changes should be given to patients who have recently started taking medications that are known to cause either or both of these problems.

Listen to the Patient

It is important to note if patients are asking leading or subtle questions about their drug therapy or their sexuality. This could be an indication that they have some concern regarding sexual problems caused by their medications. Patients may also joke about or voice curiosity or interest in the possible use of various hormones or nonprescription sexual stimulants, possibly indicating some concern about their own sexual function.

Review the Patient's Drug Therapy

If impotence or gynecomastia is suspected or documented, it will be necessary to identify one or more drugs in the patient's therapeutic regimen that might be a possible cause of the problem. Patient medication profiles can be checked and medication histories can be performed to identify any prescription or nonprescription medications that may be the cause of this problem.

Determine If the Patient Is Abusing Drugs

The abuse of alcohol is the single most common cause of drug-induced impotence and may also lead to gynecomastia in the case of severe liver disease. Other drugs of abuse such as barbiturates, narcotics, amphetamines, and tranquilizers can also cause impotence. It may be possible to restore patients' sexual potency following the alteration of their abuse behavior and discontinuation of the causative agent(s).

Provide Consultation to the Patient

If patients experience problems with impotence or gynecomastia, the health professional must attempt to understand their concerns and be willing to discuss the problem with them. If patients experience impotence resulting from the use of one or more medications, they should be dealt with in a positive manner and informed that the problem is not their failure and is likely to resolve with the alteration of their drug therapy. If they experience gynecomastia, they should be assured that the problem is not harmful, may not be noticeable to others, and is reversible following alteration of their drug therapy.

Consider Alteration of the Drug Therapy Regimen

Drug-induced impotence or gynecomastia may be diminished or eliminated by altering a patient's medication regimen. The prescriber has the option of decreasing the medication dosage, discontinuing the offending agent, or switching to a medication that may not exhibit the same problems. Patients should be instructed not to alter their drug therapy by themselves but rather leave it up to the appropriate health professionals, such as the prescriber in consultation with a pharmacist.

Consider Treatment of the Problem with a Medication

Some medications may be effective in the treatment of impotence. If the problem is the result of a hormone deficiency, hormonal therapy may be effective. If related to other diseases, such as arthritis, or heart attack, other drug therapy may be effective. If the cause is psychogenic, psychotherapy or counseling may be effective or consideration can be given to the use of various prescription or nonprescription medications that supposedly stimulate sexual activity, through either their pharmacological or their placebo effect.

Drug therapy may also be used to intervene in other conditions relating to the patient's sexuality, such as the intravaginal use of estrogen cream to halt or reverse age-related tissue changes and decreased vaginal lubrication.

REFERENCES

Aldridge, S.A. Drug-induced sexual dysfunction. *Clinical Pharmacy*, 1982, *1*, 141-147.

Carlson, H.E. Gynecomastia. *New England Journal of Medicine*, 1980, *303*, 795-799.

DiRaimondo, C.V., Roach, A.C., & Meador, C.K. Gynecomastia from exposure to vaginal estrogen cream. *New England Journal of Medicine*, 1980, *302*, 1089-1090.

Ellenberg, M. Sexual function in diabetic patients. *Annals of Internal Medicine*, 1980, *92*(2, Pt. 2), 331-333.

Horowitz, J.D., & Goble, A.J. Drugs and impaired male sexual function. *Drugs*, 1979, *18*, 206-217.

Jaffe, L. Sexual problems of the terminally ill. In E.R. Pritchard, J. Collard, J. Starr, J.A. Lockwood, A.H. Kutscher, & I.B. Seeland (Eds.), Home care: Living with dying. New York: Columbia University Press, 1979.

Judzewitsch, Jaspan, Polonsky, Weinberg et al. Aldose reductase inhibition improves nerve conduction velocity in diabetic patients. *New England Journal of Medicine*, 1983, *308*, 119-125.

Kart, C., Metress, E., & Metress, J. Aging and health: Biologic and social perspectives. Menlo Park, Calif.: Addison-Wesley, 1978.

Lemere, F., & Smith, J.W. Alcohol-induced sexual impotence. *American Journal of Psychiatry*, 1973, *130*, 212-213.

Lording, D.W. Impotence: Role of drug and hormonal treatment. *Drugs*, 1978, *15*, 144-150.

Masters, W., & Johnson, V. *Human sexual response*. Boston: Little, Brown, 1966.

Miller, D. Sexual practices and policies in long term care institutions. In R. Solnick (Ed.), *Sexuality and aging*. Los Angeles: University of Southern California Press, 1978.

O'Connor, T.W., & Scavone, J.M. Drug-related sexual dysfunction. *The Apothecary*, 1982, *94*, 20-30.

Papadopoulos, C. Cardiovascular drugs and sexuality. *Archives of Internal Medicine*, 1980, *140*, 1341-1345.

Pearlman, C. Frequency of intercourse in males at different ages. *Medical Aspects of Human Sexuality*, 1972, *6*, 92.

Pfeiffer, E., & Davis, G. Determinants of sexual behavior in middle and old age. *Journal of the American Geriatric Society*, 1972, *20*, 151-158.

Pfeiffer, E. Sexuality in the aging individual. In R. Solnick (Ed.), Sexuality and aging. Los Angeles: University of Southern California Press, 1978.

Pfeiffer, E. (Ed.). *Successful aging*. Durham, N.C.: Duke University Center for Aging and Human Development, 1974.

Renshaw, D.C. Diabetic impotence: A need for further evaluation. *Medical Aspects of Human Sexuality*, 1978, *12*, 19-25.(a)

Renshaw, D.C. Sex and drugs. *South African Medical Journal*, 1978, *54*, 322-326.(b)

Renshaw, D.C. Inflatable penile prosthesis (editorial). *Journal of the American Medical Association*, 1979, *241*, 2637-2638.

Renshaw, D.C. Sexual problems in old age, illness and disability. *Psychosomatics*, 1981, *22*, 975-985.

Rossman, I. Sexuality and aging: An internist's perspective. In R. Solnick (Ed.), *Sexuality and aging*. Los Angeles: University of Southern California Press, 1978.

Scott, F.B., Byrd, G.J., Karacan, I., Olsson, P, Beutler, L.E., & Attia, S.L. Erectile impotence treated with an implantable, inflatable prosthesis. *Journal of the American Medical Association*, 1979, *241*, 2609-2612.

Thorn, G.W. Disturbances of sexual function. In G.W. Thorn, A.A. Adams, E. Braunwald, K.J. Isselbacher, & R.G. Petersdorf, *Principles of internal medicine* (8th ed.). New York: McGraw-Hill, 1977.

Wasow, N., & Loeb, N. Sexuality in nursing homes. In R. Solnick (Ed.), *Sexuality and aging*. Los Angeles: University of Southern California Press, 1978.

Weg, R. The physiology of sexuality in aging. In R. Solnick (Ed.), *Sexuality and aging*. Los Angeles: University of Southern California Press, 1978.

Chapter 10

The Use of Unproven Remedies by the Elderly

In the olden days, charlatans and hucksters drove into towns and out of the back of their wagons sold "snake oil" and other nostrums, potions, and lotions, claiming to cure everything from arthritis to pregnancy! These and other supposed wonder drugs would have been welcomed if they could have accomplished what they had claimed, but unfortunately they could not, and, rather than being true "cures," these "miracle drugs" were more likely to contain "secret ingredients" that consisted only of coloring and molasses with a high alcoholic content, or worse yet they may have contained toxic ingredients. These practices are a far cry from today, where all of the prescription and nonprescription medications that we take are developed under the stringent guidelines of the U.S. Food and Drug Administration (FDA), with the stipulation that all such products are required to demonstrate both safety and efficacy and must be manufactured to meet the strict standards for quality, purity, and strength established by the U.S. Pharmacopeia.

There are pros and cons to the existing regulatory procedures governing the development and marketing of new drug products, and people may complain, perhaps not without justification, that the process is cumbersome, bureaucratic, and tremendously time consuming, since it may take years from the time that a medication is discovered to the time that it becomes available to the patient.

The other side of this argument realizes that although the regulatory process may be cumbersome, it is a necessary function designed to protect the American public by preventing the sale of ineffective or unsafe medications. To appreciate the importance of this function one simply has to reflect on the thalidomide tragedy that caused hundreds of serious birth defects in the late 1950s and early 1960s when this sedative was marketed in Europe but not in the United States.

In spite of the existing regulatory system, however, some medications are available today that have not been shown to be safe and effective and therefore are not approved by the FDA for human use. Some of these unproven remedies are being sold illegally, after either manufacture in the United States, or after being smuggled into this country. Some unproven remedies (e.g., DMSO) are sold legally for nonmedical purposes but used as medicines, and some of them are prescription or nonprescription medications that, although they have been approved for use in humans for specific diseases, are being used to treat diseases for which their use is unapproved. A number of unproven remedies are available in the United States and many reasons, both valid and invalid, exist for their use, but invariably the primary motivation for their use is an attempt to delay or reverse the inevitable cause of disease, the negative results of disease, or the aging process itself.

Since elderly individuals are more likely to be the consumers of these unproven remedies, it is important that persons who work with the elderly be familiar with the more commonly used compounds, what they are used for, and the reasons that people may have for using them. With this knowledge, health professionals will be better prepared to understand this process and communicate with their elderly patients or clients concerning the appropriate or inappropriate use of these unproven remedies.

THEORIES OF AGING

Before I discuss some of the specific unproven remedies that the elderly may use, I would like to review some of the existing theories of why living creatures age and what interventions are being investigated to intervene in this process.

Although many theories attempt to describe the aging process, it is important to note that the process itself is not well understood. Certain visible changes such as wrinkling of the skin, greying of hair, and other physical changes commonly accompany the aging process; however, the actual process that results in these and all of the other changes is still largely a mystery.

None of the existing theories provide us with a completely satisfactory explanation of the aging process, but they do provide some insight into that process, along with how and why it may be occurring and how drug therapy may someday slow down or even stop the process (Hayflick, 1975; Saenz & Danti, 1980; Saxon & Etten, 1978; Shock, 1977). Theories of aging include the following:

- *molecular basis of aging (or error-theory)*. This theory contends that aging may be a result of cumulative molecular errors in the synthesis of DNA and RNA, which are proteins within the nucleus of the body's cells that govern cell replication, and that the rate of occurrence of these errors is genetically controlled.
- *mutation theory*. This theory proposes that the gradual accumulation of mutations in the genetic material of the cell causes impairment or cessation of cellular function, thus leading to aging.

- *cross-linking theory*. Continuous bridging of large molecules such as cellular proteins may cause molecular immobility, resulting in impaired cellular functioning.
- *immunological theory*. The immunological alterations that are associated with aging may lessen the body's resistance to disease and consequently may lead to an autoimmune response whereby the body's defense systems attack the body itself.
- *free radical theory*. Aging may result from the detrimental effects of "free radicals," which are highly reactive fragments of molecules released in energy reactions within the body. It is postulated that these free radicals may cause oxidation reactions in various tissues, thus contributing to the aging process.
- *waste product theory*. This theory postulates that toxic compounds that are byproducts of normal cellular activity accumulate within cells, in time interfering with cellular function.
- *wear and tear theory*. This rather straightforward theory is based on the possibility that the cells, tissues, and organs of the human body may simply "wear out" over time as a result of constant use.
- *stress theory*. In this theory it is proposed that the aging process is a result of an accumulation of the effects of the stresses of living over a period of time.

INTERVENTIONS IN THE AGING PROCESS

The expected life span at birth for males in the United States is 69.5 years, while for females it is 77.2 years. The average expected life span at birth for both sexes has increased dramatically since 1900, when it was 47.3 years. Most of this increase is a result of a decrease in infant mortality, rather than a substantial increase in the oldest age that we might expect to live. Presently, a 65-year-old man can expect to live, on the average, 14.0 additional years to the age of 79, while a 65-year-old woman can expect to live 18.4 more years to age 83. In the year 1900, a 65-year-old man, on the average, lived to age 77, and women of that age could expect to live to age 77 also. While the difference in life expectancy at age 65 is significant, it is not as dramatic as one might expect and it demonstrates that if a person can survive childhood illnesses, their life expectancy today is very similar to that of 80 years ago (U.S. Department of Health and Human Services, 1981).

As we continue to conquer many of the diseases that previously prevented persons from living to old age, it is natural for us to wonder how old should humans be able to live if all diseases were conquered. It may be possible for humans to routinely live 100 years or more, for even today one century of life is attainable, with an estimated 13,000 centenarians presently living in the United States.

It is interesting to wonder what would happen to our life span if one or more of the chronic conditions commonly occurring in the elderly were conquered. What if a cure for hardening of the arteries was discovered? Certain types of heart disease and strokes would largely become diseases mentioned only in history books. How long could we expect to live then? 125 years? 150 years?

As the aging process is studied, it is logical to wonder whether the process itself can be halted, and, if so, how would that goal best be accomplished. Although we do not presently know how to slow down or reverse this process, some possible interventions have been investigated.

Transplanted Immunity

It is known that the immune mechanisms of the body function less efficiently as a person ages, possibly resulting in an increased risk of bacterial or viral infections, and perhaps even an increased risk of cancer. Since certain types of white blood cells (lymphocytes) may be largely responsible for the proper functioning of the body's immune system, it has been postulated that white blood cells could be extracted from human hosts during their teenage years and preserved, only to be reinjected into the same person during old age in an effort to revitalize the individual.

Use of a Drug to Block the Aging Hormone

If, in fact, the aging process is the result of a so-called aging hormone that is produced somewhere in the body, it might then be possible to block the effects of this hormone with a drug developed specifically for that purpose. It must be emphasized that the existence of an aging hormone has not been proven, but it is certainly an interesting possibility.

Biochemical Manipulation

With age, certain biochemical changes have been found to occur in the body. One such change is a documented decrease in the amount of the neurotransmitter acetylcholine (a chemical that is involved in the transmission of electrical impulses through nerves) in the aging brain. It has been postulated that with drug-induced biochemical manipulation of the system regulating the amount of acetylcholine in the brain, this amount could be increased, thereby reversing the memory deficits that are sometimes experienced in old age.

Cryonics

Some individuals who want to extend their lives but suffer from some presently incurable disease are resorting to having their bodies frozen to be thawed out and brought to life at some time in the future when a cure for their disease is available. The obvious drawback of this technique is that it has never been demonstrated to work in humans.

THE IMPACT OF AN EXTENDED LIFE SPAN

It is certainly interesting and exciting to consider the possibility of significantly extending our life spans, maybe even doubling or tripling them, but the mere possibility of such a development provides us with a great deal of food for thought.

Should we be interested in simply extending the length of our lives, or must we also consider the quality of our extended life spans? I doubt that anyone would look forward to a 200-year life span if the last 100 years were to be spent in a nursing home.

Just imagine the profound impact on society in general if we were able to increase significantly our life spans. What would happen to our society if 95 percent of its members were retired? Would the social security system be viable if people paid into it for 45 years and collected from it for 135 years? Would it be fair for people to live and consume resources until age 150 when each year millions of infants in third-world countries die of starvation?

Indeed, if we were ever faced with the possibility of dramatically increasing our life spans we would first be obligated to ask ourselves whether we in fact wanted to, because the ethical, political, economic, and moral issues presented would be unprecedented in the history of civilization. We would have to ask ourselves whether we wanted to live longer lives, or rather, should we simply devote our energies to living our present life span at the highest possible quality.

WHY DO PEOPLE USE UNPROVEN REMEDIES?

The reasons for using unproven remedies are many and may stem from individuals' perceptions of their own health needs, or they may be a result of the influence of others. Elderly persons may resort to using one or more unproven remedies for a variety of reasons, the result of a complex interplay between themselves, the health care system, and the influence of others.

Although some of the reasons for using unproven remedies are the result of inappropriate decisions on the part of the individuals using them, others may be motivated to use these preparations for reasons that are at least based on a rational decision-making process, even though the ultimate decision to use such a preparation may be inappropriate.

Persons choosing to use one or more of these unproven remedies should not be condemned for their decision, but rather an effort should be made to understand why they have made this choice so that we might be better able to appreciate the needs of these individuals.

Health professionals can better appreciate the use of unproven remedies if we first examine a number of the more common reasons why people would choose to use these products.

Belief in the Therapy

Patients may truly believe that the particular therapy that they have chosen to use will effectively manage or cure their disease. Their faith in this therapy may come from the testimony of others who have claimed that they have been cured by these means, or it may have evolved from their personal experience with the preparation (Vigil, 1980).

Confusion or Deception

The individual may be confused or deceived by claims made by promoters of the product. Misleading promotion may result from fanatical supporters of the product who feel that it is their "mission" to "spread the word" about this "wonder drug," or, more likely, false promotion may be an effort to encourage use of a product that could bring handsome profits to the seller or developer of the product.

Although it is true that laws exist in the United States to regulate false advertising claims made about prescription and nonprescription medications, these laws apply to "official" or "approved" medications. Misleading claims for unproven remedies may still be made and spread by word of mouth, or false claims may be made in media publicity, such as newspaper interviews of a person claiming to have discovered a "miracle drug." False claims may also be made in literature originating in other countries, where regulations concerning false advertising may be more lenient than in the United States.

Dislike of Existing Therapy

Patients may fear, or be disillusioned by, currently accepted treatment that has been offered to them. For example, patients who have a tremendous fear of surgery may resort to a remedy that offers them a cure without the need for surgery (Brown, 1975; Isler, 1974; Satchell, 1980).

Search for Youth

Since so much of Western culture glorifies youth and beauty, some persons may choose to use unproven products that claim to be able to reverse or slow down the aging process and the inevitable greying, wrinkling, or balding that many people fear (Hecht, 1980; Sansweet, 1977).

Promise of Cure

When a physician can no longer offer a patient any new therapeutic modalities in the treatment or management of a disease some patients may turn to anyone who can "promise" such a cure, even though the promise may be false (O'Neill, 1979).

Search for a "Last Resort" Cure

If patients have a disease that has not responded to the traditional and approved therapy offered by the medical community, they may resort to an unapproved remedy as a "last resort," with the attitude that they have nothing to lose.

Dissatisfaction with Regulating Agencies

Patients may feel that the FDA is "too slow" in approving a potentially lifesaving drug and is purposely withholding a valuable therapeutic agent from the American public; therefore, they may choose to use a product that has not yet been approved.

Distrust of the Health Care System

Patients may believe that physicians are against the approval of a particular new drug because it is such an effective "miracle cure" that the medical community will lose much "business " from their patients who no longer need the care of a physician.

Some patients may also think that pharmaceutical manufacturers are opposed to the approval of a new "miracle cure" because an exclusive patent and high profits cannot be obtained for the product, as is the case with DMSO or that the "wonder drug" will put pharmaceutical companies out of business by curing all diseases and eliminating the need for other medications.

I do not believe that these particular views are widely held, yet I have seen such instances in which it seemed that certain individuals honestly thought that such a collusion actually exists. I am confident that if such miracle drugs were discovered, pharmaceutical manufacturers would rush to get the drug approved for use in humans because of the tremendous profits that such a product would garner.

Dissatisfaction with the Traditional Health Care System

Some individuals may be disappointed with the "cold and clinical" atmosphere that is frequently associated with modern medicine, big hospitals, and busy physicians. This dissatisfaction may prompt the consumer to search for care that has an "active, personalized . . . home-based alternative" (Cassileth, 1982, p. 1483), as is characteristic of some of the providers of unproven remedies.

This complaint may in many instances be valid, but as providers of health care we must remain compassionate, exhibiting empathy toward patients so that we do not drive them away from proper care into the waiting arms of a huckster.

Trust in Credentials of Provider

It may be difficult for some patients to treat a "trusted" individual with skepticism, such as a person with the title of "Doctor," which of course may be unearned, or even someone with an M.D. degree; yet there are "hucksters" and "con artists" who may be medical doctors, or other types of doctors, making outlandish and unfounded claims regarding particular unproven remedies (Swanbrow, 1980).

Trust in Testimonials of Users

Actors and other famous personalities may endorse "quack" cures that they themselves believe in, thus unfairly influencing the opinions of their "fans" who may have great respect for the viewpoints of these famous personalities (Isler, 1974).

Ignorance or Gullibility

Some persons are not able to detect the difference between a qualified health professional and a "quack" who puts on a white coat and adopts the title "Doctor" (Brown, 1975).

Search for a "Miracle"

Some persons may seek a "miracle cure" for their health problems without first considering approved and recognized therapies (Brown, 1975).

Impatience

Some individuals may lack the patience to wait for the results of long-term therapy and may therefore resort to the use of remedies promising quick results (Brown, 1975).

Effectiveness of Unproven Therapy Observed

The patient may have had contact with, or heard about, an individual who responded successfully to a particular unproven remedy.

Some individuals may indeed respond to unproven remedies when used in certain conditions due to the actual effectiveness of the unproven remedy or to their response to the drug's placebo effect. In some conditions, such as headache, placebos, which are medications that contain no active ingredients, may evoke a positive response in 30 to 60 percent of the persons using them (Vogel, Goodwin, & Goodwin, 1980). Although the placebo effect is poorly understood, many health professionals will agree that the mind has a tremendous potential effect in the management and cure of numerous conditions, including many diseases that result in actual physical problems, not just figments of one's imagination.

WHAT ARE UNPROVEN REMEDIES TREATING?

Unproven remedies may be used by persons of all ages, but most of the more commonly encountered ones purport some benefit in one or more conditions associated either with old age or the aging process. The following is a description of some of these "conditions" that may be present in the elderly. After each condition there is a listing of specific unproven remedies that may be used in the treatment or management of that condition. Some of the more commonly used "remedies" listed are described in more detail later in this chapter.

Cancer

A large number of unproven methods used to supposedly detect or cure cancer have been advocated in recent years. These products or devices tend to experience a brief popularity and then fall into obscurity. The American Cancer Society has a listing of more than 60 "treatments," "diagnostic methods," and "devices" that at one time have been advocated or used in an attempt to prevent, treat, or cure cancer. A few of these are listed below. More detailed information on these and other methods can be obtained from the American Cancer Society ("Unproven Methods," 1979).

- Contreras methods
- Dotto Electronic Reactor
- fresh cell therapy
- Issels combination therapy
- Kelley Malignancy Index and ecology therapy
- laetrile
- orgone energy devices
- ultraviolet blood irradiation intravenous treatment

Old Age

Some treatments are alleged to be able to restore youthfulness to aging individuals. These compounds include

- gerovital (GH-3) (Arriola & Shimomura, 1978; Kent, 1982; Saenz & Danti, 1980)
- KH-3 (Kent, 1982)
- pangamic acid
- vitamin E
- fresh cell theory
- hormones

Arthritis

Arthritis most frequently occurs in the elderly as osteoarthritis, which generally results from wear and tear on the major joints, and also as rheumatoid arthritis, which is usually a more crippling and painful type of degenerative arthritis resulting from an autoimmune phenomenon occurring within the body, where for some reason the body reacts against its own tissue.

It must be realized that arthritis, especially the rheumatoid form, can be a painful and debilitating disease and that patients suffering from severe arthritis are frequently willing to resort to unproven remedies for some relief of their condition.

Two unproven agents that have been used are (1) DMSO (DMSO: New Hope for Arthritis?, 1980; Kastrup, 1980; DMSO Update, 1982); and (2) Gerovital (Arriola & Shimomura, 1978; Hecht, 1980; Ostfeld, Smith, & Stotsky, 1977; Saenz & Danti, 1980).

I have also seen patients who have spent large sums of money to visit arthritis clinics in Mexico with the hope of obtaining some type of therapy, or ideally cure, that was being withheld from them in the United States. To date I am unimpressed that these clinics offer anything but false hope and medication that can be obtained in the United States, the main difference being that at the Mexican clinics the patients are not told what medications they are being given, even though they are usually prescription drugs that are commonly available in the United States, and the patients end up paying a lot more for these drugs than they would have at their neighborhood pharmacy.

Cardiovascular Disease

Various types of cardiovascular diseases have been "treated" with unproven remedies, including the following:

- chelation therapy with EDTA (Swanbrow, 1980; Walker, 1980)
- gerovital (Arriola & Shimomura, 1978; Hecht, 1980; Ostfeld, Smith, & Stotsky, 1977; Saenz & Danti, 1980)
- pangamic acid (EDTA Chelation Therapy, 1978; Saenz & Danti, 1980)
- vitamin E (Editors of *Consumer Reports*, 1980; Lamy, 1980; Weg, 1978)

Memory Loss

The memory loss that is sometimes associated with aging has been "treated" with gerovital or the zen macrobiotic diet (available from the American Cancer Society).

Baldness

An expert advisory panel of the FDA has reported that the products available that supposedly stimulate hair growth or prevent baldness are ineffective. Preparations that have been used are listed below (MacCoy, 1979):

- gerovital
- ascorbic acid
- benzoic acid
- estradiol
- lanolin
- tetracaine
- wheat germ oil (for vitamin E and thiamine)

Sexual Impotence or Frigidity

Numerous "sexual stimulants" have been recommended by various proponents. Three include gerovital, the zen macrobiotic diet, and vitamin E, and more are discussed in Chapter 9.

COMMON UNPROVEN REMEDIES

Although numerous unproven "remedies" are presently available or have been popularized over the years, the names of a few have become quite familiar to many. Some of the more sensational "tabloid" publications frequently print stories alluding to the discovery of wonder "cures" for arthritis, cancer, and other maladies. Occasionally some of these unproven remedies will receive a significant amount of publicity in the more legitimate media, such as newspapers or radio, when they are embroiled in some sort of controversy, such as a debate as to whether or not they are effective or whether they should be approved by the FDA and subsequently made available for public use. The preparations laetrile and DMSO have recently received such attention, making them almost household words.

A general familiarity with some of the more commonly used unproven remedies can be helpful to anyone working closely with the elderly, since the reader may know an elderly individual who is looking for advice or information concerning one or more of these compounds. Also a familiarity with some of these preparations will help the reader to understand some of the many ramifications involved with the use of these products.

Gerovital

Dr. Anna Aslan, a Romanian physician, first experimented with gerovital (also called gerovital H-3 or GH-3) in 1949, and by 1956 she was publishing astonishing results from the gerovital treatments that she had given to her patients. In addition to retarding the aging process, it was claimed that gerovital could treat many of the afflictions that occur with increasing frequency in the elderly population, such as depression, baldness, hypertension, arthritis, ulcers, memory loss, sexual impotence and frigidity, diminishing skin and muscle tone, and arteriosclerosis.

Gerovital contains procaine hydrochloride, which is the active compound of the local anesthetic Novocaine®, in a buffered solution. It also contains minute amounts of the preservative benzoic acid and also potassium metabisulfite and disodium phosphate. Dr. Aslan claims that these additional ingredients are important, particularly the benzoic acid, because they inhibit the breakdown of procaine to its metabolites, thereby prolonging and increasing the drug's activity (Kent, 1982).

Although it would be nice to have such a medication available for our use, it appears that claims for the effectiveness of gerovital are unsubstantiated.

KH-3

KH-3 was developed in the 1960s in West Germany as an alternative to gerovital. It is supposedly effective as an antiaging drug. It differs from gerovital by the type of additives it contains, which include magnesium carbonate, sodium hydrogen phosphate, potassium chloride, magnesium hydrogen phosphate, and hematoporphyrin. As with gerovital, these additives are included to enhance the biological activity of the "active" ingredient, procaine (Kent, 1982). KH-3 is available in many countries; however, as with gerovital, its effectiveness is unconvincing.

Laetrile

Laetrile is actually the chemical amygdalin, which is produced from ground, defatted apricot kernels and concentrations of peach pits. It has also been referred to as vitamin B_{17} or Apikern and was discovered in 1920 by Dr. Ernst Krebs, Sr., during an attempt to develop a compound that would improve the flavor of bootleg whiskey. After the compound was supposedly purified by Krebs' son, Ernst Krebs, Jr., they both advocated the use of the substance as an effective treatment for cancer. Amygdalin was registered with the U.S. Patent Office in 1952, under the trade name of Laetrile, by Ernst Krebs, Jr.

Proponents of laetrile have claimed that the compound can both help prevent and cure cancer when it is used as a dietary supplement.

Krebs theorized that laetrile is effective because it contains the poison cyanide, which is released from the laetrile by an enzyme unique to cancer cells, therefore selectively killing the cancer cell. The theory continues that normal cells possess a different enzyme system that detoxifies the cyanide.

In the middle and late 1970s many of laetrile's proponents professed strong faith in the drug's effectiveness as an anticancer remedy; however, documentation of the drug's supposed effectiveness was largely anecdotal in a small number of cases.

Since that time, well-controlled scientific studies have determined that laetrile has no anticancer properties and is ineffective in the treatment of cancer (Brody, 1975).

A well-controlled clinical trial of laetrile was performed at the Mayo Clinic and three other facilities, with the results being published in the prestigious *New England Journal of Medicine* (Moertel, Fleming, Rubin, Kvols et al., 1982). The study consisted of 178 patients with cancer who received as therapy, laetrile and concurrent "metabolic therapy" consisting of diet, enzymes, and vitamins. The laetrile doses and the concurrent "metabolic therapy" were used precisely as advocated by the foremost laetrile practitioners in an effort to duplicate the laetrile therapy that cancer patients are given.

Of the 178 eligible patients who entered the study before May 1981, 152 (85 percent) had died by January 1982. The median length of survival for all patients was 4.8 months from the start of laetrile therapy (Table 10-1). In addition, several of the patients experienced symptoms of cyanide toxicity as a result of the laetrile therapy. The conclusion of this study is that laetrile is a toxic drug that is not effective as a cancer treatment.

It seems very ironic that this drug, which for years was suspected by many to be ineffective, and whose ineffectiveness is now documented, has been legalized in many states, largely as a result of compassionate, but misguided pressure on state legislators to make this "cancer remedy" available to the people of their state (Editors of *Consumer Reports,* 1980). To me, this irony represents the crucial

Table 10-1 Cancer Patient Survival Measured from the Start of Laetrile Therapy (178 Patients)

Months after start of treatment	Approximate percent of patients surviving
0	100
3	66
6	42
9	22
12	17
15	13
18	5

Source: Adapted from "A Clinical Trial of Amygdalin (Laetrile) in the Treatment of Human Cancer," by C.G. Moertel, T.R. Fleming, J. Rubin, L. Kvols et al. Reprinted by permission of the *New England Journal of Medicine*, Vol. 306, pp. 201-206, 1982.

issue concerning the use of unproven remedies by the elderly or others who suffer from uncurable or painful diseases or who are ready to grasp at any treatment that promises them hope, false or otherwise.

The following quotation by Dr. Barrie Cassileth (1982) of the University of Pennsylvania Cancer Center eloquently sums up the reasons why public support for such ineffective therapy exists.

> Patients with cancer face an invisible disease. Standard treatment regimens are similarly mysterious. Both the disease and its traditional treatment are frustratingly beyond the patient's own control. There is something to be learned from the seductive draw of alternative remedies. We may not wish to recommend wheatgrass therapy or spiritual healing in lieu of chemotherapy, but we might well consider the merits of a patient's need for involvement in their own case, their interest in helping themselves through attention to diet, their requirements for personalized attention to the self as opposed to the disease, and their needs for expiation, pardon, or explanation for their presumed role in allowing this illness to descend. (pp. 1483-1484)*

Krebiozen

Krebiozen is a drug that was originally produced by a Yugoslavian physician and was brought to the United States in 1949.

*Reprinted by permission of the *New England Journal of Medicine*, 1982, 306:24, 1483-1484.

Although thoughts of using krebiozen as an anticancer drug have essentially disappeared, the chronology of the rise and subsequent fall of the drug's popularity are extremely interesting in their similarity to that of laetrile.

Shortly after the drug was brought to the United States it was touted as a wonder drug that could cure cancer. Anecdotal case reports were publicized of people who were supposedly cured of their cancer through the use of krebiozen, and its proponents claimed that the FDA was purposely keeping their "wonder drug" away from the American public. Finally, scientific studies were performed, revealing that krebiozen lacked any anticancer effect. Actual samples of krebiozen analyzed in the United States were found to contain only mineral oil and sometimes traces of amyl alcohol and 1-methyl hydantoin (Council on Pharmacy, 1951; Szujewski, 1952).

This course of events is similar to that of laetrile in that a supposed "wonder drug" was discovered and assumed to be a new cure for cancer until proper scientific studies were performed, only to reveal that, unfortunately, the drug had no anticancer effect at all (Isler, 1974).

Pangamic Acid

In 1943, Ernst Krebs applied for a patent on this substance, which was also commonly referred to as vitamin B_{15} (Bylinski, 1976). Pangamic acid is extracted from apricot pits, and as such it appears that no such standardized chemical exists because the substance is a varied mixture of sodium (or sometimes calcium) gluconate, glycine, and diisopropylamine dichloroacetate.

Claims made concerning pangamic acid have been optimistic to say the least. It has been advocated as a panacea cure for diabetes, cancer, heart disease, hypertension, aging, senility, alcoholism, and schizophrenia. No scientific evidence exists concerning the safety or effectiveness of pangamic acid in the prevention or treatment of any human ailment (Saenz & Danti, 1980).

DMSO

DMSO is the acronym for the chemical compound dimethylsulfoxide, which was first discovered in 1866 by Alexander Saytzeff. The compound has been used for industrial purposes as a solvent and chemical reagent, and it has rather widespread popularity in veterinary medicine, in which it is used to reduce pain and inflammation in the legs of horses.

The potential for the use of DMSO as a therapeutic agent was first suggested in the 1950s by Dr. Stanley Jacob and Robert Herschler.

The compound is thought by some to hold significant promise in the treatment of a variety of musculoskeletal disorders such as arthritis and other types of muscle and joint pain and has also been proposed for use as a carrier to enhance drug absorption through the skin, since it penetrates the skin quite readily.

The reported pharmacological activity of DMSO is considerable and supposedly includes the following:

- the ability to freely penetrate cellular membranes
- antiinflammatory activity
- the ability to dissolve collagen, a protein that is found in the body
- the ability to block peripheral nerves, thus possibly causing local anesthesia (pain relief)
- the ability to dilate blood vessels
- a weak antibacterial and antifungal activity
- the ability to relax muscles (DMSO Update, 1982; Kastrup, 1980; Schultz, 1976)

When a small amount of DMSO is applied to an area of skin, such as a hand or leg, a characteristic "garliclike" odor will be present on the breath within seconds, reflecting the extremely rapid penetration through the skin and distribution throughout the body.

Although DMSO must still be classified as an "unproven remedy," I believe that its use must be looked at in a somewhat different perspective than the use of gerovital, laetrile, or krebiozen, since it does have demonstrated effectiveness in animals and does have approval by the FDA for use in humans in the treatment of interstitial cystitis, an inflammatory condition of the urinary bladder. Additionally, it does penetrate the skin very quickly, raising the possibility that it could be used to enhance drug absorption through the skin.

The fact that DMSO has many satisfied users was underscored dramatically during the DMSO hearings held by the U.S. House of Representatives Select Committee on Aging in March 1980. This published report (DMSO: New Hope for Arthritis?, 1982) includes very convincing testimony and dozens of letters supporting DMSO's therapeutic effectiveness. One of the points that is brought out is the fact that because DMSO is already a commercially available product it would not be possible for a pharmaceutical manufacturer to obtain an exclusive patent for the sale of the drug. Another related point is the fact that the compound is very inexpensive to manufacture. These two considerations indicate that no financial incentive exists for pharmaceutical companies to sell the drug, and in fact some individuals feel that pharmaceutical manufacturers would prefer that the drug not be approved because it would present stiff competition for the drugs, such as arthritis medications, on which manufacturers already hold patents.

Another unique aspect of DMSO is that it can be purchased without a prescription in many states. This is possible because, although the compound cannot be sold for human use, it can be, and is, sold for use as a "solvent." DMSO is frequently available in some gasoline service stations, health stores, and even some pharmacies, although the sale of nonprescription DMSO has been condemned by the American Pharmaceutical Association ("A.Ph.A. Policy," 1981).

Obviously, when this chemical is sold to someone for use as a solvent, there is nothing to prevent that person from using it as a medicine. However, some major potential problems are associated with that practice, primarily because of the absence of the strict labeling requirements and quality control standards that apply to medications designed for human consumption. Therefore, when DMSO intended for commercial or industrial use is purchased for medicinal purposes, there is no guarantee that the quality or strength of the product is of sufficiently high standards for human consumption. In addition, the purity of the DMSO that has not specifically been prepared for use in humans is not guaranteed, which is an especially important consideration in light of the possibility that any impurities may actually be carried into the bloodstream with the drug as it penetrates the skin.

DMSO has been used investigationally to treat a variety of disorders, including arthritis and muscle pain, but conclusive evidence of the effectiveness of the drug, especially in the long-term treatment of rheumatic disease has not been established. Some concern has been raised concerning DMSO's potential for causing cataracts; however, the available data on its toxicity overwhelmingly suggest that it is a safe substance with no major toxic effects (Schultz, 1976).

Vitamin E

Vitamin E, also called tocopherol, was first synthesized in 1938 and is currently used therapeutically to correct various anemias that result from its deficiency. Vitamin E deficiency, however, is rare, owing to its abundance in normal diets in foods including meat, poultry, eggs, cereal grains, fruits, and vegetables.

In spite of the fact that vitamin E is a nonprescription vitamin it can still be considered to be an unproven remedy because it has been suggested for unproven uses as a chemical that can delay or prevent the process of aging, in addition to being used to treat diabetes, heart disease, infertility, ulcers, and warts (Editors of *Consumer Reports,* 1980; Lamy, 1980).

It is theorized that the antioxidant activity of vitamin E limits or inhibits the synthesis of free radicals in the body, thereby reducing their age-accelerating effect (Lamy, 1980; Weg, 1978).

Some questionable evidence exists that vitamin E may provide some protection from the effects of air pollution; however, it appears unlikely that vitamin E, even in massive doses, would have an appreciable effect on the aging process. Clinical trials have also failed to demonstrate any benefits of vitamin E for miscarriages, sterility, menopausal disturbances, muscular dystrophies, cystic fibrosis, blood disorders, leg ulcers, diabetes, and a variety of cardiovascular diseases.

Fortunately, vitamin E is usually nontoxic, but large doses (more than 300 units daily) have rarely caused minor problems including nausea, diarrhea, intestinal cramps, weakness, and headaches.

EDTA

EDTA (ethylenediaminetetraacetic acid) is another prescription drug that has a dual role, one for an approved medical reason and one for an unapproved use. The drug has been used since prior to 1960 in the treatment of lead poisoning. When injected, it forms a soluble complex with the otherwise only slightly soluble lead, which can then be excreted through the kidneys.

The unapproved use of this drug lies in its purported use to reverse hardening of the arteries. The drug has been used for this purpose in the United States since 1948, and although it is not approved for treatment of atherosclerosis approximately 1,000 U.S. physicians offer this intravenous therapy (Walker, 1980).

The use of EDTA for this purpose is called chelation therapy because EDTA binds, or chelates, certain metal ions in the body, including calcium, which, according to proponents of chelation therapy, is then removed from the plaques that have been deposited on the inside of blood vessels in patients with atherosclerosis. Supposedly this will result in the breakup and reduction or removal of these plaques from the body, leading to a greater degree of elasticity in the arteries that had previously developed these plaques and become "hardened." Consequently, it is postulated that blood flow will improve through these arteries, thus relieving the symptoms of poor circulation.

Chelation therapy is not without its problems, however, largely due to the inherent toxicity of EDTA, which has resulted in serious kidney damage and even death.

Some scientific studies have been performed to assess the effectiveness of chelation therapy, indicating some potential benefit, but the studies did not use control patients to compare the possible beneficial effect of the drug with the response of patients who had not received the drug.

After a review of the research performed to evaluate the effectiveness of chelation therapy with EDTA, *The Medical Letter* has concluded that no acceptable evidence exists to indicate its effectiveness in the treatment of atherosclerosis and cautions that the drug's effects may be lethal (EDTA Chelation Therapy, 1981).

DANGERS OF UNPROVEN REMEDIES

Several drawbacks to the use of unproven remedies should be recognized by both health professionals and persons who are considering the use of such therapy.

Inappropriate Therapy

When individuals decide to use an unproven remedy they are taking a chance that they will not receive the most appropriate therapy for their disease (O'Neill, 1979). Some extremely serious and dreaded diseases, including cancer, can be treated or even cured through proper treatment, which may include drug therapy, irradiation, surgery, or perhaps even a combination of all three. In the case of cancer, the use of an unproven and ineffective "remedy" may very well mean the difference between life and death by depriving the patient of effective treatment.

Financial Expense

The financial expenditures for unproven remedies can be considerable. For example, in 1974 it was estimated that Americans spent $2 to $3 billion a year on fraudulent cancer quackery alone (Isler, 1974).

Not only might the particular therapy be expensive by itself, but expenses that are associated with such therapies, such as a trip to Romania to receive gerovital therapy or travel to Mexico to visit an arthritis clinic, can be considerable. Certainly, some individuals can afford the luxury of traveling to a foreign country to receive treatments that are unavailable to them in the United States; however, the economic considerations may have tragic implications when significant portions of one's life savings are squandered on unnecessary and ineffective therapy that is not affordable in the first place.

Toxicity

In an attempt to receive the supposed therapeutic benefit of an unproven remedy, patients may place themselves at risk of experiencing the toxicity associated with that therapy. Although some of the unproven remedies that persons use may simply be inactive and nontoxic sugar pills or colored water, others are strong chemical compounds that possess a significant potential for toxicity.

Drug Misrepresentation

Another significant problem associated with the use of unproven remedies is that the patient may be unaware of the actual content of "secret ingredients." These unknown ingredients could be potentially toxic to the patient through their inherent toxicity or as the result of a possible allergic reaction or interaction with another medication or nutrient that the patient might be consuming.

Although it may be argued that the elderly, or any citizen for that matter, should have the right to use whatever unproven remedies they care to, it is the responsibility of health professionals and others who work with the elderly to see to it that the use of these compounds does not harm the patient, through toxicity, financial disaster, or prevention of the patient from receiving appropriate therapy.

REFERENCES

A.Ph.A. policy on DMSO draws praise from FDA. *APHArmacy Weekly,* 1981, *20*(15), 61.

Arriola, E., & Shimomura, S. Gerovital as a rejuvenator or snake oil. *Drug Intelligence and Clinical Pharmacy,* 1978, *12,* 42-43.

Brody, J.E. Four cancer centers find lack of proof of any medical value in banned drug. *The New York Times,* July 21, 1975.

Brown, H. Cancer quackery: What can you do about it? *Nursing 75,* 1975, *5*(5), 24-26.

Bylinski, G. Science is on the trail of the fountain of youth. *Fortune,* July 1976, pp. 54-59.

Cassileth, B.R. After laetrile, what? *New England Journal of Medicine,* 1982, *306,* 1482-1484.

Council on Pharmacy and Chemistry. A status report on "Krebiozen." *Journal of the American Medical Association,* 1951, *147,* 864-873.

DMSO: New Hope for Arthritis? Hearing before the Select Committee On Aging, House of Representatives (Committee Publication No. 96-232). Washington, D.C.: U.S. Government Printing Office, 1980.

DMSO Update. *Senior Health News,* 1982, *4*(3), 1-2.

Editors of *Consumer Reports.* Laetrile: The political success of a scientific failure. In *Health quackery.* New York: Holt, Rinehart & Winston, 1980.

Editors of *Consumer Reports.* The vitamin E cure-all. In *Health quackery.* New York: Holt, Rinehart & Winston, 1980.

EDTA chelation therapy for arteriosclerotic heart disease. *Medical Letter,* 1981, *23*(11), 51.

Hayflick, L. Current theories of biological aging. *Federation Proceedings,* 1975, *34*(1), 9-13.

Hecht, A. Time marches on despite Gerovital. *FDA Consumer,* March 1980, pp. 16-19.

Isler, C. The fatal choice: Cancer quackery. *RN,* September 1974.

Kastrup, E.K. (Ed.). Dimethyl sulfoxide (DMSO)—renewed interest in old "wonder drug." In *Facts and Comparisons.* St. Louis: Facts and Comparisons, June 1980, p. 774.

Kent, S. The procaine "youth" drugs. *Geriatrics,* 1982, *37*(4), 32-36.

Lamy, P.P. Can aging be decelerated? In P.P. Lamy (Ed.), *Prescribing for the elderly.* Littleton, Mass.: Publishing Sciences Group, 1980.

MacCoy, B. Preventive medicine. *Senior Citizen News,* November 1979, p. 11.

Moertel, C.G., Fleming, T.R., Rubin, J., Kvols, L. et al. A clinical trial of amygdalin (Laetrile) in the treatment of human cancer. *New England Journal of Medicine,* 1982, *306,* 201-206.

O'Neill, T.P., III. Health quackery. In L.L. Sanders (Ed.), *The consumers tribune: Target the elderly.* Boston: Consumer Affairs Foundation, 1979.

Ostfeld, A., Smith, C.M., & Stotsky, B.A. The systemic use of procaine in the treatment of the elderly: A review. *Journal of the American Geriatric Society,* 1977, *25,* 1-19.

Saenz, R.V., & Danti, A.V. Pharmacological intervention of the aging process. *Pharm Index,* 1980, *22*(8), 11-16.

Sansweet, S.J. Gerovital approved by Nevada, is hailed as rejuvenator and assailed as snake oil. *Wall Street Journal,* June 2, 1977, p. 8.

Satchell, M. Mexico's "miracle" cures. *Parade*, April 1980, *20*, 4-5.

Saxon, S.V., & Etten, M.J. Theories of aging. In S.V. Saxon & M.J. Etten (Eds.), *Physical change and aging*. New York: Tiresias Press, 1978.

Schultz, H.W. DMSO. *Pharm Index*, 1976, *18*(3).

Shock, N.W. Biological theories of aging. In J.E. Birren, & K.W. Schaie (Eds.), *Handbook of the psychology of aging*. New York: Van Nostrand Reinhold, 1977.

Swanbrow, D. Is there a doctor on the air? *New West*, February 25, 1980, *25*, 35-42.

Szujewski, H.A. "Krebiozen" in treatment of cancer: Comparison with other therapy as determined by enzyme analysis. *Journal of the American Medical Association*, 1952, *148*, 929-933.

United States Department of Health and Human Services. *Health United States 1981*, DHHS Publication No. (PHS) 82-1232. Hyattsville, MD, December 1981 (U.S. GPO, 1982).

Unproven methods of cancer management. New York: American Cancer Society, 1979.

Vigil, A.A. Folk medicine: Healing with the power of the human mind. *Generations*, 1980, *5*(2), 29.

Vogel, A.V., Goodwin, J.S., & Goodwin, J.M. The therapeutics of placebo. *American Family Physician*, 1980, *22*(1), 105-109.

Walker, M. *Chelation therapy: How to prevent or reverse hardening of the arteries*. Atlanta: 76 Press, 1980.

Weg, R.B. Vitamin E, tocopherols and tocotrienols. In R.B. Weg (Ed.), *Nutrition and the later years*. Los Angeles: University of Southern California Press, 1978.

Index

A

Absorption
  changes in, 111-114
  of drugs, 106
Abuse. *See* Drug abuse
Acetaminophen, 22, 133, 141, 152
Achromycin V, 48
Addiction
  See also Alcohol
  knowledge of, 205
  and sexual dysfunction, 198
Adverse reaction. *See* Drug reactions
Advertising
  by brand name, 50-51
  consumer-oriented, 30
  and consumption, 7
  influence on physicians, 23
Aging, 2, 24
  National Institute on, 125
  and pharmacokinetic changes,
    110-120
  sexual response and, 187-189
  theories of, 210
  unproven cures for, 218
  U.S. House of Representatives
    Selected Committee on, 224
Air pollution, 225
Albumin, 116
  and drug interactions, 173

Alcohol
  and drug interactions, 68, 175
  and sexual problems, 194-195, 198
Aldactone, 192
Aldomet, 133, 137, 192, 197
Allergies
  to medication, 126
  and patient profile, 157
Aluminum hydroxide, 134, 145-146
American Cancer Society, 217
American Pharmaceutical Association,
  225
Amitriptyline, 134, 142-143, 149,
  192, 197-198
Amphetamines, 198
Ampicillin, 54, 56, 148, 174
Amygdalin, 217, 221-222
Analgesics, 20, 22, 134
  and constipation, 152
  narcotic, 133, 141
  risks of, 145
Angina, 190-191
Anorexia, 149-150
Antabuse, 174
Antacids, 20, 22, 134, 145-146, 152
Antianxiety drugs, 22, 133, 142
Antibiotics, 120
  dosing chart for, 121
  and drug interactions, 174
  and nutrient interactions, 176-180
Anticholinergic drugs, 133, 141, 193,
  198

Anticoagulants, 85, 116-117, 132-133, 138-139
Antidepressants, 142-143, 148-149, 152
   and sexual dysfunction, 192, 198
Antigout drugs, 174
Antihistamines
   effects of, 126
   and sexual dysfunction, 192
Antihypertensives
   See also Hypertension
   and sexual problems, 199
Antinuclear drugs, 52, 133, 140-141, 149, 154
   drug interactions with, 170-171
Antioxidants, 225-226
Antiparkinson drugs, 193, 198
Antipsychotics, 134, 143-144
   risks of, 148, 175, 197-198
Antispasmodics, 152
Antiulcer drugs, 193
Aphrodisiacs, 203-204
Apikern, 217, 221-222
Apresoline, 192
Artane, 193
Arthritis
   drugs for, 17-18, 21-22, 133, 138
   and DSMO, 223-225
   and sexual activity, 191-194
   unproven remedies for, 218
Aspirin, 134
   and arthritis, 18
   risks of, 145
   and strokes, 20
Assessment, of patients, 130-132
Ataxia, 151
Atherosclerosis. See Heart disease
Atropine, 133, 141, 198
Attitudes
   of patients, 27-28, 213-217
   of physicians, 24, 204-206

B

Baldness, 219

Barbituates
   reaction to, 151
   and sexual dysfunction, 198
Belladonna alkaloids, 22, 133, 141, 193
Benadryl, 126-127, 192
Benemid, 174
Benztropine, 175, 193, 198
Beta blockers, 191
Bioavailability, 45, 106
   alterations in, 55
Biochemistry, of aging, 212
Biotransformation, 107
Boston Collaborative Drug Surveillance Program, 129
Brand names, 22, 44
   See also Medications
   appearance of, 86
   and new prescriptions, 48
   patent protection for, 50-52
Bronchodilators, 118-119, 133, 140
Butazolidin, 116, 133, 138, 173

C

Calcium carbonate, 134, 145-146
Calcium channel blockers, 191
Calendars, for drug therapy, 86
Cancer
   and Krebiozen, 222-223
   and Laetrile, 221-222
   medications for, 202, 217, 221-223
   unproved cures for, 217
   uterine, 202
Cardiac disease. See Heart disease
Cardizem 191
Care. See Health care
Catapres, 19, 21, 192, 197
Cerebrovascular accident (CVA). See Strokes
Chelation therapy, 219, 226
Chemical names, of drugs, 44
Child-proof closures, 79-80
Chlordiazepoxide hydrochloride, 44
Chlorothiazide, 133, 135-137

Chlorpheniramine, 22, 192
Chlorpromazine, 134, 143-144, 149, 154, 175, 192
Chlorpropamide, 18, 21
Chlorthalidone, 192
Chlor-Trimeton, 22, 192
Chloral hydrate, 26-27
Cimetidine, 52, 133, 140-141, 149, 154, 170-171, 193
Clearance, of drugs, 107
Clinoral, 22
Clonidine, 19, 21, 192, 197
Codeine, 133, 141
    and constipation, 152
    in Tylenol, 32
Cogentin, 175, 193, 198
Communication, with patients, 96-98
Compliance, to drug therapy, 65-80
Confusion, in patients, 148-149
Constipation, 152
Consumers
    See also Patients
    and drug costs, 52-53
    education of, 60-61, 74, 77, 80
    and generic drugs, 43-44, 46-50, 57
    references for, 101-104
    U.S. Bureau of Consumer Protection, 53
Corgard, 192
Corticosteroids, 18, 21, 133, 139-140
Costs
    of drug compliance, 73
    of generic drugs, 52, 60-61
    of health care, 7-11, 29
    of polypharmacy, 35
    of prescription drugs, 47
Coumadin, 85, 116-117, 132-133, 138-139, 170-177, 179
Creatine clearance, 120
Cryonics, 212-213
CVA. *See* Strokes
Cystitis, 224

D

Dalmane, 133, 142, 151, 156
Deltasone, 133, 139-140
Demerol, 116
Depression
    See also Antidepressants
    as drug reaction, 149-150
Dexedrine, 198
Diabetes, 18
    drugs for, 21, 189
Diabinese, 18, 21
Diagnosis
    and drug therapy, 159
    and polypharmacy, 36
Diarrhea, 152
Diazepam, 22, 133, 142, 151
Dietitians
    and drug interactions, 182-183
    role in drug therapy, 163
Digitalis compounds, 17
Digoxin, 22, 37, 55, 66, 113, 120, 132-135, 149-150, 168, 170, 173, 180, 193
Dilantin, 55
Diltiazem, 191
Diphenhydramine, 126-127, 192
Dipyridamole, 20-21
Discharge rates, by age, 9
Disease
    age as, 24, 211-212
    and drug consumption, 15, 21
    and sexuality, 189-196
Disopyramide, 193
Disulfiram, 174
Diuretics, 17, 59, 66
    adverse reactions to, 132, 135-137
    and hypertension, 19, 21
    and sex, 191-192
    weakness reaction of, 150-151
Diuril, 133, 135-137
DMSO
    as therapeutic agent, 223
    as unproven remedy, 215, 218, 220
Donnatal, 22, 133, 141, 193

Dosage
    and aging, 105-122
    forms of, 72-73
    inappropriate, 34-39
    loading, 108
    maintenance, 108
    overdoses, 23-24, 126-127
    patient education in, 85-87
    role of nurse in, 159
Doxepin, 192
Drowsiness, 151
Drug absorption. *See* Absorption
Drug abuse, 23-24, 198
    See also Addiction
Drug-alcohol interactions, 175
Drug distribution, 173
Drug metabolism, 117-118
Drug reactions, 33, 38-39
    See also Drug interactions
    adverse, 34-35, 38, 72, 89,
        125-164
    allergies and, 126, 157
    in the elderly, 110-122, 167-180
    monitoring of, 148-152
    and noncompliance, 66-68
    patient reporting of, 94
Drug therapy
    and aging, 105-122
    patient's compliance with, 65-80
    and patient education, 83-104
    polypharmacy reactions of, 147
    review of, 37-39, 130-132,
        157-163, 205
    sexual implications of, 185-206
Drugs. *See* Medications
Dyrenium, 22

E

Economics. *See* Costs
EDTA. *See* Chelation therapy
Education
    See also Training
    of the elderly, 83-104

medication references for, 101-104
    of patients, 74, 77, 80
Elavil, 134, 142-143, 149, 192,
    197-198
Elderly
    communication problems of, 96-98
    definition of, 2
    drug consumption patterns of, 7-39
    health problems of, 15-20
    life expectancy of, 211-212
    medication problems of, 3, 95-97,
        167-180
    noncompliance to therapy of, 65-80
    physiological changes in, 2, 105,
        110-120, 210-211
    and polypharmacy, 32-39
    sexual dysfunction of, 185-205
Elixophyllin, 118
Empirin, 133, 141
Estrogens, 202
Ethylalcohol, 174
Eutonyl, 177
Eutron, 177
Excretion, 107, 118-120
    and drug interactions, 152, 174
Ex-Lax, 22
Eye drops, 20

F

Family, role of, 28-29, 94-95,
    163-164
FDA. *See* U.S. Food and Drug
    Administration
Feosol, 113
Ferrous sulfate, 113
Flurazepam, 19, 21, 122, 133, 142,
    151, 156
Foods
    and dietitians, 182-183, 163
    and drug interactions, 176-180
Formularies, 47
Fulvicin, 177
Furadantin, 177, 180
Furosemide, 59, 66, 133, 135-137,
    150

G

Garamycin, 120
Gastrointestinal drugs, 52
  risks of, 133, 140-141, 152
Generic drugs, 44
  See also Medications
  appearance of, 5, 43-63, 86
  availability of, 60-61
  common, 22
  disadvantages of, 57-59
Generic equivalence, 45
  versus therapeutic, 55-57
Gentamicin, 120
Geriatrics, 1
  physician training in, 24
  research in, 122
Gerontology
  See also Geriatrics
  societies and organizations, 1, 125
  training for, 2-3, 24
Gerovital, 218, 220
Glaucoma, 20-21
Glycoside digoxin, 33
  See also Digoxin
Griseofulvin, 177
Guanethidine, 197
Gynecomastia
  drug-induced, 192-193, 200-202
  professionals and, 204-205

H

Haldol, 134, 144, 152, 192
Half-life, 107
Haloperidol, 134, 144, 152, 192
Health care
  access to, 29
  costs of, 7-11, 35, 47, 52, 60-61, 73
  dissatisfaction with, 215-216
  and the elderly, 15-20
  environment of, 8-9, 30-33, 36-39
  long-term, 7-8

Health professionals
  drug therapy role of, 70-74, 77-78, 148-152, 156-164, 180-183
  as prescribers, 51, 160
  as team members, 1-5, 89-93
Heart disease, 16-17
  angina, 190-191
  and EDTA, 226
  medications for, 133-135, 168-171
  and sexual dysfunction, 190-191, 193
  unproven remedies for, 218-219
High blood pressure. *See* Hypertension
Home remedies, 209-228
Hormones
  and aging, 188-189, 210-212, 218
  replacement therapy, 202-203
  and sex, 200
Hydralazine, 192
Hydrochlorothiazide, 19, 21-22, 133, 135-136, 150
Hydrodiuril, 19, 21-22, 133, 135-136, 150, 192
Hygroton, 192
Hypertension
  drugs for, 18-19, 21-22, 133, 137, 199
  and sexual functioning, 192, 197
Hypokalemia, 150-151
Hysterectomy, 195

I

Ibuprofen, 18, 21
Illness. *See* Disease
Imipramine, 192, 197
Immunity, transplanted, 212
Impotence
  and drug therapy, 196-198
  suggestion of, 204
Inderal, 118, 191-192
Indocin, 18, 21, 133, 138, 146
Indomethacin, 18, 21, 133, 138, 146
Insurance, effect of, 30

In vitro testing, 45, 56
In vivo testing, 45, 55
Ismelin, 197
Isoptin, 191

K

Kaolin-pectin, 33
Kaopectate, 33
KH-3 antiaging drug, 220
Krebiozen, 222-223

L

Labeling
  auxiliary prescription, 90
  of drugs, 77-80
Laetrile, 217, 221-222
Lanoxin, 55, 66, 91, 113, 120,
  132-135, 149-150, 168, 170, 173,
  193
Lasix, 19, 21-22, 59, 66, 150
Laws, antisubstitution, 46-50
Laxatives, 20, 22, 134, 146
Liability
  of pharmacists, 59
  of prescribers, 20-24, 29, 51, 58,
  156, 160

M

Maalox, 22, 152
Magnesium-aluminum hydroxide,
  22, 152
Magnesium-aluminum hydroxide-
  simethicone, 22
Magnesium hydroxide, 134, 145-146,
  152
MAO inhibitors, 177
Mastectomy, 195
Medicare/Medicaid
  and drug therapy, 37
  Supplemental Medical Insurance
  option, 11-13

Medications
  See also Drug reactions; Generic
  drugs
  adverse effects of, 125-164
  analgesics, 20, 22, 133-134, 141,
  152
  antacids, 20, 22, 134, 145-146,
  152
  antibiotics, 120-121, 174, 176-180,
  anticholinergics, 133, 141, 193,
  198
  anticoagulants, 85, 116-117,
  132-133, 138-139
  antidepressants, 142-143, 148-149,
  152
  antigout, 174
  antihistamines, 7, 126, 192
  antinuclear, 52, 133, 140-141, 149,
  154, 170-171
  antioxidants, 225-226
  antiparkinson, 193, 198
  antipsychotics, 134, 143-144, 148,
  175, 197-198
  antispasmodics, 152
  antiulcer, 193
  for anxiety, 22, 133, 142
  for arthritis, 17-18, 21-22, 133,
  138
  bronchodilators, 118-119, 133, 140
  calendars for, 86
  chemical equivalence of, 44
  consumption patterns of, 7-39
  costs of, 9-11, 29, 35, 47, 52,
  60-61, 73
  dependency on, 27-28, 32-39
  for diabetes, 18, 21, 189
  discontinuance of, 34-35, 67
  diuretics, 17, 59, 66, 132,
  135-137, 150-151, 191-192
  dosages of, 2-3, 34-39, 72-73,
  85-87, 105-122, 159
  education about, 83-104
  gastrointestinal, 52, 133, 140-141,
  152
  for heart diseases, 17, 133-135,

168-171, 190-191, 193, 218-219, 226
history of, 37-39, 130-132, 157-163
for hypertension, 18-19, 21-22, 133, 137, 199
labeling of, 77-80, 90
laxatives, 20, 22, 134, 146
nonprescription, 9, 14-15, 20-22, 134, 145-146, 217-228
overdoses of, 23-24, 126-127
patents on, 50-52
patient noncompliance with, 65-80
and polypharmacy, 32-39
p.r.n. orders, 26-27
problems with, 13-14, 33, 38-39, 125-164, 167-183
safety closures of, 78-80
sedatives, 133, 141-142, 175
and sexual dysfunction, 185-206, 219
sleep-inducing, 133, 141-142, 151, 156
storage of, 88
substitution of, 45
and toxicity, 36-38, 55, 116, 173-174, 176, 179-180, 204, 221, 226-227
U.S. Food and Drug Administration standards for, 46-50, 54, 56, 59, 168-169, 209-215, 224
Medicines. *See* Medications
Mellaril, 192, 197
Memory loss, 219
Mental disorders, 195
See also Antipsychotics
Meperidine, 116
Metabolism, 107
and drug interactions, 174
of the elderly, 117-118
metabolic therapy, 221
Methyldopa, 19, 21-22, 133, 137, 192, 197
Milk of magnesia, 22
Miracle cures, 209, 216

Moisturizing creams, 22
Morbidity, 146
Morphine, 198
Mortality, 146-147
Motility, intestinal, 112-113
Motrin, 18, 21
Multiple source product, 45
Mylanta, 22

N

Nadolol, 192
Names, of drugs, 44-45
See also Brand names; Generic names
Narcotics, 198
and sexual function, 192
Nardil, 177
Nebcin, 120
Nembutal, 133, 141-142, 151, 198
Nifedipine, 191
Nitrofurantoin, 177, 180
Nitroglycerin, 191
Nitrostat, 191
Noctec, 26-27
Noncompliance
to drug therapy, 65-80
and interactions, 171
Nonprescription drugs, 9, 14-15
adverse reactions to, 134, 145-146
common, 20-22
unproven remedies, 217-228
Norpace, 193
Nurses
drug therapy role of, 26-27, 39, 159-160, 182
and generic drugs, 58
and medication education, 91
Nutrient-drug interactions, 176-177
Nursing homes
cost of, 7-8
drug consumption in, 30-32
and polypharmacy, 32-33, 36-39
population of, 8

O

Oral hypoglycemics, 18, 21
Orinase, 18, 21
Osteoarthritis, 17-18
  See also Arthritis
Overdoses, 23-24, 126-127
  Overmedication. *See* Polypharmacy
Over-the-counter drugs. *See*
  Nonprescription drugs
Oxycodone, 152

P

Pangamic acid, 223
Panmycin, 48
Paraprofessionals. *See* Health
  professionals
Parnate, 177
Patents, 50-52
Patients
  See also Consumers
  attitudes of, 27
  compliance of, 65-80
  creatine clearance of, 120
  with disabilities, 95-96
  and drug abuse, 32-39
  and drug interactions, 167-180
  education of, 83-104
  family of, 28-29, 94-95, 163-164
  insurance plans of, 30
  medication history profile of,
    37-39, 130-132, 157-163
  reactions to drugs, 133-164
  rights and responsibilities of, 43,
    93-94
  sexual dysfunctions of, 185-204
Penicillin, 157
Pentobarbital, 115, 133, 141-142, 151
Percodan, 152
Persantine, 20-21
Pharmaceutical industry
  American Pharmaceutical
    Association, 225
  advertising by, 23, 50

  and bioavailability, 55
  drug packaging by, 77-80
  Pharmaceutical Manufacturers
    Association, 53
  review process of, 53-54
Pharmacies
  displays in, 99
  licensing of, 60
Pharmacists
  and drug interactions, 181
  and generic drugs, 54, 58-59
  as pharmacokineticist, 105-109
  role of, 4-5, 25-26, 83, 91-92,
    161-163
Pharmacokinetics, 2
  changes due to age, 110-120
  and drug interactions, 181-182
  science of, 105-110
Pharmacology, 2-3
Phenolphthalein, 22
Phenylbutazone, 116, 133, 173
Phenytoin, 55, 151
Physical therapists, 1, 163
Physicians
  and brand name prescribing, 50-51
  costs of, 9
  and drug interactions, 180-181
  and generic drugs, 43-44, 47
  influence of, 20-24, 29, 58, 171
  patient education by, 90-91
  role of, 156
Physiology
  of aging, 2, 105, 110-120, 210-211
  of menopause, 188-189, 202
  sex and drug therapy, 185-206
Pilocar, 20-21
Pilocarpine, 20-21
Piroxicam, 18, 21
Placebo effects, 203
Politics, of drugs, 43-44
Polycillin, 148, 174
Polycillin-PRB, 174
Polypharmacy, 32-39
Potassium
  chloride, 22

deficiency of, 150-151
  supplemental, 17
Prednisone, 133, 139-140
Premarin, 202
Prescribers, 51, 160
Prescriptions
  See also Medications
  adverse reactions to, 132-146
  auxiliary labels, 90
  as contracts, 24
  cost of, 9-11
  failure to fill, 67
  patterns of consumption, 11-14
  and physicians, 20-24
  and polypharmacy, 32-39
  refill of, 88
P.r.n. medications, 26-27
  appropriate use of, 160
Pro-Barthine, 149, 152
Probenecid, 174
Procardia, 191
Professionals. *See* Health professionals
Propantheline, 149, 152
Propranolol, 19, 21-22, 34, 118, 133-135, 191-192
Proprietary name. *See* Brand names
Prostate disorders, 195
Protein binding, 116
Prothesis, penile, 197
Psychotropics. *See* Antipsychotics

Q

Quinidine, 168, 173
Quinoro, 168, 173

R

Regulation. *See* U.S. Food and Drug Administration
Reimbursement, for drugs, 30
Renal function, 120
Reporting, of drug reactions, 160

Resources, consumer-oriented, 101-104
Resperine, 22, 133, 138, 192
Review, of drug therapy, 37-39, 130-132, 157-163, 205
Rheumatoid arthritis, 17, 21
  See also Arthritis

S

Safety
  See also U.S. Food and Drug Administration
  in packaging, 78-80
Secobarbital, 151
Seconal, 151
Sedatives
  and drug interactions, 175
  hypnotics, 133, 141-142
Senior citizens. *See* Elderly
Serpasil, 22, 133, 138, 192
Sexual dysfunction
  drug-induced, 185-206
  unproved remedies for, 219
Sinequam, 192
Skin preparations, 20
Sleep-inducers, 133, 141-142
  geriatric dosages of, 156
  risks of, 151
Slow-K, 22
S.M.I. *See* Medicare/Medicaid
Sodium bicarbonate, 134, 145-146
Spironolactone, 192
Statistics
  on adverse reactions, 128-130
  on generic drug use, 48-49
  on health care costs, 7-11
Storage, of drugs, 88
Strokes, 19-21
Sulindac, 22
Sumycin, 48
Symptoms, of drug reactions, 146-152

T

Tagamet, 52, 133, 140-141, 149,
  154, 170-171, 193
Testing, of drugs, 45, 55-56
Testosterone derivatives, 202-203
Tetracycline, 48
Theo-Dur, 22
Theophylline, 22, 118-119, 133,
  140
Therapeutic equivalence, 55-57
Thiazide diuretics, 192, 198
Thioridazine, 192, 198
Thorazine, 134, 143-144, 149, 154,
  175, 192
Timolol, 20-21
Timoptic, 20-21
Tobramycin, 120
Tobutamide, 18, 21
Tofranil, 192, 197
Toxicity
  of aphrodisiacs, 204
  and bioavailability, 55
  cyanide, 221
  and drug interactions, 173-174, 176
  of medications, 36, 38
  and nutrient interactions, 179-180
  and protein binding, 116
  and unproven remedies, 227
  of Vitamin E, 226
Trade name. *See* Brand names
Training
  in geriatrics, 2-3
  of physicians, 21, 241
Tremors, 152
Trends
  in generic drug use, 48-50
  in geriatric care, 8
Triamterine, 22

Trihexphenidyl, 193
Tylenol # 3, 32, 133, 141, 152

U

Urinary retention, 152, 195
U.S. Bureau of Consumer
  Protection, 53
U.S. Federal Trade Commission, 53
U.S. Food and Drug Administration
  (FDA), 46, 54, 61
  and DSMO approval, 224
  and generic equivalence, 56
  guidelines of, 209, 215
  and new drug approval, 49, 59
  patient education by, 93
  testing procedures of, 45, 55-56,
    168-169
United States Pharmacopeia (USP)
  advisory panel of, 1
  consumer resources of, 101-102

V

Vaginal creams, 202
Valium, 22, 133, 142, 151
Verapamil, 191
Vitamins, 20
  as unproven remedies, 217-219
  Vitamin E, 225-226
Volume of distribution, 106

W

Warfarin, 85, 116-117, 132-133,
  138-139, 170-171, 173, 177, 179
Weight, and drugs, 114-117

About the Author

William Simonson received his Bachelor of Science degree in Pharmacy from the University of Rhode Island and his Doctor of Pharmacy degree from the University of Michigan, where he also completed a residency program in hospital pharmacy.

His pharmacy experiences include teaching and consulting in major medical centers, pharmacy practice in a small community pharmacy, and working as a nursing home consultant pharmacist.

Dr. Simonson is presently an Associate Professor of Pharmacy in the School of Pharmacy at Oregon State University, where much of his teaching, research, and service has been devoted to the field of aging. In his present position he has published numerous articles about the use and misuse of medications by the elderly and has been involved in the development of a variety of university level geriatrics courses for both pharmacy students and students of other disciplines who have an interest in gerontology.